Cities, Towns *and* Communities
of
Georgia

Between 1847-1962
8500 Places *and the* County *in which* Located

Compiled by:
Marion R. Hemperley
Deputy Surveyor General of Georgia

Southern Historical Press, Inc.
Greenville, South Carolina

Copyright 1980 by:
The Rev. Silas Emmett Lucas, Jr.

All rights reserved. No part of this publication may be reproduced, stored in a retrieval system or transmitted in any form or by any means without the prior permission of the publisher.

SOUTHERN HISTORICAL PRESS, INC.
PO BOX 1267
Greenville, SC   29601

ISBN #978-0-89308-153-1

Printed in the United States of America

PREFACE

The etymological study of place or town names in Georgia is still in its infancy although interest is growing day by day by those interested in the origins of our state names. It is well to note that place names are ALL names appearing on maps, including towns, rivers, and all geographical or man-made features. Municipal names are, of course, somewhat more limited in that they have to either appear on maps as towns or to be included in some type of digest or list. The compiler has not made an overall systematic study of all the towns herein listed, but has simply been intrigued for a number of years with Georgia's wide variety of town names. One study has been published on Georgia place names as a whole which includes many town and city names (Kenneth K. Krakow, **Georgia Place-Names**. [Macon: Winship Press, 1975]).

The late Dr. John H. Goff noted many of our unique names and wrote a series of articles on them. These articles were reprinted, with a minimum of editing, in one volume in 1975 (Francis Lee Utley and Marion R. Hemperley, ed., **Placenames of Georgia**. [Athens: University of Georgia Press, 1975]). Although Dr. Goff's primary interest were those words of Indian origin or derivation, his studies included all names in Georgia, including those of towns and cities. The compiler of this list was very fortunate to have been associated with Dr. Goff for a number of years and to have helped him in his studies of Georgia names. Dr. Goff first pointed out the different categories and explained how they were used, and without his help and inspiration this work would not have been compiled.

The following classifications are made by the compiler only and are in no way official state opinions. They are simply offered as guides to anyone seeking to classify particular names of interest.

It has been stated that Georgia has the largest percentage of Indian names remaining within her borders of any state in the U.S. There is a very good reason for this fact. For one hundred years, 1732-1832, Georgia had a common border with the Cherokee and Creek Indians, as well as a number of sub-tribes. As the Indians were removed from an area by a cession of land, the whites moved in and, in many cases, retained the Indian names found therein. The list of Indian names for our towns is long, and only a few will be listed here. We have a Coosa, the Cherokee name for an ancient Creek town, as well as Coosawattee, which translates into Old Coosa. There is Nicojack, Osceola, Philima, and Settendown, all names for Indian men as well as Waleska, a Cherokee maiden (all Indian women are recorded as beautiful maidens). We have towns and cities named for our major rivers, which all bear Indian names, Ocmulgee, Oconee, Ogeechee, Ohoopee, Savannah, Chattahoochee, and others. Tallahassee in Appling is Creek for Old Town, while Sutalee in Cherokee County is Cherokee for the numeral six. An interesting name, Walkee, is a Creek Indian word borrowed from the Spanish "waca" meaning cow. When the Spanish introduced cattle into the Indian nations, the latter had no word for the animals and adopted the Spanish name. We have Fowlstown and Sandtown, which are English translations of Indian town names. In the Cherokee section of Georgia we have three towns by the name, Yonah, which is the Cherokee word for bear. One of the most picturesque names in our state is Willacoochee, which translates into "little river." To conclude this category, we have towns named for Indian nations or tribes, as Chehaw, Cherokee, Modoc, Omaha, Pawnee, and Shawnee.

Americans have many of their places and towns named after foreign cities, countries, and objects, indicating an interest in or a migration from those places. Georgia is no exception as the following examples will indicate. Dividing the foreign names into different groups, the cities will be first. We have two Aberdeens, an Amsterdam, Athens, Havana, Rome, and Paris. In addition, we have two each of Bethlehem, Damascus, and Jerusalem, indicating an unusual interest in the Holy Land. We have three Berlins, three Warsaws, and five Waterloos.

Many foreign countries are represented in Georgia town names. There is Arabia in Thomas, Ceylon in Camden, Corsica in Candler, Egypt in Effingham (and a Nile in Brooks), Germany in Rabun, Mexico in Clinch, Spain in Brooks, and Sweden in Pickens. We have two each of Armenia, India, and Peru, as well as four Bermudas. Not to be outdone by foreign city and country names, Georgians have named many of their towns after foreign objects and places. There is, in addition to the Nile mentioned above, a Rhine in Dodge and Sahara in Richmond. Spanish names probably dominate the foreign field in Georgia, with Santa Luca in Gilmer, and Satilla in Appling, Wayne, and Pierce. The latter name is a corruption of the Spanish, St. Illa and is one of the oldest names in Georgia, dating back to the Spanish rule in southeast Georgia. In addition to Spanish Creek in Charlton, we have three Rios, a Rio Vista, Rico, Villa, and Villa Rica throughout the state.

Not to be outdone in the foreign field, we have towns by the names of English, French, Japanese, Orient, and Welch.

One of the more unusual foreign names in Georgia is Subligna, from the two Latin words, "sub" and "ligna," meaning underwood. The town was so named by a resident of that area, Dr. Underwood, who incorporated and named the town in 1870.

We have a number of colors in our town names. There is a Golden in Brooks, Gray in Jones, Green in Bulloch, and a total of 24 towns that have "red" in them. In addition, we have 37 "white" places in Georgia.

At least five other states are represented, indicating an interest in those states. We have Dakota in Turner, Kansas in Carroll, Nebraska in both Columbia and Richmond, and Oregon in Cobb. Chattooga, Heard, and Meriwether each have a Texas in them. It is interesting to note that all states named are west and northwest of Georgia, indicating a desire to migrate to, or at least an unusual interest in those areas.

The months and seasons are represented in Georgia's town names. We have a June in Dawson, May in Clinch, as well as Spring in Henry and Winter in Laurens. In addition, there is a Winter's in Oglethorpe and Winterville in both Oglethorpe and Clarke.

Even the mythical gods are depicted. There is a Vulcan in Walker and Venus in Stewart (as well as Valentine in Echols). In addition, there is a Sprite in Floyd.

One major category of Georgia names are those of commercial and industrial origin. To commemorate the jug manufacturing in eastern Georgia, we had a Jug Factory in Jackson and Jug Tavern in Walton. The latter became today's Winder. We also have a Commerce in Jackson, Farmers in Meriwether, Planter in Madison, and Shipyard in Chatham. In addition to Saw Mill in Chattooga, we have Saw Dust in Columbia. There is also a Scienceville in Stewart, Turpentine Farm in Worth, as well as three Vineyards over the state. Mechanics Hill in Richmond and Mechanicsville in both Gwinnett and Jasper fit in this category of industrial names.

Americans have always named their places and towns for politicians and Georgia was no exception. We have Napoleon in Union, Polk in the same county, Russell in Barrow, Ben Hill in Fulton, Schley in Colquitt and Schley, Taliaferro in Chattooga, Toombs in Richmond and Toombsboro in Wilkinson. In addition we have Van Buren in both Jones and Pike, and Wrightsville, named for John B. Wright, state senator, as the county seat of Johnson County.

Georgia also has named many of her towns for prominent men whom she has admired. We have three towns by the name of Pulaski, honoring the Revolutionary hero of Savannah, and Rossville in Walker, named for the Cherokee Chief John Ross. In Floyd County we have Vanns Valley, named for mixed-blood Cherokee David Van. John Wesley is well remembered in Georgia as there are four towns by his surname in the state.

One of the largest categories of town names is that of things, objects, or items. The list is long and contains many interesting names of which only a few will be given. We have Anvil Block in Clayton, Beehive in Dodge, Fence in Gwinnett, Furnace in Walker, Labor in Carroll, as well as Match in Elbert. In addition, we have Moonlight in Echols, Moon in Walker, and Twilight in Miller. There is a Pin in Paulding, Shot in Emanuel, Signboard in Liberty, Toy in Houston, Wax in Floyd, as well as the Indian money, Wampun, in Haralson. Other interesting names in this category are Yacht and Cyclone in Screven, Package in Macon, Hat in Tift, and Hatoff in Laurens.

One group of interesting names is that of rustic Americanisms which are purely local in nature. The U.S. is the only place in the world with names of that type, and Georgia has her full share. We have Hells Gate in Baker, Hatchet Landing in Douglas, Getup in Walker, as well as Republican in McDuffie and States Rights in Oglethorpe. Screven and Telfair both have a Temperance. Rough and Ready in Clayton was a very tough place in early days, with a number of saloons therein. Many years ago, the name was changed to Mountain View, and only lately the town has gone out of existence altogether.

Many towns and cities have been named for trees and plants found therein. Examples are Crabapple in Fulton, Fig in Jones, Magnolia in Pulaski and Sumter, Spruce in Rabun, and just plain Tree in Towns. We have a total of 42 towns with the name "pine" in them and 43 with "oak," all scattered over the state. In addition, many flowers are represented. We have a Daisy in Evans, Hyacinth in Ben Hill, Mistletoe in Columbia, Tulip in Chattooga, and Violet in Meriwether. In addition, we have a total of 20 places with "rose" in the name, as Rosebud in Gwinnett and Heard and Rose in Lamar.

Many animals are represented in Georgia's town names. Since the list is long, only a few will be discussed here. We have Alligator in Telfair, Crow in Whitfield, Fawn in Henry, Crawfish in Douglas, as well as Fish in Polk. There is a Parrott in Terrell, Peacocks in Washington, Shad in Floyd, and Snake in Fannin. In Rabun we have a Tiger to remind us that we once had mountain lions here in Georgia which were usually called tigers. Three of our counties have Buffalos representing those large animals which once roamed our state as they later did in the far west. To conclude this list, we have Horse Head in Houston, Jay Bird Springs in Dodge, as well as Possum Trot in Bartow and Owl Hollow in Walker.

Minerals have played an important part in the naming of our towns. We have Asbestos in White, Cement in Bartow, Clay in Lincoln, Dirt in Chattooga, as well as Flint in Mitchell. Polk has a Hematite, while Washington has a Kaolin. There is Marble in Colquitt, Quartz in Rabun, and Ore Bank in Polk, as well as Oreburg in Floyd. Over the state is a total of 29 "rock" places. Grady and Laurens each have a Lime Sink, while Polk has a Lime Branch and Hall has just plain Lime. Three of our counties, Chattahoochee, Dade, and Hall, each have a Sulphur Springs.

Georgia has had a large number of good and bad names throughout the years. Each category has its place in this study and both will be discussed, commencing with the good or optimistic places. We have Comfort in Greene, Good Hope in Walton, Heartease in Berrien, Hopeful in Mitchell, as well as Hope in Floyd and Pike. There is a Joy in Rabun, and Barrow and Walton each have a Paradise. Peace is in Baker, Plentitude in Jones, Success in Screven, Benevolence in Randolph, while Social Circle is in Walton and Social Hill in Cherokee. In addition, we have seven New Hopes across the state.

The bad or pessimistic names of Georgia are some of the most picturesque of all the names noted. We have Bogerville in Jasper, Cheap in Banks, Gip in Irwin, Grab All in Walton, and Hard Money in Webster. There is a Hardup in Baker, Help in Franklin, Hush in Gwinnett, and Shakerag in Fulton. Jasper has a Trickem, while Carroll, Whitfield, and Gwinnett each have a Trickum, spelled with a "u." To conclude this category, there is a Troublesome in Echols and a Poverty Hill in Jones.

Finally, there are some town names in Georgia that do not fit any of the regular categories. Many of these are named for their location, as Between in Walton, so named because it is located equidistant between Monroe and Loganville. Another name of that type is Middle Ground in Screven. Not only was there a town of that name, but that whole district was known as the Middle Ground District. Both received their names from the fact they were located between the Savannah and Ogeechee Rivers. There is a total of seven Midways across Georgia, and a Six Mile in Floyd. We have a Spot in Forsyth, Tiptop in Harris, and just plain Top in Jenkins.

There is a New in Chattooga, Philadelphia in Putnam, Stay in Lumpkin, Stop in Fayette, Tax in Henry and Talbot, Tell in Fulton, and Time in Hall. Probably the most unusual name in Georgia is Nameless in Laurens. It is said to have originated when, after a number of names had been submitted in vain to the Post Office Department, a resident made the statement, "We have a town that is nameless." That designation stuck and a Post Office was established there from 1886 through 1901.

Marion R. Hemperley
Atlanta, Georgia
March 1, 1980

This list of some 8,500 Georgia cities, towns and communities has been compiled due to the increasing demand for information on the many dead or non-existent municipalities of that state. Many historians, georgraphers, anthropologists, genealogists, and others, find town names on old letters or other documents and desire to know their locations. For the first time, this can be accomplished with a degree of accuracy as this list will place that town in a county, most of which have remained relatively constant.

This study had been compiled from records on file in the Georgia Surveyor General Department consisting of maps, indexes, gazeteers, and a list of post offices, all covering the period, 1847-1962. That time span was selected because detailed maps and the other materials are available showing a large number of towns. No attempt has been made to list completely all the towns and cities of Georgia shown on the large collection of maps on file in the Surveyor General Department. Only the best and most detailed were used and the towns recorded, with a county location given for each. It was found that, in many cases, a town was shown on more than one map and, while each source was carefully checked, no attempt was made in this study to record all entries for any one name. Only a single listing has been given, except when a discrepancy appeared in the spelling or a derivation of the name given.

The creation of new counties and county line changes have presented rather peculiar problems for the compiler of this list. As has been noted, town names were taken from several sources of varying dates. If a name appeared in a county other than that of the original entry, a new recording was made although this does not necessarily mean the new entry is a different town. New counties have been created from parts of one or more existing counties and, in addition, counties exchanged parcels of land. Towns, therefore, could change counties but not necessarily their location. No attempt has been made to trace the movement of county boundaries, as this was beyond the scope of the compiler due to time. In early periods of Georgia's history, a post office would sometimes move from one location to another, perhaps across county lines, yet retain the same name. Again, no attempt has been made to trace that migration and additional research is needed to determine if they are, indeed, the same.

Alone with each entry and the county of location, a reference date is given. That date shows the source of that particular entry and is given in order that a more precise location may be ascertained if desired. The date does not necessarily mean that a town or city was not in existence before or after the date shown. For instance, most of the many towns listed in 1920 remain in existence today, although some are mere crossroads and not cities or town as such.

A special effort has been made to include all the present-day towns and cities of Georgia in order that the list may prove more useful to anyone not wholly familiar with that state.

The following sources, most of which can be checked at libraries having map collections, have been used in compiling this list.

1. Map of the State of Georgia, compiled under the direction of his Excellency, George W. Crawford, by William Bonner, Civil Engineer, Milledgeville, 1847. This map is referred to in the text as "1847."

2. Wight, Willard E., Georgia Post Offices, 1859, unpublished manuscript, compiled by Dr. Wight in 1962, a copy of which is on file in the Georgia Surveyor General Department. This list is hereinafter referred to as "1859."

3. Map of the State of Georgia, compiled by J. R. Butts, 1859, Revised by A. G. Butts, 1870, Macon. This map referred to as "1870."

4. Standard Directory Company [compilers and publishers], Georgia State Gazetteer and Business Directory, 1881-1882, 1881, Atlanta. This is an excellent book and contains much additional information on the cities and towns of that period. This book is referred to as "1881."

5. Rand McNally & Company, Indexed County and Railroad Pocket Map and Shipper's Guide of Georgia, 1894, Chicago and New York. The Surveyor General Department has a copy of the shipper's guide or gazetteer only and not the pocket map. This gazetteer is referred to as "1894."

6. New Commercial and Census Map of Georgia, National Map Company, Indianapolis, Indiana, undated but circa 1920. This fine map includes an index of towns and was the base map used in this study. Referred to in the text as "1920."

7. Georgia Pocket Map [with gazetteer included], Rand McNally and Company, Chicago, 1962. This map and index referred to as "1962."

Aaron, Bulloch Co. (1920)

Aaron, Jefferson Co. (1920)

Abac, Tift Co. (1962);
P.O. name for Abraham
Baldwin College.

Abba, Irwin Co. (1962)

Abbeville, Wilcox Co. (1920)

Abbottsford, Troup Co.
(1920).

Abel, Houston Co. (1920)

Abercorn Heights, Chatham
Co. (1962); part of
Savannah.

Aberdeen, Emanuel Co.
(1894)

Aberdeen, Fayette Co.
(1920)

Abernethys, Haralson Co.
(1920)

Abilene, Carroll Co.
(1920)

Abner, Spalding Co. (1881)

Abraham Baldwin College,
Tift Co. (1962); R.R.
name for Abac.

Absalom, Hall Co. (1920)

Abt, Floyd Co. (1962)

Academy, Jackson Co. (1920)

Accommodation, Hall Co.
(1894)

Achord, Dodge Co. (1920)

Achords, Montgomery Co.
(1894)

Ackert, Fayette Co. (1920);
P.O. name is Inman.

Acorn, Habersham Co. (1920)

Acree, Dougherty Co. (1920)

Acree, Worth Co. (1894)

Acton, Harris Co. (1920)

Acworth, Cobb Co. (1920)

Ada, Dooly Co. (1894)

Adabelle, Bulloch Co.
(1962)

Adair, Murray Co. (1920)

Adairsville, Bartow Co.
(1920)

Adam, Richmond Co. (1920)

Adams, Lee Co. (1920);
P.O. name is Enterprise
(1881).

Adams, Irwin Co. (1847)

Adams, Wilcox Co. (1859)

Adamson, Heard Co. (1920)

Adams Park, Fulton Co.
(1962); part of Atlanta.

Adams Park, Twiggs Co. (1962)

Adamsville, Fulton Co. (1881)

Adamsville, Cass (Bartow)
Co., (1847)

Adamsville, Gordon Co.
(1881)

Adasburg, Wilkes Co. (1920)

Adel, Berrien Co. (1894)

Adel, Cook Co. (1920)

Adelaide, Bulloch Co. (1920)

Adelaide, Mitchell Co. (1962)

Adgateville, Jasper Co.
(1920)

Adlai, Brooks Co. (1920)

Adolphus, Franklin Co. (1920)

Adrian, Emanuel and Johnson
Cos. (1920)

Adventure, Richmond Co.
(1920)

Aerial, Habersham Co. (1920)

Afton, Berrien Co. (1881); also known as William Store (1881)

Afton, Dawson Co. (1920)

Agate, Floyd Co. (1920); R.R. name for Cunningham.

Agnes, Lincoln Co. (1920)

Agricola, Glascock Co. (1920)

Ai, Gilmer Co. (1920)

Aid, Franklin Co. (1920)

Aiken, Effingham Co. (1881)

Aikenton, Jasper Co. (1920)

Ailey, Montgomery Co. (1920)

Aimar, Long Co. (1920)

Ainslie, Bleckley Co. (1962)

Airline, Hart Co. (1920); also spelled Airline (1870)

Akes, Polk Co. (1920); P.O. name is Berry.

Akin, Bulloch Co. (1894)

Akin, Stephens Co. (1920)

Akin, Wayne Co. (1920)

Akridge, Grady Co. (1920)

Arkridge, Mitchell Co. (1920)

Alabama Junction, Chatham Co. (1962)

Alaculsy, Murray Co. (1920)

Alamo, Wheeler Co. (1920)

Alapaha, Berrien Co. (1920)

Albany, Baker Co. (1847)

Albany, Dougherty Co. (1920)

Allen, Richmond Co. (1894)

Allenhurst, Liberty Co. (1920)

Allen Rock Pond, Decatur Co. (1870)

Allens, Richmond Co. (1920)

Allens Mills, Carroll Co. (1920)

Allentown, Wilkinson Co. (1920)

Allenville, Berrien Co. (1920)

Aller, Houston Co. (1881)

Allgood's Mill, Haralson Co. (1894)

Alliance, Decatur Co. (1894)

Alliance, Jasper Co. (1920)

Allie, Meriwether Co. (1920)

Alligator, Telfair Co. (1881)

Allon, Crawford Co. (1920)

Alma, Bacon Co. (1920)

Alma, Decatur Co. (1894)

Alma, Gilmer Co. (1859)

Almira, Jefferson Co. (1920)

Almon, Newton Co. (1920)

Alnwick, Chatham Co. (1920)

Alonzo, Telfair Co. (1920)

Alpha, Worth Co. (1894)

Alpharetta, Milton (Fulton) Co. (1920)

Alphonso, Macon Co. (1920)

Alphine, Chattooga Co. (1920)

Alps, Meriwether Co. (1920)

Alston, Montgomery Co. (1920)

Alstons, Stewart Co. (1920)

Altamaha, Tattnall Co. (1920)

Altavista, Butts Co. (1894)

Alta Vista, Muscogee Co. (1962); part of Columbus.

Altimira, Hancock Co. (1870)

Altman, Dooly Co. (1894)

Altman, Screven Co. (1962)

Altmera, Hancock Co. (1881); also known as Fair Play

Alto, Habersham and Banks Cos. (1920); also known as Lulah (1881)

Alton, Milton (Fulton) Co. (1920)

Alton, Tattnall Co. (1920)

Alva, Jasper Co. (1920)

Alvaton, Meriwether Co. (1920)

Alvin, Madison Co. (1920)

Amandaville, Elbert Co. (1859)

Amandaville, Hart Co. (1881)

Amason, Bibb Co. (1920)

Amboy, Turner Co. (1920)

Ambrose, Coffee Co. (1920)

Amco. Jasper Co. (1962)

Americus, Sumter Co. (1920)

Amerson, Washington Co. (1920)

Ami, Forsyth Co. (1859)

Amicalola, Dawson Co. (1920)

Amity, Lincoln Co. (1920)

Amoskeag, Dodge Co. (1894)

Amsterdam, Decatur Co. (1920)

Amys Creek, Habersham Co. (1881); also known as Mauldin.

Amzi, Murray Co. (1920)

Anandale, Habersham Co. (1920)

Anchor, Wayne Co. (1894)

Andalusia, Randolph Co. (1920)

Anderson, Chatham Co. (1920)

Anderson, Laurens Co. (1881)

Anderson, Randolph Co. (1859)

Anderson, Sumter Co. (1894)

Anderson City, Worth Co. (1962)

Andersons Corner, Mitchell Co. (1962)

Andersonville, Cobb Co. (1847)

Andersonville, Sumter Co. (1920)

Andes, Baldwin Co. (1920)

Andrews, Heard Co. (1894)

Anguilla, Glynn Co. (1920)

Anita, Bulloch Co. (1920)

Anna, Baker Co. (1920)

Annie, Lowndes Co. (1894)

Anniedelle, Floyd Co. (1920)

Anoia, Wilkes Co. (1920)

Anon, Oglethorpe Co. (1894)

Anthony, McDuffie Co. (1920)

Anthony Shoals, Elbert Co. (1859)

Antioch, Campbell (Fulton) Co. (1870)

Antioch, Meriwether Co. (1870)

Antioch, Oglethorpe Co. (1881); also known as Solomonville.

Antioch, Polk Co. (1962)

Antioch, Stewart Co. (1881); also known as Hannahatchee.

Antioch, Troup Co. (1920)

Antioch, Twiggs Co. (1881)

Anvil Block, Clayton Co. (1881)

Apalachee, Morgan Co. (1920)

Apez, Mitchell Co. (1894)

Apple Blossom, Butts Co. (1894)

Appleton, Montgomery Co. (1894)

Apple Valley, Jackson Co. (1920)

Appling, Columbia Co. (1920)

Appling Camp Ground, Appling Co. (1870)

Aquavia, Hart Co. (1920)

Arabi, Crisp Co. (1920)

Arabi, Dooly Co. (1894)

Arabia, Thomas Co. (1881)

Aragon, Polk Co. (1920)

Aragon Station, Polk Co. (1920)

Arara, Jasper Co. (1881)

Arara, Putnam Co. (1894)

Arcade, Hall Co. (1881)

Arcade, Jackson Co. (1920)

Arcadia, Hall Co. (1881)

Arcadia, Liberty Co. (1920); R.R. name is Dorchester

Arch, Forsyth Co. (1920)

Arch City, Gordon Co. (1962)

Archer, Walker Co. (1962)

Archery, Webster Co. (1962)

Archery, Webster Co. (1962)

Arco, Glynn Co. (1962); census name is Dock Junction

Arcola, Bulloch Co. (1920)

Arden, Bryan Co. (1920)

Ardmore, Effingham Co. (1920)

Ardsley Park, Chatham Co. (1962); part of Savannah.

Argo, Fannin Co. (1894)

Argo, Hall Co. (1881)

Argyle, Ware Co. (1881)

Argyle, Clinch Co. (1920)

Argyle, Decatur (now Seminole) Co. (1870)

Arien, Bulloch Co. (1920)

Arkwright, Bibb Co. (1962); also known as Holton.

Arles, Sumter Co. (1920)

Arlington, Calhoun Co. (1920)

Armacolola, Lumpkin Co. (1847)

Armcork, Bibb Co. (1962)

Armena, Lee Co. (1920)

Armenia, Screven Co. (1881)

Armour, Fulton Co. (1920)

Armstrong, Wilkes Co. (1920)

Armuchee, Floyd Co. (1920)

Army Depot, Clayton Co. (1962); also known as Atlanta General Depot.

Army Pilot School, Dougherty Co. (1962); part of Turner Air Force Base.

Arnall, Coweta Co. (1920)

Arnco Mills, Coweta Co. (1962)

Arnett, Decatur Co. (1870)

Arnold, Cherokee Co. (1894)

Arnold, Dougherty Co. (1881)

Arnold, Hancock Co. (1847)

Arnold, Milton (Fulton) Co. (1920)

Arnold, Ware Co. (1881)

Arnold Mill, Cherokee and Fulton Cos. (1962)

Arnolds, Thomas Co. (1962)

Arnoldsville, Oglethorpe Co. (1920)

Arp, Banks Co. (1920)

Arp, Irwin Co. (1920)

Arraratt, Putnam Co. (1870)

Arrieville, Johnson Co. (1920)

Arrington, Worth Co. (1920)

Arrowood, Fulton Co. (1894)

Artesia, Worth Co. (1920)

Arthur, Laurens Co. (1881)

Artic, Warren Co. (1894)

Asa, Twiggs Co. (1920)

Asbestos, White Co. (1920)

Asbury, Troup Co. (1920); also known as Harrisonville.

Asbury Chapel Academy, Houston Co. (1847)

Ascalon, Walker Co. (1920)

Ashburn, Glynn Co. (1847)

Ashburn, Turner Co. (1920)

Ashburn, Worth Co. (1894)

Ashford Park, DeKalb Co. (1920)

Ashintilly, McIntosh Co. (1962)

Ashland, Forsyth Co. (1870)

Ashland, Franklin Co. (1920)

Ashley, Ben Hill Co. (1920)

Ashley, Wilcox Co. (1894)

Ashton, Bel Hill Co. (1920)

Ashwood, Berrien Co. (1920)

Aska, Fannin Co. (1920)

Astor, Clayton Co. (1881); formerly known as Forest Station, name changed March 1881; now known as Forest Park.

Astoria, Ware Co. (1920)

Asylum, Baldwin Co. (1920); P.O. name is Midway.

Atco, Bartow Co. (1920)

Athens, Clarke Co. (1920)

Athol, Monroe Co. (1894)

Athon, Putnam Co. (1920)

Atkinson, Brantley Co. (1962)

Atkinson, Camden Co. (1881)

Atkinson, Wayne Co. (1894)

Atlanta, Fulton Co. (1920)

Atlanta General Depot, Clayton Co. (1962); also known as Army Depot.

Atlanta Heights, Fulton Co. (1894)

Atlanta Junction, Floyd Co. (1920)

Atlanta Naval Station, DeKalb Co. (1962); another name for Naval Air Station; base moved to Dobbins Air Force Station, Cobb Co. in 1959.

Atlanta Shops, Fulton Co. (1894)

Atlanta Yard, Fulton Co. (1894)

Atlantic, Twiggs Co. (1920)

Att, Worth Co. (1920)

Attapulgus, Decatur Co. (1920)

Attica, Jackson Co. (1920)

Atwater, Upson Co. (1920)

Atwood, Ware Co. (1920)

Aubrey, Heard Co. (1920)

Auburn, Gwinnett Co. (1859)

Auburn, Barrow Co. (1920)

Auburn Hill, Franklin Co. (1859)

Aucilla, Thomas Co. (1881)

Audaston, Hancock Co. (1847)

Audubon, Gordon Co. (1920)

Augusta, Richmond Co. (1920)

Aults, Telfair Co. (1920)

Auraria, Lumpkin Co. (1920)

Austell, Cobb Co. (1920)

Austin, Morgan Co. (1920)

Autney, McDuffie Co. (1920)

Autreyville, Colquitt Co. (1920)

Autry, Hall Co. (1962)

Auvil, Berrien Co. (1920)

Ava, Berrien Co. (1881)

Ava, Lowndes Co. (1859)

Avalanta, Putnam Co. (1870)

Avalanta Eatonton Factory, Putnam Co. (1870)

Avalon, Stephens Co. (1920)

Avalon, Franklin Co. (1881)

Avalona, Putnam Co. (1881)

Avans, Dade Co. (1920)

Avant, Pierce Co. (1894)

Avants, Wheeler Co. (1920)

Aventon, Randolph Co. (1881)

Avera, Jefferson Co. (1920)

Avirett, Decatur Co. (1894)

Avondale, Bibb Co. (1920)

Avondale, Chatham Co. (1962); part of Savannah.

Avondale, DeKalb Co. (1962); R.R. name for Avondale Estates.

Avondale, McDuffie Co. (1962)

Avondale, Muscogee Co. (1962); part of Columbus.

Avondale Estates, DeKalb Co. (1962); P.O. name for Avondale.

Avon Park, Chatham Co. (1962); part of Savannah.

Axson, Atkinson Co. (1920)

Ayersville, Habersham Co. (1881)

Ayersville, Stephens Co. (1920)

Aylmer, Bartow Co. (1920)

Azalea, Habersham Co. (1894)

Azalia, Screven Co. (1894)

Babb, Henry Co. (1920)

Babcock, Miller Co. (1920)

Babcock Station, Miller Co. (1920); P.O. known as Boykin (1920); also known as Babcock (1962).

Bachelot, Brantley Co. (1920)

Bachlot, Charlton Co. (1894)

Bacon, Lamar Co. (1920)

Baconton, Mitchell Co. (1920)

Bacot, Long Co. (1920)

Baden, Brooks Co. (1920)

Bahima, McIntosh Co. (1894)

Bailey, Ware Co. (1881)

Baileys, Bryan Co. (1920)

Baileys Mill, Bibb Co. (1847)

Baileys Mill, Cherokee Co. (1881)

Bailey's Mills, Camden Co. (1894)

Bailey's Mills, Cherokee Co. (1894)

Baileys Park, Bleckley Co. (1920)

Bain, Pike Co. (1894)

Bainbridge, Decatur Co. (1920)

Bainbridge Junction, Decatur Co. (1894)

Bairdstown, Oglethorpe Co. (1920)

Bait, Miller Co. (1920)

Baker, Hall Co. (1881)

Baker, Paulding Co. (1920)

Bakers Ferry, Elbert Co. (1881)

Baker Village, Muscogee Co. (1962); part of Columbus.

Bald Hill, Chattahoochee Co. (1870)

Bald Spring, Franklin Co. (1859)

Baldwin, Habersham Co. (1920)

Baldwinville, Talbot Co. (1920)

Bales, Laurens Co. (1920)

Baleys Bluff, Camden Co. (1847)

Balcom, Jones Co. (1920)

Ball Ground, Cherokee Co. (1920)

Ball Ground, Murray Co. (1962)

Balloon, Clinch Co. (1894)

Balloon, Coffee Co. (1881)

Balloon, Atkinson Co. (1920)

Balls Church, Wilkinson Co. (1920)

Baltimore, Wilkes Co. (1962); part of Washington

Bamah, Monroe Co. (1894)

Bamberg, Echols Co. (1920)

Bamboo, Wayne Co. (1894)

Bancroft, Early Co. (1920)

Bancroft, Franklin Co. (1881)

Bandanna, Montgomery Co. (1920)

Bandy, Lowndes Co. (1920)

Bankston, Monroe Co. (1870)

Banksville, Banks Co. (1920)

Banner, Liberty Co. (1894)

Banning, Carroll Co. (1920)

Bannister, Cherokee Co. (1920)

Bannockburn, Berrien Co. (1920)

Barbers, Colquitt Co. (1920)

Barbers Creek, Jackson Co. (1881)

Barclay, Wayne Co. (1920)

Barcom Academy, Screven Co. (1870)

Barefoot, Towns Co. (1920)

Barfield, Lowndes Co. (1962)

Barge, Carroll Co. (1920)

Barges, Stewart Co. (1920)

Bark Camp, Burke Co. (1870)

Barkers, Chattooga Co. (1920)

Barkers, Fannin Co. (1894)

Barker Spring, Upson Co. (1962)

Barkers Store, Floyd Co. (1881)

Barksdale, Washington Co. (1920)

Barkwood, Fannin Co. (1920)

Barnard, Chatham Co. (1894)

Barnes, Douglas Co. (1920)

Barnesdale, Cook Co. (1962)

Barnes Still, Echols Co. (1920)

Barnesville, Pike Co. (1859)

Barnesville, Lamar Co. (1920)

Barnetfield, Bibb Co. (1920)

Barnett, Warren Co. (1920); also known as Cumming and Double Wells (1881).

Barnetts, Whitfield Co. (1881); R.R. name for Cove City; also known as Carbondale.

Barnett, Shoals, Oconee Co. (1920)

Barney, Brooks Co. (1920)

Barnsley, Bartow Co. (1920)

Barretts, Lowndes Co. (1920)

Barrettsville, Lumpkin Co. (1847)

Barrettsville, Dawson Co. (1920)

Barrineau, Berrien Co. (1920)

Barrington, McIntosh Co. (1920)

Barron's, Jones Co. (1894)

Barrons Lane, Macon Co. (1920)

Barrows Bluff, Coffee Co. (1920)

Bartlett, Macon Co. (1920)

Bartlett, Bibb Co. (1920)

Bartletts Ferry, Harris Co. (1962)

Bartonville, Wilcox Co. (1920)

Barton Woods, DeKalb Co. (1962)

Bartow, Chatham Co. (1894)

Bartow, Bartow Co. (1920)

Bartow, Jefferson Co. (1920); also known as Spiers (1881).

Bartow Iron Works, Bartow Co. (1881)

Barwick, Brooks Co. (1920)

Barwick Station, Thomas Co. (1920)

Bascobel, Jackson Co. (1881); also known as Centre and Center.

Bascom, Screven Co. (1920); also known as Bascoms Academy (1881).

Bascoms Academy, Screven Co. (1881); another name for Bascoms.

Base, Butts Co. (1894)

Bass Ferry, Floyd Co. (1920)

Bassett, Bulloch Co. (1962)

Bastonville, Glascock Co. (1920)

Bateman, Houston Co. (1847)

Batesville, Cherokee Co. (1920)

Batesville, Habersham Co. (1881); former name of Soque.

Bath, Jefferson Co. (1847)

Bath, Richmond Co. (1847)

Batson, Laurens Co. (1920)

Battey State Hospital, Floyd Co. (1962)

Battlefield, Walker Co. (1894)

Battle Ground, Cherokee Co. (1894)

Battle Ground, Johnson Co. (1881)

Battle Ground, Wilcox Co. (1870)

Battlehill, Fulton Co. (1920)

Battle Park, Muscogee Co. (1962); part of Ft. Benning.

Baugh Siding, Gordon Co. (1920)

Baughs Mountain, Gordon Co. (1881)

Baughville, Talbot Co. (1920)

Bauxite, Floyd Co. (1920)

Baxley, Appling Co. (1920)

Baxter, Union Co. (1920)

Bay, Colquitt Co. (1920)

Bayard, Harris Co. (1920)

Bayboro, Colquitt Co. (1920)

Bay Branch, Emanuel Co. (1881)

Bay Creek, Gwinnett Co. (1881)

Bayley, Camden Co. (1881)

Bayview, Liberty Co. (1894)

Bayview, Long Co. (1920)

Bazemore, Screven Co. (1881); also known as Brier Creek.

Beach, Ware Co. (1920)

Beachton, Grady Co. (1920)

Beacon Heights, Morgan Co. (1962)

Beall, Talbot Co. (1920)

Bealls, Putnam Co. (1920)

Beall Springs, Glascock Co. (1920); R.R. name for Belle Springs.

Bealwood, Muscogee Co. (1920)

Belle Springs, Glascock Co. (1920); P.O. name for Beall Springs.

Bear Creek, Coffee Co. (1920)

Bear Creek, Henry Co. (1881); another name for Hampton.

Beards Bluff, Liberty Co. (1894)

Beards Creek, Liberty Co. (1881)

Beards Creek, Long Co. (1920)

Beasley, Jefferson Co. (1894)

Beathoney, Milton (Fulton) Co. (1894)

Beatrice, Stewart Co. (1920)

Beatum, Chattooga Co. (1920)

Beaufort, Randolph Co. (1881)

Beaulieu, Chatham Co. (1962)

Bearmont, Catoosa Co. (1920)

Beauxite, Wilkinson Co. (1920)

Beaverdale, Whitfield Co. (1920)

Beaver Dam, Gwinnett Co. (1962)

Beckham, Early Co. (1894)

Bede, Wilcox Co. (1894)

Bedford Heights, Richmond Co. (1962); part of Augusta.

Beding, Washington Co. (1881)

Bee, Coweta Co. (1920)

Bee, Wilcox Co. (1894)

Beech Creek, Haralson Co. (1881)

Beech Grove, Franklin Co. (1881)

Beech Grove, Walker Co. (1894)

Beech Hill, Wilkinson Co. (1920)

Beechwood, Crawford Co. (1920)

Beehive, Dodge Co. (1920)

Beeckroms Cross Roads, Calhoun Co. (1859)

Beeks, Pike Co. (1920)

Bela, Campbell (Fulton) Co. (1894)

Bel Air, Richmond Co. (1920); also spelled Belair (1881).

Belcher, Decatur Co. (1870)

Belfast, Bryan Co. (1920)

Belfast Station, Bryan Co. (1920)

Belknap, Bryan Co. (1894)

Bell, Elbert Co. (1920)

Bellefont, Muscogee Co. (1920)

Belleville, Evans Co. (1962); R.R. name for Bellville.

Belleville, McIntosh Co. (1920)

Belle Vista, Glynn Co. (1920)

Bellmont, Hall Co. (1894)

Bell Springs, Glascock Co. (1894)

Bellton, Hall and Banks Cos. (1962); annexed to Lula in 1956.

Bellview, Bibb Co. (1962); part of Macon.

Bellview, Miller Co. (1962)

Bellville, Evans Co. (1920); P.O. name for Belleville (1962).

Bellville, Tattnall Co. (1894)

Bellville Factory, Richmond Co. (1847)

Bellvue, Talbot Co. (1847)

Bellwood, Fulton Co. (1894)

Belmont, Hall Co. (1920)

Belmont Hills, Cobb Co. (1962); part of Smyrna.

Beloit, Lee Co. (1920)

Beloteville, Lowndes Co. (1920)

Belt Junction, DeKalb Co. (1920)

Belt Junction, Fulton Co. (1894)

Belt Line Junction, Fulton Co. (1920)

Belton, Franklin Co. (1859)

Beltwood, Burke Co. (1894)

Belvedere-Decatur, DeKalb Co. (1962)

Belvedere Park, DeKalb Co. (1962); part of South Decatur.

Belvidere, Hancock Co. (1881)

Belvue, Putnam Co. (1881)

Bemiss, Lowndes Co. (1920)

Ben, Dooly Co. (1894)

Ben, Pulaski Co. (1920)

Ben Butts, Hancock Co. (1847)

Bender, Laurens Co. (1920)

Benderburg, Whitfield Co. (1894)

Benefit, White Co. (1920)

Benevolence, Randolph Co. (1920)

Bengall, Bulloch Co. (1881)

Ben Hill, Fulton Co. (1920); also known as Mt. Gilead Cross Roads (1881).

Ben Lomond, Hancock Co. (1847)

Bennett, Ware Co. (1881)

Bennetts, Wayne Co. (1870)

Bennetts Still, Wayne Co. (1920)

Bennettsville, Wayne Co. (1859)

Bennie, Carroll Co. (1920)

Benning Hills, Muscogee Co. (1962); part of Columbus.

Benning Park, Muscogee Co. (1962); part of Columbus.

Bennock's, Richmond Co. (1894)

Bennocks Mill, Richmond Co. (1920)

Benshoe, Harris Co. (1920)

Bentley, Haralson Co. (1920)

Bentley, Union Co. (1920)

Berea, Madison Co. (1920)

Berkeley Lake, Gwinnett Co. (1962)

Berkley, Madison Co. (1920); P.O. name is Carlton.

Berkshire, Gwinnett Co. (1881)

Berlene, Carroll Co. (1920)

Berlin, Banks Co. (1881)

Berlin, Colquitt Co. (1920)

Berlin, Lowndes Co. (1894)

Bermuda, Seminole Co. (1920)

Bermuda, Calhoun Co. (1920)

Bermuda, DeKalb Co. (1962)

Bermuda, Gwinnett Co. (1920)

Berne, Camden Co. (1881)

Berner, Monroe Co. (1920)

Bernice, Lincoln Co. (1920)

Bernita, Twiggs Co. (1920)

Berrien, Heard Co. (1847)

Berrien, Pickens Co. (1881)

Berrien, Tattnall Co. (1894)

Berry, Polk Co. (1920);
R.R. name is Akes.

Berry Hill, Floyd Co. (1920)

Berrys, Effingham Co. (1920)

Berryton, Chattooga Co.
(1920)

Berryville, Effingham Co.
(1894)

Bersheba, Henry Co. (1881)

Berwin, Floyd Co. (1920)

Berzelia, Columbia Co.
(1920)

Bessie, Wilkes Co. (1920)

Bessleton, Washington Co.
(1894)

Bests, Bartow Co. (1920)

Bethany, Baker Co. (1962)

Bethany, Greene Co. (1847)

Bethany, Jefferson Co.
(1881); another name
for Wadley.

Bethany, Morgan Co. (1920)

Bethel, Dooly Co. (1870)

Bethel, Effingham Co.
(1920)

Bethel, Glynn Co. (1881);
another name for Hazlehurst
(1881) [both Bethel and
Hazlehurst shown on map
of 1847].

Bethel, Jasper Co. (1962)

Bethel, Rabun Co. (1920)

Bethel, Randolph Co. (1920)

Bethel, Talfair Co. (1870)

Bethel, Wilkinson Co. (1881);
another name for Irwinton.

Bethlehem, Barrow Co. (1920)

Bethlehem, Walton Co. (1894)

Bethlehem, Forsyth Co. (1859)

Between, Walton Co. (1920)

Beulah, Laurens Co. (1920)

Beulah, Lincoln and Wilkes
Cos. (1962)

Beverly, Chatham Co. (1847)

Beverly, Elbert Co. (1920)

Beverly, Wilkinson Co. (1894)

Beverly Hills, Walker Co.
(1962)

Bexar, Coweta Co. (1847)

Bexton, Doweta Co. (1920)

Bibb City, Muscogee Co.
(1920)

Bickley, Ware Co. (1920)

Bie, Hart Co. (1859)

Big Creek, Forsyth Co. (1920)

Bigenoch, Cherokee Co. (1920)

Big Indian, Houston Co. (1920)

Bigoak, Twiggs Co. (1920)

Big Sandy, Wilkinson Co.
(1962)

Big Sandy, Twiggs Co. (1920)

Big Savanna, Dawson Co.
(1894); also spelled
Big Savannah (1881).

Big Savannah, Dawson Co.
(1881); also spelled
Big Savanna (1894).

Big Shanty, Cobb Co. (1881);
another name for Kennesaw.

Big Spring, Hancock Co.
(1881)

Big Spring, Troup Co. (1920)

Big Wahoo, Hall Co. (1870)

Bill, Montgomery Co. (1894)

Billarp, Douglas Co. (1920)

Bill Davis, Burke Co. (1962)

Billow, Carroll Co. (1920)

Billvan, Toombs Co. (1920)

Biltmore Estates, DeKalb Co. (1962)

Binford, Tattnall Co. (1920)

Bingen, Decatur Co. (1920)

Bingham, Jeff Davis Co. (1920)

Bio, Hart Co. (1920)

Birdford, Tattnall Co. (1881)

Birdie, Spalding Co. (1920)

Birds Mill, Coffee Co. (1870)

Birds Spur, Effingham Co. (1920)

Birdsville, Burke Co. (1881)

Birdville, Burke Co. (1894)

Birmingham, Milton (Fulton) Co. (1920)

Birmont, Fulton Co. (1920)

Bishop, Oconee Co. (1920)

Bissel, Pulaski Co. (1894)

Black, Bulloch Co. (1920)

Black Creek, Screven Co. (1881)

Black Jack, Talbot Co. (1920)

Black Point, Camden Co. (1847)

Blacks, Upson Co. (1920)

Blacksboro, Upson Co. (1962)

Blackshear, Pierce Co. (1920)

Blackshear Place, Hall Co. (1962)

Blackshears Mill, Laurens Co. (1881)

Black Spring, Baldwin Co. (1881)

Blacks Switch, Habersham Co. (1962)

Blacksville, Henry Co. (1962)

Blacksville, Treutlen Co. (1920)

Blackville, Habersham Co. (1894)

Blackwells, Cobb Co. (1920)

Blackwood, Gordon Co. (1962)

Bladen, Glynn Co. (1920)

Bladen, Stewart Co. (1881)

Bladen Creek, Stewart Co. (1859)

Blaine, Habersham Co. (1894)

Blaine, Pickens Co. (1920)

Blairs Trap Shoal, Lee Co. (1847)

Blairsville, Union Co. (1920)

Blair Village, Fulton Co. (1962)

Blakely, Early Co. (1920)

Blalock, Fayette Co. (1894)

Blalock, Rabun Co. (1920; also known as Persimmon (1962).

Blanchard, Muscogee Co. (1881)

Blanche, Cobb Co. (1920)

Bland, Bulloch Co. (1962)

Blanford, Effingham Co. (1920)

Bland Villa, Crisp Co. (1962)

Blandy, Baldwin Co. (1962)

Blanton, Lowndes Co. (1920)

Blarney, Appling Co. (1920)

Blassingame, Colquitt Co. (1920)

Bliss, Bulloch Co. (1894)

Bliss, Jenkins Co. (1920)

Blitch, Bulloch Co. (1920)

Blitchton, Bryan Co. (1920)

Blocker, Long Co. (1920)

Bloodworth, Wilkinson Co. (1920)

Bloom, Decatur Co. (1894)

Bloomfield, Bibb Co. (1962); part of Macon.

Bloomfield, Worth Co. (1859)

Bloomfield Gardens, Bibb Co. (1962); part of Macon.

Bloomingdale, Chatham Co. (1920)

Blossom, Rockdale Co. (1920)

Blount, Monroe Co. (1920)

Blountsville, Jones Co. (1881)

Blowing Cave, Decatur Co. (1847)

Blowing Spring, Walker Co. (1894)

Blowing Springs, Walker Co. (1962)

Bloys, Bulloch Co. (1920)

Blue Creek, Habersham Co. (1859)

Blue Creek, White Co. (1881)

Blue Ridge, Fannin Co. (1920)

Blue Ridge, Gilmer Co. (1859)

Blue Spring, Baker Co. (1847)

Blue Spring, Dougherty Co. (1870)

Blue Spring, Gordon Co. (1881); also known as Millers and Millers Station.

Blue Spring, Morgan Co. (1847)

Blue Springs, Dougherty Co. (1894)

Blue Springs, Morgan Co. (1894)

Blue Water, Laurens Co. (1881); also known as Reedy Springs.

Blueville, Marion Co. (1920)

Bluff, Gordon Co. (1920)

Bluff Spring, Talbot Co. (1847)

Bluffton, Butts Co. (1894)

Bluffton, Clay Co. (1920)

Blun, Emanuel Co. (1920)

Blundale, Emanuel Co. (1920)

Blystone, Coffee Co. (1920)

Blythe, Richmond Co. (1920)

Blythe Station, Burke Co. (1894)

Boardtown, Gilmer Co. (1881); also known as Santa Luca and Burkhorn.

Boardtree, Cherokee Co. (1881)

Boaz, Appling Co. (1920)

Bob Lee, Newton Co. (1894)

Bobo, Oconee Co. (1894)

Bochee, Bartow Co. (1920)

Bodine, Bibb Co. (1920)

Bogart, Oconee Co. (1920)

Bogerville, Jasper Co. (1894)

Boggs, Madison Co. (1920)

Bohannon, Echols Co. (1920)

Cohler, Columbia Co. (1920)

Bohrman, Colquitt Co. (1920)

Boito, Taylor Co. (1920)

Boldspring, Franklin Co. (1920)

Bold Spring, Walton Co. (1962)

Bolen, Ware Co. (1920)

Boling, Cherokee Co. (1894)

Bolingbroke, Monroe Co. (1920); also known as Colaparche (1881).

Bolivar, Bartow Co. (1920)

Boliver, Bartow Co. (1894)

Boliver, Wilkes Co. (1894)

Bolton, Fulton Co. (1920); also known as Boltonville and Fulton (1881).

Boltonville, Fulton Co. (1881); also known as Fulton; R.R. name is Bolton (1881).

Bona Bella, Chatham Co. (1962)

Bonaire, Houston Co. (1920)

Bonami, Hart Co. (1894)

Bonaventure, Chatham Co. (1847)

Bonaventure, Glynn Co. (1847)

Bond, Bibb Co. (1920)

Bond, Clayton Co. (1894)

Bonds, Crawford Co. (1920)

Bonds, Twiggs Co. (1962)

Bonds Mill, Lee Co. (1847)

Bonds Mills, Baker Co. (1859)

Bonds Mills, Twiggs Co. (1881)

Bone, Floyd Co. (1962)

Boneville, McDuffie Co. (1920)

Bonner, Carroll Co. (1894)

Bonners Mine, Carroll Co. (1881)

Bonnie, Fannin Co. (1920)

Bonny Doon, Jefferson Co. (1881)

Bonnyman, Pierce Co. (1920)

Boody, Floyd Co. (1920)

Bookersville, Wilkes Co. (1881)

Booth, Grady Co. (1920)

Booth, Jackson Co. (1894)

Bostick, Jefferson Co. (1881)

Bostick, Talbot Co. (1881)

Boston, Screven Co. (1881)

Boston, Thomas Co. (1920)

Bostwick, Morgan Co. (1920)

Botan, Houston Co. (1920)

Botsford, Sumter Co. (1881)

Bourne, Chatham Co. (1920)

Bowater, Meriwether Co. (1962)

Bowden, Carroll Co. (1920)

Bowdon Junction, Carroll Co. (1920)

Bowdre, Hall Co. (1881); formerly known as Lomonville.

Bowens Mill, Wilcox Co. (1881); also known as House Creek.

Bowens Mill, Ben Hill Co. (1920)

Bowenville, Carroll Co. (1881)

Bowenville, Irwin Co. (1847)

Bowenville, Wilcox Co. (1870)

Bower, Decatur Co. (1920)

Bowers, Crawford Co. (1894)

Bowersville, Franklin Co. (1859)

Bowersville, Hart Co. (1920)

Bowles Place, Richmond Co. (1962); part of Augusta.

Bowling, Oglethorpe Co. (1920)

Bowling Green, Oglethorpe Co. (1881)

Bowls, Gordon Co. (1894)

Bowman, Elbert Co. (1920)

Box Spring, Muscogee Co. (1870)

Boxspring, Talbot Co. (1920); also spelled Box Springs (1962).

Box Springs, Talbot Co. (1962); also spelled Boxspring (1920)

Boxville, Montgomery Co. (1847)

Boxwood, Wilkinson Co. (1920)

Boyd, Screven Co. (1920)

Boydville, Grady Co. (1920)

Boyettville, Decatur Co. (1894)

Boyettville, Seminole Co. (1920)

Boykin, Miller Co. (1920); R.R. name is Babcock Station.

Boynton, Catoosa Co. (1920)

Boys Estate, Glynn Co. (1962)

Bracksboro, Echols Co. (1894)

Braden, Gwinnett Co. (1920)

Bradley, Jones Co. (1920)

Bradleys, Tattnall Co. (1920)

Brady, Burke Co. (1881)

Brag, Bulloch Co. (1920)

Braganza, Ware Co. (1920)

Bramblett, Rabun Co. (1894)

Bran, DeKalb Co. (1920)

Branch, Paulding Co. (1881)

Branchville, Laurens Co. (1894)

Branchville, Mitchell Co. (1920)

Brandon, Walton Co. (1894)

Branhams Store, Bulloch Co. (1870)

Brannons, Cherokee Co. (1920)

Brantley, Marion Co. (1920)

Braselton, Jackson Co. (1920)

Brasstown, Towns Co. (1881)

Brasstown, Union Co. (1859)

Braswell, Paulding Co. (1920)

Brayton, Floyd Co. (1920)

Bremen, Haralson Co. (1920)

Brent, Monroe Co. (1920)

Brentwood, Wayne Co. (1920)

Brest, Mitchell Co. (1920)

Brewer, Effingham Co. (1881); also known as Browns.

Brewer, Long Co. (1920)

Brewers, Polk Co. (1894)

Brewton, Laurens Co. (1920)

Brewtons Mill, Tattnall Co. (1870)

Brewtons Mills, Tattnall Co. (1870)

Brice, Floyd Co. (1920)

Briceville, Floyd Co. (1894)

Brickstone, McIntosh Co. (1920)

Brick Store, Newton Co. (1881)

Brick Yard, Floyd Co. (1894)

Bridge, Emanuel Co. (1894)

Bridge, Treutlen Co. (1920)

Bridgeboro, Worth Co. (1920)

Bridges, Spalding Co. (1920)

Bridgetown, Coffee Co. (1894)

Brier Creek, Screven Co. (1881); also known as Bazemore.

Brierwood Estates, Cobb Co. (1962)

Briggston, Lowndes Co. (1920)

Bright, Dawson Co. (1920)

Bright Star, Douglas Co. (1881)

Brighton, Douglas Co. (1920)

Brighton, Tift Co. (1920)

Brighton Mills, Monroe Co. (1962)

Brinson, Decatur Co. (1920)

Brinsonville, Burke Co. (1881); also known as Cushingville.

Brinsonville, Jenkins Co. (1920)

Brisbron, Irwin Co. (1920)

Briscoe, Floyd Co. (1920)

Bristan, Coffee Co. (1920)

Bristol, Pierce Co. (1920)

Broad, Wilkes Co. (1920)

Broadfield, Glynn Co. (1920); P.O. name is Evelyn.

Broadhurst, Wayne Co. (1920)

Broad River, Elbert Co. (1881)

Broadtree, Cherokee Co. (1894)

Brobston, Glynn Co. (1920)

Brobston, Morgan Co. (1894)

Brock, Haralson Co. (1894)

Brockton, Jackson Co. (1962)

Brogdon, Fayette Co. (1920)

Broken Arrow, Walton Co. (1881)

Bromley, Toombs Co. (1920)

Bronco, Walker Co. (1920)

Bronwood, Terrell Co. (1920)

Brooker, Coffee Co. (1894)

Brooker, Jeff Davis Co. (1920)

Brookfield, Berrien Co. (1881)

Brookfield, Tift Co. (1920)

Brookhaven, DeKalb Co. (1962)

Brookhaven, Muscogee Co. (1962); part of Columbus.

Brookland, Evans Co. (1920)

Brooklet, Bulloch Co. (1920)

Brookline, Madison Co. (1881)

Brooklyn, Stewart Co. (1920)

Brookman, Glynn Co. (1920)

Brookmont, Cobb Co. (1920)

Brooks, Fayette Co. (1920); also known as Brooks Station and Goodson (1881).

Brooks, Worth Co. (1859)

Brooks Crossing, Clarke Co. (1962)

Brooks Station, Fayette Co. (1881); also known as Brooks (1920) and Goodson (1881).

Brooksville, Fayette Co. (1894)

Brooksville, Randolph Co. (1962); also spelled Brookville (1881).

Brookton, Hall Co. (1920)

Brookton, Jackson Co. (1920)

Brookville, Randolph Co. (1881); also spelled Brooksville (1962).

Brookville, Worth Co. (1881)

Brookwood, Fulton Co. (1962)

Broom, Polk Co. (1894)

Broomtown, Chattooga Co. (1881)

Broughton, Jasper Co. (1920)

Broughton, Morgan Co. (1894)

Broughtonville, Morgan Co. (1894)

Bowndale, Pulaski Co. (1920)

Browning, Polk Co. (1894)

Browning, Wilcox Co. (1920)

Brownlee, Grady Co. (1962)

Browns, Baldwin Co. (1962)

Browns, Bartow Co. (1920)

Browns, Cobb Co. (1859)

Browns, Effingham Co. (1881); also known as Brewer.

Browns, Henry Co. (1894)

Browns, Terrell Co. (1881); R.R. name for Powers.

Brown's Bridge, Forsyth Co. (1894)

Browns Crossing, Baldwin Co. (1920)

Browns Lane, Macon Co. (1881); also known as Marthasville.

Browns Mill, Terrell Co. (1870)

Brownsville, Paulding Co. (1920)

Browntown, Brantley Co. (1920)

Brownwood, Morgan Co. (1962)

Brownwood University, Troup Co. (1847)

Broxton, Coffee Co. (1920)

Bruce, Montgomery Co. (1894)

Bruce, Wheeler Co. (1920)

Brumby, Walker Co. (1920)

Brundage, Jones Co. (1920)

Brunswick, Glynn Co. (1920)

Brunswick and Western Junction, Dougherty Co. (1894)

Brushy, Spalding Co. (1920)

Brushy Creek, Burke Co. (1920)

Bruton, Laurens Co. (1894)

Brutus, Laurens Co. (1894)

Bryan, Bryan Co. (1881); another name for Eden.

Bryan, Gwinnett Co. (1894)

Bryant, Fannin Co. (1894)

Bryants White Bluff, Pulaski Co. (1870)

Bryantville, Cobb Co. (1894)

Buchalters, Floyd Co. (1920)

Buchanan, Fulton Co. (1894)

Buchanan, Haralson Co. (1920)

Buchanan, Talbot Co. (1847)

Buck, Coweta Co. (1920)

Buckcreek, Screven Co. (1920); also spelled Buck Creek (1859).

Buck Eye, Laurens Co. (1859)

Buckhead, Fulton Co. (1962); part of Atlanta.

Buckhead, Morgan Co. (1920)

Buckhorn, Gilmer Co. (1881); also known as Santa Luca and Boardtown.

Buckhorn, Laurens Co. (1920)

Buckingham, Carroll Co. (1920)

Buck's Still, Wayne Co. (1894)

Bud, Paulding Co. (1920)

Budapest, Haralson Co. (1962)

Budville, Cherokee Co. (1894)

Buena Vista, Marion Co. (1920)

Buff, Gordon Co. (1894)

Buffalo, Carroll Co. (1859)

Buffalo, Hart Co. (1920)

Buffalo, Wayne Co. (1881); P.O. name is Mount Pleasant.

Buffington, Cherokee Co. (1920)

Buford, Gwinnett Co. (1920)

Buford, Randolph Co. (1870)

Bulah, Hancock Co. (1881)

Bullards, Twiggs Co. (1920)

Bull Creek, Screven Co. (1859)

Bull Creek, Tattnall Co. (1881)

Bullhead Bluff, Camden Co. (1847)

Bullinger, Candler Co. (1920)

Bullochville, Meriwether Co. (1920)

Bull Sluice, Columbia Co. (1847)

Bulo, Cherokee Co. (1881)

Bunkley, Camden Co. (1894)

Burbages Mill, Pierce Co. (1881)

Burch, Charlton Co. (1920)

Buren, Union Co. (1920)

Burke, Burke Co. (1894)

Burke, Lee Co. (1894)

Burketts, Bibb Co. (1920)

Burlington, Union Co. (1920)

Burnet, Glynn Co. (1847)

Burnett, Gilmer Co. (1920)

Burnett, Wayne Co. (1920)

Burney Hill, Colquitt Co. (1920)

Burney Hill, Cook Co. (1962)

Burns, Twiggs Co. (1894)

Burnside, Chatham Co. (1962)

Burnt Fort, Camden Co. (1920)

Burnt Hickory, Douglas Co. (1920)

Burnt Mountain, Pickens Co. (1881)

Burnt Stand, Carroll Co. (1859)

Burnt Stand, Haralson Co. (1894)

Burrell, Burke Co. (1881)

Burrell, Ware Co. (1859)

Burroughs, Chatham Co. (1920)

Burton, Burke Co. (1881); another name for Midville.

Burton, Jefferson Co. (1894)

Burton, Rabun Co. (1920); also known as Powellsville (1881).

Burtsboro, Lumpkin Co. (1920)

Burwell, Carroll Co. (1920)

Busbayville, Houston Co. (1881)

Busby, Lincoln Co. (1894)

Busbyville, Houston Co. (1894)

Bush, Wilcox Co. (1920)

Bushboro, Pulaski Co. (1894)

Bushnell, Coffee Co. (1920)

Bushville, Banks Co. (1920)

Bushville, Franklin Co. (1859)

Bussey, Lincoln Co. (1920)

Bussey, Meriwether Co. (1894)

Busseys Store, Chattahoochee Co. (1920)

Butler, Cobb Co. (1920)

Butler, Taylor Co. (1920)

Butts, Emanuel Co. (1894)

Butts, Jenkins Co. (1920)

Buzzard Roost, Twiggs Co. (1881)

Byers Crossroads, Carroll Co. (1962)

Bynum, Union Co. (1920)

Bynum, Bacon Co. (1920)

Byrd, Floyd Co. (1920)

Byrds Mill, Coffee Co. (1881); also known as Durhams Mills.

Byrds Spur, Harris Co. (1920)

Byromville, Dooly Co. (1920)

Byron, Baker Co. (1847)

Byron, Dougherty Co. (1870)

Byron, Houston Co. (1920); also known as Jackson (1881).

Byron, Peach Co. (1962)

Cabaniss, Monroe Co. (1894)

Cabbage Bluff, Glynn Co. (1847)

Cabin Bluff, Camden Co. (1881)

Cabiniss, Monroe Co. (1920); also known as Gullettsville (1881).

Cad, Fannin Co. (1920)

Cadiz, Franklin Co. (1920)

Cadley, Warren Co. (1920)

Cadwell, Laurens Co. (1920)

Cage, Webster Co. (1920)

Cagle, Paulding Co. (1920)

Cains, Gwinnett Co. (1920); another name for Hog Mountain (1881).

Cairo, Decatur Co. (1847)

Cairo, Grady Co. (1920)

Cairo, Thomas Co. (1894)

Caldwell, Floyd Co. (1894)

Caldwell, Union Co. (1920)

Caldwell, Wilkes Co. (1881)

Caleb, Gwinnett Co. (1920)

Calhoun, Gordon Co. (1920)

Calhoun, Lumpkin Co. (1847)

Calhouns Mills, Montgomery Co. (1870)

Cailie, Bulloch Co. (1920)

Callafield, Early Co. (1920)

Callaway, Mitchell Co. (1870)

Calvary, Decatur Co. (1894)

Calvary, Grady Co. (1920)

Calvin, Jasper Co. (1920)

Camak, Warren Co. (1920)

Camden, Camden Co. (1894)

Cameo, Meriwether Co. (1920)

Cameron, Screven Co. (1920)

Camerons Mill, Telfair Co. (1881); another name for Cobbville.

Camilla, Mitchell Co. (1920)

Campagne, Towns Co. (1920)

Campania, Columbia Co. (1920)

Campbell, Jones Co. (1920)

Campbell Factory, Campbell (Fulton) Co. (1870)

Campbellton, Campbell (Fulton) Co. (1920)

Camp Benning, Chattahoochee Co. (1920)

Campcreek, Union Co. (1920); also spelled Camp Creek (1894).

Camp Gordon. Was prior name for Fort Gordon, located in Richmond, Columbia, McDuffie, and Jefferson Cos. (1962).

Camp Ground, Greene Co. (1847)

Camp Ground, Hancock Co. (1847)

Camp Hope, Bibb Co. (1847)

Camp Mills, Gwinnett Co. (1881)

Camp Pinkney, Camden Co. (1847)

Camp Pinkney, Charlton Co. (1881)

Camps, Telfair Co. (1920)

Camps, Walton Co. (1894)

Camp Stewart. Was prior name for Fort Stewart, located in Liberty, Bryan, Evans, Long, and Tattnall Cos. (1962).

Campton, Walton Co. (1920)

Campus, Clarke Co. (1962); part of Athens.

Camp Yonah, Stephens Co. (1920)

Candler, Hall Co. (1920)

Candy, Oconee Co. (1920)

Canecreek, Lumpkin Co. (1920)

Cane Creek, Meriwether Co. (1870)

Cane Creek, Walker Co. (1859)

Cane Point, Troup Co. (1847)

Caney Bay, Pierce Co. (1881)

Cannonville, Troup Co. (1920)

Canoe, Candler Co. (1920)

Canon, Franklin Co. (1920)

Canoochee, Emanuel Co. (1920)

Canoochee Station, Emanuel Co. (1894)

Cannons Point, Blynn Co. (1847)

Canton, Cherokee Co. (1920)

Canton Copper Mines, Cherokee Co. (1894)

Cap, Irwin Co. (1894)

Capel, Grady Co. (1920)

Capron, Dooly Co. (1920)

Capstan, Heard Co. (1920)

Captolo, Screven Co. (1920)

Carbondale, Whitfield Co. (1920); R.R. name is Barnetts (1881), also known as Cove City (1881).

Cardsville, Jones Co. (1881); also spelled Cardville (1920)

Cardville, Jones Co. (1920); also spelled Cardsville (1881).

Carey, Greene Co. (1920)

Carithers Mill, Walton Co. (1962)

Carl, Barrow Co. (1920)

Carl, Gwinnett Co. (1894)

Carlan, Banks Co. (1920)

Carlisle, Gilmer Co. (1894)

Carlos, Bulloch Co. (1894)

Carlton, Madison Co. (1920); R.R. name is Berkley.

Carlyle, Hancock Co. (1920)

Carmel, Meriwether Co. (1920)

Carmel Junction, Newton Co. (1894)

Carmichael, Cobb Co. (1962)

Carne, Dodge Co. (1894)

Carnegie, Randolph Co. (1920)

Carnesville, Franklin Co. (1920)

Carnigan, McIntosh Co. (1962)

Carnot, Banks Co. (1920)

Carns Mill, Pickens Co. (1920); P.O. name is Keasley.

Carolina, Gwinnett Co. (1962)

Caroline, Marion Co. (1920)

Caroline Park, Muscogee Co. (1962); part of Columbus.

Carroll, Douglas Co. (1920)

Carrolls, Newton Co. (1894)

Carrollton, Carroll Co. (1920)

Carrs, Hancock Co. (1962); also known as Carrs Station (1920)

Carrs Station, Hancock Co. (1920); also known as Carrs (1962).

Carruth, Madison Co. (1920)

Carse of Cowrie, Glynn Co. (1847)

Carsonville, Talbot Co. (1847)

Carsonville, Taylor Co. (1920)

Carswell, Jefferson Co. (1920)

Cartecay, Gilmer Co. (1920)

Carter Acres, Muscogee Co. (1962); part of Columbus.

Carter Bridge, Clinch Co. (1881)

Carterets Point, Glynn Co. (1847)

Carters, Murray Co. (1920)

Carters, Stewart Co. (1920)

Carters Grove, Taliaferro Co. (1962)

Carters Mill, Appling Co. (1881)

Carters Ridge, Clinch Co. (1859)

Cartersville, Bartow Co. (1920)

Carticay, Gilmer Co. (1859)

Caruso, Spalding Co. (1962)

Caruthers Mill, Walton Co. (1962)

Carver Village, Chatham Co. (1962); part of Savannah.

Cary, Bleckley Co. (1920)

Cary, Pulaski Co. (1894)

Cascade, Fulton Co. (1920)

Cascade Heights, Fulton Co. (1962); part of Atlanta.

Cascade Hills, Muscogee Co. (1962); part of Columbus.

Cash, Gordon Co. (1920)

Cason, Wilcox Co. (1881)

Cass, Bartow Co. (1962)

Cassandra, Walker Co. (1920)

Cass Station, Bartow Co. (1920)

Cassville, Bartow Co. (1920)

Castle Park, Lowndes Co. (1962); part of Valdosta.

Cataula, Harris Co. (1920)

Cat Creek, Lowndes Co. (1920)

Cater, Glynn Co. (1847)

Cates, Brooks Co. (1920)

Cathey, Floyd Co. (1894)

Catie, Carroll Co. (1894)

Catlett, Walker Co. (1962)

Catlin, Laurens Co. (1920)

Catoosa, Catoosa Co. (1881); P.O. name is Catoosa Springs.

Catoosa, Dawson Co. (1870)

Catoosa Platform, Catoosa Co. (1870)

Catoosa Springs, Catoosa Co. (1881); R.R. name is Catoosa.

Catoosa Springs, Walker Co. (1859)

Caustons Bluff, Chatham Co. (1847)

Cauthan, Elbert Co. (1920)

Cauthen, Elbert Co. (1962)

Cave, Bartow Co. (1920); R.R. name is Bests.

Cavenda, Lumpkin Co. (1894)

Cavender, Lumpkin Co. (1881)

Cave Spring, Floyd Co. (1920)

Cawthon, Greene Co. (1920)

Cawthon, Hancock Co. (1881)

Cecil, Berrien Co. (1894)

Cecil, Cook Co. (1920)

Cedar Branch, Campbell (Fulton) Co. (1859)

Cedar Creek, Tattnall Co. (1881)

Cedar Crossing, Toombs Co. (1962)

Cedar Grove, Walker Co. (1920)

Cedar Hill, Dooly Co. (1847)

Cedar Hill, Gwinnett Co. (1881)

Cedar Hill, Johnson Co. (1881)

Cedar Park, Talfair Co. (1894)

Cedarridge, Whitfield Co. (1920)

Cedar Rock, Warren Co. (1962)

Cedar Rock Academy, Meriwether Co. (1870)

Cedar Shoal, Newton Co. (1881)

Cedar Shoal Factory, Newton Co. (1847)

Cedar Springs, Early Co. (1920)

Cedartown, Paulding Co. (1847)

Cedartown, Polk Co. (1920)

Cedar Valley, Paulding Co. (1847)

Cedar Valley, Polk Co. (1881)

Celanese Village, Floyd Co. (1962)

Celeste, Wilkes Co. (1920)

Cement, Bartow Co. (1920)

Cenchat, Walker Co. (1920)

Cenoby, Fulaske Co. (1920)

Centaur, Bibb Co. (1962)

Centennial, Morgan Co. (1962)

Center, Decatur Co. (1894)

Center, Heard Co. (1894)

Center, Jackson Co. (1920); also known as Bascobel and also spelled Centre (1881).

Center, Talbot Co. (1894)

Center Hill, Fulton Co. (1962); part of Atlanta.

Center Point, Carroll Co. (1962)

Centerpost, Walker Co. (1920)

Centerside, White Co. (1894)

Center Valley, Murray Co. (1894)

Center Village, Charlton Co. (1894)

Center Village, Jackson Co. (1870)

Centerville, Houston Co. (1962)

Centerville, Gwinnett Co. (1920); also spelled Centreville (1881)

Centerville, Talbot Co. (1962)

Centralhatchee, Heard Co. (1920)

Central Junction, Bibb Co. (1894)

Central Junction, Chatham Co. (1920)

Central Point, Carroll Co. (1859)

Central Railroad Junction, Bibb Co. (1920; another name for Macon Junction).

Central Springs, Chattahoochee Co. (1962)

Centre, Jackson Co. (1881); also spelled Center (1920) and also known as Bascobel (1881).

Centre, Talbot Co. (1881)

Centre Valley, Murray Co. (1881)

Centre Village, Charlton Co. (1881)

Centerville, Gwinnett Co. (1881); also spelled Centerville (1920).

Centreville, Wilkes Co. (1859)

Century, Lee Co. (1920)

Ceres, Crawford Co. (1920)

Cerlastae, Columbia Co. (1920)

Ceylon, Camden Co. (1920)

Chalk Cut, Bibb Co. (1894)

Chalker, Washington Co. (1920)

Chalybeate, Meriwether Co. (1920); also known as Chalybeate Springs (1881 & 1962).

Chalybeate Springs, Meriwether Co. (1962); also known as Chalybeate (1920).

Chamberlain, Walker Co. (1962)

Chambers, Floyd Co. (1920)

Chambell, DeKalb Co. (1920)

Chambliss, Sumter Co. (1962)

Chambliss, Terrell Co. (1962)

Chambliss, Webster Co. (1920)

Chance, Houston Co. (1920)

Chanceville, Carroll Co. (1859)

Chapelhill, Campbell Co. (1859)

Chapelhill, Douglas Co. (1920); also spelled Chapel Hill (1881) and also known as Holly Springs (1881).

Chapman, Lowndes Co. (1920)

Chappel, Lamar Co. (1920)

Chappel, Monroe Co. (1894)

Charing, Taylor Co. (1920)

Charles, Stewart Co. (1920)

Charles, Toombs Co. (1962)

Charlotte, Montgomery Co. (1920); R.R. name is Charlottesville.

Charlotte, Union Co. (1920)

Charlottesville, Montgomery Co. (1920); R.R. name for Charlotte.

Charlton, Charlton Co. (1920)

Charme, Cherokee Co. (1920)

Chaseville, Gordon Co. (1881)

Chaseville, Murray Co. (1859)

Chastain, Thomas Co. (1920)

Chatfield, Wilkes Co. (1920)

Chatham, Chatham Co. (1920)

Chatham City, Chatham Co. (1962); part of Garden City.

Chatillon, Floyd Co. (1962)

Chatsworth, Murray Co. (120)

Chattahoochee, Fulton Co. (1920)

Chattahoochee, Muscogee Co. (1920)

Chatterton, Coffee Co. (1920)

Chattoogaville, Chattooga Co. (1920)

Chauncey, Dodge Co. (1920)

Chauncey, Pulaski Co. (1920)

Cheap, Banks Co. (1920)

Cheatham, Jones Co. (1920)

Chechero, Rabun Co. (1920)

Cheeck, Cook Co. (1920)

Cheese, Columbia Co. (1894)

Cheevertown, Baker Co. (1894)

Chehaw, Lee Co. (1962)

Chelsea, Chattooga Co. (1920)

Cheney, Chattooga Co. (1894)

Chennault, Lincoln Co. (1920)

Chenuba, Lee Co. (1847)

Chenuba, Terrell Co. (1859)

Chenuva, Stewart Co. (1881)

Cherbury, DeKalb Co. (1847)

Cherbury, Fulton Co. (1870)

Cherokee, Cherokee Co. (1920)

Cherokee Corner, Oglethorpe & Clarke Cos. (1847)

Cherokee Heights, Bibb Co. (1962); part of Macon.

Cherokee Hill, Chatham Co. (1847)

Cherokee Mills, Cherokee Co. (1881)

Cherrylog, Gilmer Co. (1920); also spelled Cherry Log (1859) & also known as Whitepath (1881).

Chesnut Flat, Walker Co. (1859); also spelled Chestnutflat (1920)

Chesnut Gap, Gilmer Co. (1859)

Chesnut Mountain, Hall Co. (1859); also spelled Chestnut Mountain (1920)

Chestatee, Forsyth Co. (1881)

Chester, Dodge Co. (1920)

Chester, Gwinnett Co. (1881)

Chestlehurst, Fayette Co. (1920)

Chestnutflat, Walker Co. (1920); also spelled Chesnut Flat (1859).

Chestnutgap, Fannin Co. (1920); also spelled Chestnut Gap (1870).

Chestnut Grove, Hancock Co. (1847)

Chestnut Hill, Hall Co. (1847)

Chestnut Mountain, Hall Co. (1920); also spelled Chesnut Mountain (1859).

Chicasawhatchee, Terrell Co. (1881); also spelled Chickasawhatchee (1962).

Chickamauga, Walker Co. (1920)

Chickamauga Battle Field, Walker Co. (1894)

Chickapin Grove, Gwinnett Co. (1859); also spelled Chincapin Grove (1881).

Chickawawhatchee, Terrell Co. (1962); also spelled Chicasawhatchee (1920).

Chickasawhatchie, Lee Co. (1859)

Chicopee, Hall Co. (1962)

Childs, Henry Co. (1920)

Childsville, Franklin Co. (1881)

Childsville, Hart Co. (1894)

Chinahill, Telfiar Co. (1920)

Chincapin Grove, Gwinnett Co. (1881); also spelled Chickapin Grove (1859).

Chipeta, Fannin Co. (1920)

Chipley, Harris Co. (1920); also known as Goodmans Cross Roads (1881); name changed to Pine Mountain in 1950 (1962).

Chippewa Terrace, Chatham Co. (1962); part of Savannah.

Chiversville, Washington Co. (1894)

Choestoe, Union Co. (1920)

Choice, Gwinnett Co. (1881)

Chokee, Lee Co. (1920)

Chopped Oak School House, Gilmer Co. (1920)

Christian, Echols Co. (1920)

Christopher, Chattahoochee Co. (1920)

Christopher, Union Co. (1920)

Chubbtown, Floyd Co. (1920)

Chula, Irwin Co. (1894)

Chula, Tift Co. (1920)

Chulio, Floyd Co. (1920)

Church, White Co. (1920)

Church Hill, Marion Co. (1870)

Church Hill, Webster Co. (1894)

Cicada, Cobb Co. (1894)

Cisco, Murray Co. (1920)

City Village, Muscogee Co. (1962); part of Columbus.

Clara, Fulton Co. (1894)

Clare, Screven Co. (1920)

Clarence, Terrell Co. (1920)

Clark, Bulloch Co. (1894)

Clark, Hall Co. (1920)

Clarksdale, Cobb Co. (1962)

Clarkesville, Habersham Co. (1920); another spelling of Clarksville (1962).

Clarkesville Station, Habersham Co. (1920)

Clarking, Charlton Co. (1920)

Clarks Battle Ground, Walton Co. (1847)

Clarks Bluff, Glynn Co. (1847)

Clarksboro, Jackson Co. (1920)

Clarks Mill, Crawford Co. (1881)

Clarkston, DeKalb Co. (1920)

Clarksville, Habersham Co. (1962); another spelling for Clarkesville (1920)

Claud, Houston Co. (1920)

Claude, Washington Co. (1894)

Claxton, Evans Co. (1920)

Clay, Lincoln Co. (1894)

Claybed, Houston Co. (1962)

Clayhill, Lincoln Co. (1920); also spelled Clay Hill (1859).

Claymont, Wilkinson Co. (1920)

Clayton, Rabun Co. (1920)

Claytonville, Dougherty Co. (1894)

Clayville, Rabun Co. (1920)

Clearview, Chatham Co. (1962); part of Savannah.

Cleaton, Walton Co. (1962)

Cleburn, Fulton Co. (1894)

Cleburne, Fulton Co. (1920)

Cleghorn, Muscogee Co. (1881)

Clem, Carroll Co. (1920)

Clements, Catoosa Co. (1894)

Clementsville, Worth Co. (1881)

Clemeth, Union Co. (1881)

Cleola, Harris Co. (1920); R.R. name is Oak Mountain.

Cleone, Macon Co. (1894)

Clermont, Hall Co. (1920)

Cleveland, White Co. (1920); also known as Yonah (1881) and Mount Yonah (1881).

Cleveland, Meriwether Co. (1847)

Clifford, Bartow Co. (1920)

Clifford, McDuffie Co. (1920)

Clifton, Chatham Co. (1894)

Clifton, Bryan Co. (1920)

Clifton, DeKalb Co. (1920)

Clifton, Tattnall Co. (1894)

Clifton Mills, Miller Co. (1881)

Climax, Decatur Co. (1920)

Clinch, Hall Co. (1920)

Clinchem, Hall Co. (1881)

Clinchfield, Houston Co. (1962)

Clinch Haven, Clinch Co. (1894)

Cling, Appling Co. (1894)

Clinton, Jones Co. (1920)

Clinton Station, Jones Co. (1870)

Clipper, Pickens Co. (1920)

Clito, Bulloch Co. (1920)

Clock, Wayne Co. (1894)

Clopine, Peach Co. (1962)

Clopton, Putnam Co. (1920); also known as Cloptons Mills (1881).

Cloptons Mills, Putnam Co. (1881); also known as Clopton (1920).

Cloudland, Chattooga Co. (1920)

Clover, Fayette Co. (1962)

Cloverdale, Dade Co. (1881)

Cloverdell, Clayton Co. (1920)

Clubview Heights, Muscogee Co. (1962); part of Columbus.

Cluese, Columbia Co. (1920)

Clyatt Corner, Brooks Co. (1920)

Clyatteville, Lowndes Co. (1962); another spelling of Clyattville (1920).

Clyatts, Coffee Co. (1920)

Clyattville, Lowndes Co. (1920); also spelled Clyatteville (1962).

Clyde, Bryan Co. (1920)

Clyo, Effingham Co. (1920)

Coal Mountain, Forsyth Co. (1920)

Coal Spring, Wilkinson Co. (1881)

Coastline, Clinch Co. (1920)

Coates, Pulaski Co. (1920)

Cobb, Sumter Co. (1920)

Cobb, Carroll Co. (1920)

Cobbham, McDuffie Co. (1920)

Cobb's Creek, Tattnall Co. (1894)

Cobbtown, Tattnall Co. (1920)

Cobbville, Telfair Co. (1920); also known as Camerons Mill (1881).

Cochran, Pulaski Co. (1870)

Cochran, Bleckley Co. (1920); formerly known as Dykesboro (1881).

Cochran Field, Bibb Co. (1962)

Cochrans Cross Roads, Harris Co. (1847)

Cochran's Mills, Mitchell Co. (1894)

Coe, Tattnall Co. (1920)

Coffee, Bacon Co. (1920)

Coffee, Pierce Co. (1894)

Coffee Bluff, Chatham Co. (1962)

Coffinton, Stewart Co. (1920)

Cogburn, Dawson Co. (1920)

Cogdell, Clinch Co. (1920)

Cohutta, Whitfield Co. (1920)

Cohutta Springs, Murray Co. (1920)

Coker, Milton (Fulton) Co. (1920)

Colaparche, Monroe Co. (1881); another name for Bolingbroke (1881).

Colbert, Madison Co. (1920)

Coldbrook, Chatham Co. (1920)

Cold Spring, Meriwether Co. (1847)

Cold Watch, Elbert Co. (1859)

Coldwater, Elbert Co. (1920)

Cole, Paulding Co. (1920)

Cole, Terrell Co. (1894)

Cole City, Dade Co. (1920)

Coleman, Hancock Co. (1920)

Coleman, Randolph Co. (1920)

Colemans Depot, Randolph Co. (1881)

Colemans Lake, Emanuel Co. (1962)

Colerain, Camden Co. (1847)

Colerain, Chatham Co. (1847)

Colerain, Walker Co. (1920)

Coles, Randolph Co. (1920)

Colesburg, Camden Co. (1920)

Coles Crossing, Fannin Co. (1920); P.O. name is Cutcane.

Colespur, Emanuel Co. (1920)

Coley, Pulaski Co. (1881); R.R. name for Longstreet; also known as Coleys Station.

Coleys Station, Pulaski Co. (1881); another name for Coley.

Colfax, Bulloch Co. (1920)

Colfax, Marion Co. (1894)

Colgans Still, Ware Co. (1920)

Colhords Mill, Pierce Co. (1881); also known as Exeter.

Colima, Gordon Co. (1920)

Coll, Decatur Co. (1962)

College, Chatham Co. (1894)

College, Peach Co. (1962); part of Fort Valley.

Collegeboro, Bulloch Co. (1962); another name for Georgia Southern.

College Park, Fulton and Clayton Cos. (1920)

Collier, Monroe Co. (1894)

Colliers, Lamar Co. (1920)

Colliers, Monroe Co. (1962)

Collingsworth Institute, Talbot Co. (1847)

Collins, Tattnall Co. (1920)

Collinsville, DeKalb Co. (1962)

Colon, Clinch Co. (1920)

Colonial Place, Dougherty Co. (1962)

Colquitt, Miller Co. (1920)

Colquitt, Montgomery Co. (1847)

Colton, Mitchell Co. (1920)

Columbia Mine, Columbia Co. (1859)

Columbus, Muscogee Co. (1920)

Columbus Factory, Muscogee Co. (1881)

Colwell, Fannin Co. (1920)

Combs, Taliaferro Co. (1920)

Comer, Madison Co. (1920)

Comfort, Greene Co. (1894)

Commerce, Jackson Co. (1920)

Commissary Hill, Calhoun Co. (1920)

Commissioner, Wilkinson Co. (1881)

Commodore, Tattnall Co. (1881)

Comolli, Elbert Co. (1962)

Compton, Jasper Co. (1847)

Campton, Stewart Co. (1859)

Conap, Habersham Co. (1962)

Conasauga, Gilmer Co. (1920)

Concord, Baker Co. (1847)

Concord, Calhoun Co. (1870)

Concord, Dawson Co. (1881)

Concord, Forsyth Co. (1870)

Concord, Jasper Co. (1881)

Concord, Meriwether Co. (1870)

Concord, Pike Co. (1920)

Concord, Schley Co. (1962)

Concordia, Elbert Co. (1881)

Condor, Laurens Co. (1920)

Coney, Crisp Co. (1920)

Coinston, Murray Co. (1920)

Conkling, Hancock Co. (1920)

Conley, Clayton Co. (1920)

Conley, Tattnall Co. (1894)

Connells Mill, Berrien Co. (1881)

Connesauga, Gilmer Co. (1894)

Connesauga, Murray Co. (1881)

Constantine, Jackson Co. (1920)

Constitution, DeKalb Co. (1920)

Conyers, Rockdale Co. (1920)

Coodes, Campbell (Fulton) Co. (1920)

Coody, Dodge Co. (1894)

Coody's Landing, Chattahoochee Co. (1894)

Coogles Mill, Macon Co. (1881)

Cooks Law Office, Elbert Co. (1859)

Cooks Store, Appling Co. (1881)

Cooks Town, Wilcox Co. (1881)

Cooksville, Heard Co. (1920)

Coolidge, Thomas Co. (1920)

Cool Spring, Colquitt Co. (1962)

Coolspring, Wilkinson Co. (1920); also spelled Cool Spring (1859)

Coon Bottom, Brantley Co. (1920)

Cooper, Baldwin Co. (1962); also known as Coopers.

Cooper, Hart Co. (1920)

Cooper, Jackson Co. (1881); another name for Nicholson

Cooper Heights, Walker Co. (1920)

Coopers, Baldwin Co. (1962); also known as Cooper.

Coopers, Houston Co. (1870)

Coopers Gap, Lumpkin Co. (1881)

Coopers Spur, Baldwin Co. (1920)

Coosa, Floyd Co. (1920)

Coosa Creek Union Co. (1894); also spelled Coosacreek (1920)

Coosaville, Floyd Co. (1894)

Coosawattee, Gordon Co. (1881)

33

Coosawattee, Murray Co. (1859)

Coosawattee Old Town, Murray Co. (1847)

Copeco, Baldwin Co. (1920)

Copeland, Catoosa Co. (1920)

Copeland, Telfair Co. (1859)

Copeland, Dodge Co. (1920)

Copeland, Harris Co. (1920)

Copeland, Walker Co. (1894)

Copper Mine, Paulding Co. (1920)

Cora, Newton Co. (1920); also known as Kings (1962).

Corbetts, Colquitt Co. (1920)

Corbin, Bartow Co. (1894)

Cordele, Crisp Co. (1920)

Cordele, Dooly Co. (1894)

Cordova, Colquitt Co. (1881)

Cordray, Calhoun Co. (1920)

Corea, Early Co. (1920)

Corea, Miller Co. (1962)

Corinth, Heard Co. (1920)

Corinth, Sumter Co. (1847)

Cork, Butts Co. (1920)

Cornelia, Habersham Co. (1920)

Cornell, Fulton Co. (1920)

Cornucopia, Hancock Co. (1847)

Cornucopia, Jones Co. (1881); also known as Grab All.

Corsica, Candler Co. (1920)

Corsica, Tattnall Co. (1894)

Cortez, Wilcox Co. (1920)

Cost, Banks Co. (1894)

Costello, Walker Co. (1920)

Cottage Mill, Chattahoochee Co. (1859); also known as Cottage Mills (1920)

Cottage Mills, Chattahoochee Co. (1920); also known as Cottage Mill (1859).

Cottle, Berrien Co. (1920)

Cotton, Mitchell Co. (1920)

Cotton Bluff, Pulaski Co. (1870)

Cotton Bluff, Lee Co. (1847)

Cottondale, Terrell Co. (1920)

Cotton Hill, Clay Co. (1881)

Cotton Hill, Randolph Co. (1847)

Cotton Mill, Randolph Co. (1894)

Cotton Yard, Bibb Co. (1894)

Council, Clinch Co. (1920)

County Line, Barrow Co. (1962)

County Line, Campbell (Fulton) Co. (1859)

Countyline, Carroll Co. (1920); also spelled County Line (1894).

County Line, Stewart Co. (1962)

County Line, White Co. (1920)

County Line, Whitfield Co. (1881); also known as Red Clay and State Line.

Coupers Point, Glynn Co. (1847)

Coursey, Emanuel Co. (1894)

Courtesy, Floyd Co. (1881)

Courtney, Emanuel Co. (1920)

Cove City, Whitfield Co. (1881); P.O. name for Barnetts; also known as Carbondale.

Covena, Emanuel Co. (1920)

Coverdale, Turner Co. (1920)

Covington, Newton Co. (1920)

Covington Junction, Newton Co. (1894)

Covington Mills, Newton Co. (1920)

Cowan, Morgan Co. (1920)

Cowart, Bibb Co. (1894)

Cowarts, Early Co. (1894)

Cowart's, Emanuel Co. (1894)

Cow Creek, Clinch Co. (1859)

Cowell, Fannin Co. (1920)

Cow Pens, Walton Co. (1920); also spelled Cowpens (1847).

Cox, Dodge Co. (1894)

Cox, McIntosh Co. (1920)

Coxs Crossing, Clayton Co. (1962)

Coy, Douglas Co. (1920)

Crabapple, Milton (Fulton) Co. (1920)

Crackers Neck, Greene Co. (1847)

Crackling, Banks Co. (1881)

Craft, Cobb Co. (1920)

Craftsville, Elbert Co. (1881)

Craig, Gwinnett Co. (1920)

Crain, Heard Co. (1920)

Crandall, Murray Co. (1920)

Crane-Eater, Gordon Co. (1881)

Cravey, Telfair Co. (1920)

Crawfish, Douglas Co. (1920)

Crawfish Springs, Walker Co. (1881); also spelled Crawfish Spring (1894).

Crawford, Grady Co. (1920)

Crawford, Johnson Co. (1881)

Crawford, Oglethorpe Co. (1920); also known as Lexington Station (1881).

Crawfords, Monroe Co. (1881)

Crawfordville, Taliaferro Co. (1920)

Crawley's, Crawford Co. (1894)

Crayton, Fannin Co. (1881)

Craytonia, Fannin Co. (1920)

Creatwood, Cobb Co. (1962)

Creek Junction, Jefferson Co. (1920)

Creek Stand, Macon Co. (1859)

Creighton, Cherokee Co. (1920)

Crenshaw, Berrien Co. (1920)

Crescent, McIntosh Co. (1920)

Crest, Upson Co. (1920)

Crest View, Richmond Co. (1962)

Creswell, Spalding Co. (1881); another name for Vaughn.

Crews, Ware Co. (1920)

Cribb, Emanuel Co. (1894)

Crisp, Irwin Co. (1894)

Crispen, Glynn Co. (1847)

Crispen Island, Glynn Co. (1894)

Critic, Elbert Co. (1920)

Crochet, Meriwether Co. (1894)

Cromers, Franklin Co. (1920)

Crosby, Habersham Co. (1881)

Crosland, Colquitt Co. (1920)

Cross Anker, Campbell (Fulton) Co. (1881)

Cross Creek, Pulaski Co. (1881)

Crossing, Franklin Co. (1894)

Cross Keys, Bibb Co. (1881)

Crosskeys, DeKalb Co. (1920); also spelled Cross Keys (1881).

Crossplains, Carroll Co. (1920); also spelled Cross Plains (1894)

Cross Plains, Murray Co. (1847)

Crossroads, Hall Co. (1920)

Crossroads, Hart Co. (1962)

Crossroads, Liberty Co. (1962)

Crossville, Dawson Co. (1881)

Crossville, Lumpkin Co. (1859)

Crouch, Meriwether Co. (1920)

Crow, Whitfield Co. (1920)

Crowder, Troup Co. (1920)

Crowders Crossing, Meriwether Co. (1920)

Crow Harbor, Camden Co. (1881)

Crown Cotton Mill, Whitfield Co. (1962); part of Dalton.

Crowsville, Paulding Co. (1920)

Crump, Franklin Co. (1920)

Crumps, Bibb Co. (1920)

Cruse, Gwinnett Co. (1920)

Crutchfield, Jones Co. (1920)

Crystal Springs, Floyd Co. (1920)

Crystal Valley, Muscogee Co. (1962)

Cuba, Early Co. (1894)

Cuba, Forsyth Co. (1920)

Cubana, Thomas Co. (1894)

Culbreath, Columbia Co. (1847)

Culloden, Monroe Co. (1920)

Culloden Station, Monroe Co. (1920)

Culver, Hancock Co. (1847)

Culverton, Hancock Co. (1920)

Culverton Station, Hancock Co. (1870)

Cumberland, Camden Co. (1920)

Cumming, Forsyth Co. (1920)

Cumming, Warren Co. (1881); also known as Double Wells and Barnett.

Cumslo, Jones Co. (1920)

Cunningham, Floyd Co. (1920); P.O. name is Agate.

Cupid, Jasper Co. (1894)

Cureton, Dade Co. (1881); also known as Dademont.

Curran, Marion Co. (1920)

Curry, Wheeler Co. (1920)

Currys Mill, Glascock Co. (1881)

Currys Mills, Washington Co. (1859)

Curryville, Gordon Co. (1920)

Curtis, Carroll Co. (1881)

Curtis, Fannin Co. (1920)

Curtis, Newton Co. (1894)

Curtright, Greene Co. (1881)

Cushingville, Burke Co. (1881); also known as Brinsonville.

Cushingville, Jenkins Co. (1920)

Cusseta, Chattahoochee Co. (1920)

Custer Terrace, Muscogee Co. (1962); part of Fort Benning.

Cutcane, Fannin Co. (1920); R.R. name is Coles Crossing

Cuthbert, Randolph Co. (1920)

Cuthbert Junction, Randolph Co. (1920)

Cut Off, Walton Co. (1881)

Cutright, Greene Co. (1859)

Cutting, Clinch Co. (1920)

Cuyler, Bryan Co. (1920)

Cuyler, Effingham Co. (1894)

Cyclone, Screven Co. (1920)

Cycloneta, Irwin Co. (1894)

Cyclonetta, Tift Co. (1920)

Cypress, Pulaski Co. (1894)

Cypress Mills, Glynn Co. (1962)

Cyrene, Decatur Co. (1920)

Cyrus, Worth Co. (1881)

Dabney, DeKalb Co. (1894)

Dache, Gwinnett Co. (1894)

Dacula, Gwinnett Co. (1920)

Dademont, Dade Co. (1881); also known as Cureton.

Daffin, Screven Co. (1920)

Daffin Heights, Chatham Co. (1962); part of Savannah.

Dahlonega, Lumpkin Co. (1920)

Daisy, Evans Co. (1920)

Daisy, Tattnall Co. (1894)

Dakota, Dooly Co. (1894)

Dakota, Turner Co. (1920)

Dale, Walton Co. (1920)

Dale, Chatham Co. (1920)

Dales Mill, Wayne Co. (1881)

Dallas, Paulding Co. (1920)

Dalton, Whitfield Co. (1920)

Damascus, Early Co. (1920)

Damascus, Gordon Co. (1962)

Dames Ferry, Monroe Co. (1920)

Dame's Mills, Clinch Co. (1894)

Danburg, Wilkes Co. (1920); also spelled Danburgh (1859).

Danburgh, Wilkes Co. (1859); also spelled Danburg (1920).

Dand, Atkinson Co. (1920)

Dandy, Hall Co. (1920)

Danforth, Jefferson Co. (1894)

Daniel, Bryan Co. (1962)

Daniels, Polk Co. (1894)

Daniel Siding, Bryan Co. (1920)

Daniels Mills, Douglas Co. (1920)

Daniels Mills, Heard Co. (1870)

Daniel Springs, Greene Co. (1962)

Danielsville, Madison Co. (1920)

Daniel Village, Richmond Co. (1962)

Danton, Tattnall Co. (1920)

Danville, Sumter Co. (1881)

Danville, Twiggs Co. (1920)

Daphne, Crisp Co. (1920)

Darbys, Columbia Co. (1847)

Darien, McIntosh Co. (1920)

Darien Junction, McIntosh Co. (1894)

Dark Corner, Campbell Co. (1859)

Dark Corner, Douglas Co. (1881)

Dark Corner, Lincoln Co. (1847)

Darlot, Liberty Co. (1881)

Darnell, Lowndes Co. (1894)

Darr Homes, Dougherty Co. (1962)

Darrow, Dougherty Co. (1920)

Darsey, Grady Co. (1920)

Dart, Glynn Co. (1847)

Darts Mills, Coffee Co. (1881); also known as McDonalds Mill.

Dasher, Houston Co. (1894)

Dasher, Lowndes Co. (1920)

Dates, Emanuel Co. (1920)

Daton, Echols Co. (1894)

David, Glascock Co. (1962)

Davie, Hall Co. (1894)

Davis, Bulloch Co. (1920)

Davis, Carroll Co. (1920)

Davis, Dougherty Co. (1881)

Davis, Walker Co. (1894)

Davis, Worth Co. (1894)

Davisboro, Washington Co. (1920)

Davis Creek, Forsyth Co. (1859)

Davis Crossroads, Walker Co. (1962)

Davis Mills, Wilcox Co. (1881)

Davis Spur, Harris Co. (1920)

Daviston, Talbot Co. (1847)

Daviston, Taylor Co. (1859)

Davistown, Taylor Co. (1881)

Davittes, Polk Co. (1920)

Dawesville, Thomas Co. (1962)

Dawnville, Whitfield Co. (1920)

Dawson, Habersham Co. (1881)

Dawson, Terrell Co. (1920)

Dawson, Thomas Co. (1870)

Dawsonville, Dawson Co. (1920)

Day, Paulding Co. (1920)

Days, Oglethorpe Co. (1894)

Days Crossroads, Clay Co. (1962)

Dayton, Echols Co. (1920)

Deadwylers, Madison Co. (1920)

Deals, Bulloch Co. (1894)

Deals, Emanuel Co. (1920)

Dean, Evans Co. (1920)

Dean, Haralson Co. (1881); also known as Wolf Pen Cross Roads.

Dean, Tattnall Co. (1894)

Deans Still, Pierce Co. (1920)

Deanwood, Ware Co. (1962); census name is Hebardsville.

Dearing, Columbia Co. (1847)

Dearing, McDuffie Co. (1920); also known as Lombardy (1881).

Deatons, Polk Co. (1920)

Debbie, Colquitt Co. (1920)

DeBoise, Pulaski Co. (1870)

Debruce, Richmond Co. (1920)

Decatur, DeKalb Co. (1920)

Decatur Junction, Floyd Co. (1894)

Decora, Gordon Co. (1920)

Dedrich, Wilkinson Co. (1962); also spelled Dedrick (1920).

Dedrick, Wilkinson Co. (1920); also spelled Dedrich (1962).

Deenwood, Ware Co. (1920)

Deepstep, Washington Co. (1920)

Deercourt, Stephens Co. (1920)

Deerland, DeKalb Co. (1962)

Deerland, Fulton Co. (1920)

Deer Land, Worth Co. (1859)

Deerland Park, DeKalb Co. (1962)

Dees, Lowndes Co. (1920)

Deitzen, Houston Co. (1920)

Dekle, Thomas Co. (1881)

Dekle, Emanuel Co. (1894)

Deland, Macon Co. (1920)

Delano, Oconee Co. (1894)

Delay, Jackson Co. (1859)

Delay, Upson Co. (1881)

Delhi, Wilkes Co. (1962)

Delia, Haralson Co. (1920)

Delight, Bibb Co. (1894)

Delight, Telfair Co. (1920)

Dellwood, Emanuel Co. (1920)

Delmar, Cobb Co. (1920)

Delmar, Lowndes Co. (1920)

Deloach, Troup Co. (1920)

Deloach, Bulloch Co. (1920); R.R. name is Denmark.

Delray, Upson Co. (1920)

Delta, Macon Co. (1920)

Delzel, Twiggs Co. (1920)

Demorest, Habersham Co. (1920)

Demotte, Colquitt Co. (1920)

Dempsey, Dodge Co. (1881)

Denins, Putnam Co. (1870)

Denmark, Bulloch Co. (1920); P.O. name is Deloach.

Denmark, Crawford Co. (1920)

Dennard, Houston Co. (1920)

Dennis, Murray Co. (1920)

Dennis, Putnam Co. (1920); P.O. name is Nona.

Denson, Twiggs Co. (1870)

Denton, Coffee Co. (1894)

Denton, Jeff Davis Co. (1920)

Denver, Heard Co. (1920)

Depot, Oglethorpe Co. (1847)

Deptford, Chatham Co. (1962); part of Savannah.

Depue, Dodge Co. (1920)

Derby, Troup Co. (1894)

De Soto, Floyd Co. (1881)

De Soto, Paulding Co. (1859)

Desoto, Sumter Co. (1920)

De Soto Park, Floyd Co. (1962)

Desser, Seminole Co. (1920)

Devereaux, Hancock Co. (1920)

Devereaux Station, Hancock Co. (1881)

Devore, Milton (Fulton) Co. (1920)

Dewberry, Hall Co. (1920)

Dewey, Bartow Co. (1920)

Dewey Rose, Elbert Co. (1962); R.R. name for Dewy Rose.

Dewitt, Mitchell Co. (1920)

Dewsville, Baker Co. (1894)

Dewy Rose, Elbert Co. (1962); also spelled Dewyrose (1920); P.O. name for Dewey Rose (1962).

Dexter, Laurens Co. (1920)

Diadem, Elbert Co. (1894)

Dial, Fannin Co. (1920)

Diamond, Gilmer Co. (1920)

Diamond Hill, Madison Co. (1962)

Dickensons Store, Decatur Co. (1881); also known as Johnsons Landing, Steam Mill, and Navy Yard.

Dickerson, Clinch Co. (1920)

Dickey, Calhoun Co. (1920)

Dickey, Walker Co. (1962)

Dickeys Farm, Coffee Co. (1920)

Dicksons, Walker Co. (1894)

Dicksons Mill, Pierce Co. (1881)

Diffie, Decatur Co. (1920); R.R. name is West Bainbridge.

Digbey, Spalding Co. (1920)

Dillard, Rabun Co. (1920)

Dillon, Walker Co. (1881)

Dillon, Dade Co. (1920)

Dillon, Thomas Co. (1920)

Dime, Baker Co. (1920)

Dinglewood, Muscogee Co. (1962); part of Columbus.

Dink, Bulloch Co. (1920)

Dink, Putnam Co. (1894)

Dinsmore, Milton (Fulton) Co. (1920)

Dip, Hall Co. (1894)

Dirt, Chattooga Co. (1894)

Dirt Seller, Chattooga Co. (1920)

Dirt Town, Chattooga Co. (1881)

Divide, Polk Co. (1920)

Dix, Chattooga Co. (1920)

Dixie, Brooks Co. (1920); also known as Groverville (1881).

Dixie, Newton Co. (1962)

Dixie Heights, Dougherty Co. (1962)

Dixie Union, Ware Co. (1962)

Dixon, Dawson Co. (1881)

Dixonia, Ware Co. (1881)

Dixons, Stewart Co. (1920)

Dobbins Air Force Base, Cobb Co. (1962).

Dobbs, Hart Co. (1894)

Doboy, McIntosh Co. (1881)

Dock, Bulloch Co. (1920)

Dock Junction, Glynn Co. (1920); census name for Arco (1962).

Docks, Glynn Co. (1920)

Doctortown, Wayne Co. (1920); also spelled Doctor Town (1894).

Dodd, Habersham Co. (1920)

Dodge, Walker Co. (1920)

Dodgen, Cobb Co. (1920)

Dodo, Laurens Co. (1894)

Dodson, Coweta Co. (1920)

Doehead, Washington Co. (1894)

Doerun, Colquitt Co. (1920)

Dogsboro, Morgan Co. (1894)

Dogwood, Walker Co. (1847)

Doles, Worth Co. (1920)

Dominitz, Chatham Co. (1920)

Don, Harris Co. (1881)

Don, Polk Co. (1894)

Donald, Long Co. (1920)

Donalson, Laurens Co. (1894)

Donalsonville, Decatur Co. (1894)

Donalsonville, Seminole Co. (1920)

Donegal, Bulloch Co. (1920)

Dong, Worth Co. (1920)

Donovan, Johnson Co. (1920)

Donovan, Washington Co. (1894)

Doogan, Murray Co. (1920)

Dooling, Dooly Co. (1920)

Doolittle, Coweta Co. (1920)

Dora, Fannin Co. (1920)

Doraland, Decatur Co. (1962)

Doraville, DeKalb Co. (1920)

Dorchester, Liberty Co. (1920)

Dorchester Station, Liberty Co. (1920); P.O. name is Arcadia.

Dorminey, Ben Hill Co. (1920)

Dormineys Mill, Irwin Co (1881)

Dormineys Mill, Ben Hill Co. (1920)

Dorsett, Douglas Co. (1920)

Dorsey, Clayton Co. (1920)

Dorsey, Morgan Co. (1920)

Dosaga, Dougherty Co. (1962)

Dosia, Tift Co. (1920)

Doswell, Effingham Co. (1920)

Dot, Carroll Co. (1920)

Dot, Colquitt Co. (1894)

Dotsy, Terrell Co. (1894)

Double Branches, Lincoln Co. (1920)

Double Bridge, Upson Co. (1881); also spelled Double Bridges (1859).

Double Bridges, Upson Co. (1859); also spelled Double Bridge (1881).

Double Cabins, Henry Co. (1847)

Double Cabins, Spalding Co. (1870)

Doublerun, Wilcox Co. (1920)

Double Shoals, Morgan Co. (1870)

Double Wells, Warren Co. (1881); also known as Barnet and Cumming.

Doudy, Madison Co. (1881)

Dougherty, Dawson Co. (1920)

Dougherty, Dougherty Co. (1962)

Dougherty Junction, Dougherty Co. (1962)

Douglas, Coffee Co. (1920)

Douglasville, Douglas Co. (1920)

Douville, Decatur Co. (1920)

Dove Creek, Elbert Co. (1962); also spelled Doves Creek (1881).

Dovedale, Baldwin Co. (1920)

Dover, Glynn Co. (1847)

Dover, Greene Co. (1881)

Dover, Screven Co. (1920)

Dover, Terrell Co. (1870)

Doverel, Terrell Co. (1920)

Doves Creek, Elbert Co. (1881); also spelled Dove Creek (1962).

Dow, Milton (Fulton) Co. (1920)

Dowdy, Madison Co. (1894)

Dowell, Dougherty Co. (1920)

Downer, Troup Co. (1894)

Downing, Coffee Co. (1894)

Downs, Washington Co. (1894)

Dozier, Miller Co. (1894)

Dradys, Wayne Co. (1881); another name for Jesup.

Draketown, Haralson Co. (1920)

Drake Town, Paulding Co. (1859)

Dranesville, Marion Co. (1920)

Drawdy, Wayne Co. (1920)

Drayton, Dooly Co. (1920)

Dresden, Coweta Co. (1920)

Dreskolls, Carroll Co. (1920)

Drew, Forsyth Co. (1920)

Drew, Lee Co. (1870)

Drewryville, Spalding Co. (1920)

Drews Mill, Lee Co. (1870)

Drexel, Morgan Co. (1920)

Driskoll, Carroll Co. (1962)

Drone, Burke Co. (1920)

Druid Hills, DeKalb Co. (1962)

Drummond, Washington Co. (1881)

Drybranch, Bibb Co. (1920)

Drycreek, Chattooga Co. (1920)

Dry Lake, Thomas Co. (1881)

Dry Lake, Brooks Co. (1870)

Drypond, Jackson Co. (1920)

Duane Street, Banks Co. (1881)

Duane Street, Habersham Co. (1859)

Duane Street, Hall Co. (1870 & 1881)

Dubignon, Glynn Co. (1847)

Dublin, Butts Co. (1847)

Dublin, Laurens Co. (1920)

Dubois, Dodge Co. (1920)

Ducan, Houston Co. (1920)

Duck, Union Co. (1894)

Duck Creek, Walker Co. (1881)

Ducker, Dougherty Co. (1920)

Ducktown, Forsyth Co. (1920)

Dudley, Laurens Co. (1920)

Due, Fannin Co. (1920)

Due West, Cobb Co. (1962)

Duffie, Mitchell Co. (1962)

Duffie, Wilcox Co. (1894)

Dugdown, Haralson Co. (1920)

Duggers, Taylor Co. (1920)

Dugroad, Pickens Co. (1920)

Duke, Ware Co. (1894)

Dukesville, Glynn Co. (1881); another name for Mount Pleasant.

Dukesville, Heard Co. (1894)

Duluth, Gwinnett Co. (1920)

Dumas, Webster Co. (1920)

Dunagan, Hall Co. (1920)

Dunbar, Houston Co. (1920)

Cuncan, Cobb Co. (1920)

Duncanville, Thomas Co. (1881)

Dundee, Fayette Co. (1920)

Dungannon, Campbell (Fulton) Co. (1920)

Dungeness, Camden Co. (1894)

Dunham, Liberty Co. (1920)

Dunlap, Oglethorpe Co. (1920)

Dunlap, Wilcox Co. (1920)

Dunn, Murray Co. (1881)

Dunn Store, Murray Co. (1962)

Dunwoody, DeKalb Co. (1920)

DuPont, Clinch Co. (1920); also known as Lawton (1881).

Dupont Junction, Clinch Co. (1920)

Durand, Meriwether Co. (1920)

Durango, Ware Co. (1920)

Durant, Franklin Co. (1920)

Durden, Brooks Co. (1920)

Durden, Emanuel Co. (1881)

Durdenville, Emanuel Co. (1894)

Durham, Walker Co. (1920)

Durham Junction, Walker Co. (1894)

Durhams Mills, Coffee Co. (1881); also known as Byrds Mill.

Durst, Richmond Co. (1920)

Duval, Montgomery Co. (1894)

Duval, Terrell Co. (1894)

Duvetom, Clinch Co. (1920)

Dwight, Washington Co. (1894)

Dyas, Monroe Co. (1920)

Dye, Elbert Co. (1920)

Dyke, Gilmer Co. (1920)

Dyke, Floyd Co. (1920)

Dykes, Floyd Co. (1894)

Dykesboro, Bleckley Co. (1881); former name of Cochran.

Dykes Store, Floyd Co. (1881)

Dykesville, Thomas Co. (1894)

Dyson, Wilkes Co. (1920)

Eagle Cliff, Walker Co. (1920)

Eagle Grove, Elbert Co. (1847)

Eagle Grove, Hart Co. (1920)

Eagle Pond, Lee Co. (1920)

Eanes, Chatham Co. (1962)

Early, Floyd Co. (1920)

Earnest, Carroll Co. (1920)

Earnest, Fayette Co. (1894)

Easons, Burke Co. (1962)

East Albany, Dougherty Co. (1962); part of Albany.

Eastanollee, Stephens Co. (1920)

East Armuchee, Walker Co. (1962)

East Atlanta, DeKalb Co. (1962); part of Atlanta.

Eastburn, White Co. (1920)

East Dublin, Laurens Co. (1962)

East Ellijay, Gilmer Co. (1920); R.R. name is Ellijay Station.

East End, DeKalb Co. (1920)

Easterling, Liberty Co. (1920)

East Griffin, Spalding Co. (1962)

East Highlands, Muscogee Co. (1962); part of Columbus.

East Juliette, Jones Co. (1962)

Eastlake, DeKalb Co. (1920)

East Macon, Bibb Co. (1894)

Eastman, Dodge Co. (1920)

Eastman Mills, Dodge Co. (1962)

East McRae, Telfair Co. (1920)

East Moultrie, Colquitt Co. (1962); part of Moultrie.

East Newnan, Coweta Co. (1962)

Easton, Fulton Co. (1920)

East Point, Fulton Co. (1920)

East Resaca, Gordon Co. (1881)

East Rome, Floyd Co. (1920)

East Tennessee, Virginia & Georgia Crossing, Glynn Co. (1894)

East Tennessee, Virginia & Georgia Junction, Fulton Co. (1894)

East Thomaston, Upson Co. (1920)

Eastville, Oconee Co. (1920)

East Warrenton, Warren Co. (1962)

East Wood, DeKalb Co. (1962); part of Atlanta.

Eastwood, Thomas Co. (1859)

Eatonton, Putnam Co. (1920)

Eatonton Factory, Putnam Co. (1847)

Eatonton Junction, Baldwin Co. (1894)

Ebener, Monroe Co. (1870)

Ebenezer, Chattooga Co. (1894)

Ebenezer, Dooly Co. (1881)

Ebenezer, McIntosh Co. (1870)

Ebenezer, Effingham Co. (1847)

Ebenezer, Monroe Co. (1870)

Ebenezer, Morgan Co. (1847)

Ebernezer, Walton Co. (1962)

E. Butts, Dooly Co. (1870)

Echaconnee, Bibb Co. (1847)

Echeconnee, Houston Co. (1920)

Echeconnee, Peach Co. (1962)

Echo, Bulloch Co. (1894)

Echo, Early Co. (1881)

Echo, Jenkins Co. (1920)

Echodell, Early Co. (1894)

Echols, Forsyth Co. (1894)

Echols, Spalding Co. (1962)

Echols Mill, Walton Co. (1847)

Echota, Gordon Co. (1920)

Eckert, Walker Co. (1920)

Economy, Upson Co. (1920)

Ector, Meriwether Co. (1920)

Eden, Bryan Co. (1881); another name for Bryan.

Eden, Effingham Co. (1920)

Edenfield, Irwin Co.(1881)

Edgar, Whitfield Co. (1894)

Edgars, Wilkinson Co. (1962)

Edge, Walker Co. (1920)

Edgehill, Glascock Co. (1920)

Edgemere, Chatham Co. (1962); part of Savannah

Edgewood, DeKalb Co. (1881)

Edgewood, Muscogee Co. (1962); part of Columbus.

Edie, Richmond Co. (1920)

Edinburg, Elbert Co. (1847); also spelled Edinburgh (1881).

Edinburgh, Elbert Co. (1881); also spelled Edinburg (1847).

Edison, Calhoun Co. (1920)

Edith, Clinch Co. (1920)

Edman, Meriwether Co. (1962)

Edna, Cobb Co. (1920)

Edna, Toombs Co. (1920); R.R. name is Petross.

Edna, Wilcox Co. (1894)

Edny, Dooly Co. (1894)

Edom, Gilmer Co. (1859)

Edward, Warren Co. (1894)

Edwards, Lee Co. (1920)

Edwardsville, Fulton Co. (1881); also known as Gradyville.

Edwin, Oglethorpe Co. (1894)

Edy, Lowndes Co. (1894)

Elbeck, Chattahoochee Co. (1920)

Effie, Whitfield Co. (1920)

Egan, Fulton Co. (1920)

Egypt, Effingham Co. (1920)

Elberta, Houston Co. (1962)

Elberton, Elbert Co. (1920)

Elder, Oconee Co. (1920)

Eldora, Bryan Co. (1920)

Eldorado, Berrien Co. (1894)

Eldorado, Tift Co. (1920); R.R. name for Fender (1962).

Eldorendo, Decatur Co. (1920)

Eleanor, Bibb Co. (1859)

Eleanor, Decatur Co. (1920)

Electric Mound, Taliaferro Co. (1894)

Elery, Heard Co. (1920)

Eleven Mile Turnout, Glynn Co. (1894)

Elgin, Butts Co. (1920)

Eli, Banks Co. (1920)

Eli, Decatur Co. (1894)

Eliam, Elbert Co. (1894)

Elind, Jefferson Co. (1894)

Elizabeth, Cobb Co. (1920)

Elizafield, Glynn Co. (1847)

Elko, Houston Co. (1920)

Ellabell, Bryan Co. (1962); R.R. name for Ellabelle.

Ellabelle, Bryan Co. (1962); P.O. name for Ellabell.

Ella Gap, Gilmer Co. (1920)

Ella Park, Camden Co. (1894)

Ellaville, Schley Co. (1920)

Ellejay, Gilmer Co. (1859); another spelling for Ellijay (1920).

Ellen, Appling Co. (1920)

Ellenton, Colquitt Co. (1920)

Ellenwood, Clayton Co. (1920)

Ellerbeetown, Upson Co. (1962)

Ellerslie, Harris Co. (1920)

Ellijay, Gilmer Co. (1920); also spelled Ellejay (1859).

Ellijay Station, Gilmer Co. (1920); P.O. name is East Ellijay.

Elliott, Appling Co. (1920)

Ellis, Columbia Co. (1894)

Ellis, Jeff Davis Co. (1920)

Elliston, Laurens Co. (1920)

Ellsworth, Union Co. (1920)

Elm, Colquitt Co. (1920)

Elmer, Screven Co. (1894)

Elmina, Telfair Co. (1920)

Elmira, Appling Co. (1894)

Elmo, Coffee Co. (1894)

Elmo, Early Co. (1920)

Elmo, Chatham Co. (1920)

Elmodel, Baker Co. (1920)

Elmore, Burke Co. (1920)

Elmore, Talbot Co. (1870)

Elmview, Marion Co. (1920)

Elmwood, Laurens Co. (1920)

Elmwood, Twiggs Co. (1881)

Elna, Paulding Co. (1859)

Elpino, Grady Co. (1920)

Elsie, Laurens Co. (1894)

Elsie, Ware Co. (1894)

Elton, Campbell (Fulton) Co. (1881)

Elton, Decatur Co. (1881)

Elton, Tattnall Co. (1894)

Elway, Walker Co. (1920)

Elwood, Richmond Co. (1920)

Elza, Tattnall Co. (1920)

Embee, Walton Co. (1920)

Embry, Paulding Co. (1920)

Emerald Spring, Wilcox Co. (1870)

Emerich, Dooly Co. (1920)

Emerson, Bartow Co. (1920)

Emerson Park, Ware Co. (1962)

Emersons, Brooks Co. (1920)

Emily, Carroll Co. (1920)

Emit, Bulloch Co. (1920)

Emma, Dawson Co. (1920)

Emmalane, Jenkins Co. (1920)

Emmallane, Emanuel Co. (1894)

Emmet, Wilkinson Co. (1847)

Emory, DeKalb Co. (1962)

Emory, Hall Co. (1894)

Emory College, Newton Co. (1870)

Emory University, DeKalb Co. (1920)

Empire, Dodge Co. (1920)

Empire Mills, Campbell Co. (1859)

Empress, Brooks Co. (1920); P.O. name is Shore.

Enal, Bulloch Co. (1920)

Endicott, Bulloch Co. (1894)

Enecks, Screven Co. (1920)

Engle, Fayette Co. (1894)

English, Colquitt Co. (1894)

English, Sumter Co. (1920)

English Eddy, Tattnall Co. (1894)

Englishville, Macon Co. (1920)

Enigma, Berrien Co. (1920)

Ennis, Baldwin Co. (1962)

Ennis, Johnson Co. (1920)

Enoch, Murray Co. (1920)

Enon, Jasper Co. (1881)

Enon, McIntosh Co. (1870)

Enongrove, Heard Co. (1920); also spelled Enon Grove (1859).

Enon Store, Heard Co. (1894)

Enterprise, Lee Co. (1881); R.R. name is Adams.

Enterprise, Morgan Co. (1920)

Enterprise, Oglethorpe Co. (1962)

Entrekins Mills, Carroll Co. (1881); another name for Mount Zion.

Enu, Meriwether Co. (1881); also known as Enu Mills.

Enu Mills, Meriwether Co. (1881); also known as Enu.

Enville, Wayne Co. (1894)

Eolia, Towns Co. (1870)

Ephesus, Douglas Co. (1894)

Epping, Montgomery Co. (1920)

Epworth, Fannin Co. (1920)

Erastus, Banks Co. (1920)

Erastus, Franklin Co. (1859)

Erick, Montgomery Co. (1894)

Erick, Wheeler Co. (1920)

Erie, Heard Co. (1920)

Erin, Meriwether Co. (1859)

Ernest, Clinch Co. (1962)

Erwin, Gordon Co. (1920)

Esco, Oglethorpe Co. (1920)

Eskay, Lowndes Co. (1962)

Esla, Bulloch Co. (1920)

Esmond, Spalding Co. (1920)

Eson, Polk Co. (1920); P.O. name is Esom Hill.

Esom Hill, Polk Co. (1920); R.R. name is Esom.

Esquiline, Muscogee Co. (1920)

Essie, Richmond Co. (1894)

Estelle, Walker Co. (1920); P.O. name is Shaw.

Ester, Franklin Co. (1894)

Ester, Stephens Co. (1920)

Estill, Chatham Co. (1920)

Ethel, Hall Co. (1881)

Ethel, Johnson Co. (1894)

Etheridge, Elbert Co. (1920); also spelled Ethridge (1962).

Ethridge, Elbert Co. (1962); also spelled Etheridge (1920).

Ethridge, Jones Co. (1920)

Etna, Haralson Co. (1894)

Etna, Macon Co. (1859)

Etna, Polk Co. (1920)

Etna Furnace, Polk Co. (1894)

Eton, Murray Co. (1920)

Etowah, Bartow Co. (1920)

Etowah, Floyd Co. (1920)

Etowah Cliffs, Cass (Bartow) Co. (1847)

Etowah Iron Works, Cass (Bartow) Co. (1847)

Etowah Valley, Cass (Bartow) Co. (1847)

Etta, Paulding Co. (1920)

Ettaville, Crawford Co. (1881)

Ettrick, Twiggs Co. (1920)

Eubanks, Columbia Co. (1920)

Eudora, Jasper Co. (1920)

Eugene, Miller Co. (1920)

Euharlee, Bartow Co. (1881); also spelled Euharley (1859).

Euharley, Bartow Co. (1859); also spelled Euharlee (1881).

Eula, Jasper Co. (1920)

Eulonia, McIntosh Co. (1920)

Eunice, DeKalb Co. (1920)

Eunice, Dodge Co. (1894)

Euno, White Co. (1894)

Eureka, Dooly Co. (1920)

Eureka Mills, Elbert Co. (1881)

Eureka Springs, Screven Co. (1920)

Eutaw, Randolph Co. (1870)

Euthtilloga, Chattooga Co. (1847); also known as Euthtilloga Springs (1870).

Euthtilloga Springs, Chattooga Co. (1870); also known as Euthtilloga (1847)

Eva, Houston Co. (1920)

Eva, Telfair Co. (1881)

Evans, Columbia Co. (1920); P.O. name is Evens.

Evan's Mills, DeKalb Co. (1894)

Evansville, Macon Co. (1881)

Evansville, Troup Co. (1920)

Evelyn, Colquitt Co. (1920)

Evelyn, Glynn Co. (1920); R.R. name is Broadfield.

Evens, Columbia Co. (1920); R.R. name is Evans.

Everett, Crawford Co. (1870)

Everett, Glynn Co. (1920); P.O. name is Everett City.

Everett City, Glynn Co. (1920); R.R. name is Everett.

Everett Springs, Floyd Co. (1920); also known as Everetts Springs (1881).

Everetts Springs, Floyd Co. (1881); also known as Everett Springs (1920).

Everetts Station, Crawford Co. (1881)

Evergreen, Irwin Co. (1881)

Evergreen, Ben Hill Co. (1920)

Evermay, Meriwether Co. (1920)

Eves, Bartow Co. (1920)

Eves, Floyd Co. (1894)

Ewell, Newton Co. (1894)

Ewing, Clinch Co. (1920)

Excelsior, Candler Co. (1920)

Excelsior, Bulloch Co. (1881); also known as Red Branch.

Exeter, Pierce Co. (1881)

Exley, Chatham Co. (1894)

Exley, Effingham Co. (1920)

Experiment, Spalding Co. (1920)

Exposition Mills, Fulton Co. (1894)

Exum, Macon Co. (1894)

Faceville, Decatur Co. (1920)

Falls Creek, Gilmer Co. (1881)

Fain, Union Co. (1920)

Fairburn, Campbell (Fulton) Co. (1920)

Fairchild, Decatur Co. (1894)

Fairchild, Seminole Co. (1920)

Faircloth, Mitchell Co. (1920)

Fairfax, Ware Co. (1920)

Fairfield, Wayne Co. (1920)

Fairfield, Chatham Co. (1962); part of Savannah.

Fairfield, Wilcox Co. (1920)

Fairhope, McIntosh Co. (1920)

Fairhope Junction, McIntosh Co. (1920)

Fair Mount, Gordon Co. (1920); also spelled Fairmount (1962).

Fair Oaks, Cobb Co. (1962)

Fairplay, Douglas Co. (1962)

Fair Play, Hancock Co. (1881); also known as Altmera (1881); also spelled Fairplay (1847).

Fairplay, Morgan Co. (1920)

Fairplay, Taliaferro Co. (1847)

Fairview, Butts Co. (1894)

Fairview, Chattooga Co. (1920)

Fair View, Franklin Co. (1881); also spelled Fairview (1859)

Fairview, Fulton Co. (1894)

Fairview, Stephens Co. (1962)

Fair View, Mitchell Co. (1881)

Fairview, Walker Co. (1962)

Fairway Oaks, Chatham Co. (1962); part of Savannah.

Fairy, Murray Co. (1920)

Fairyland, Walker Co. (1962)

Faith, Fulton Co. (1894)

Fales, Coffee Co. (1920)

Fall Creek, Clay Co. (1859)

Falls Creek, Gilmer Co. (1881)

Fambro, Gordon Co. (1920)

Fancy Bluff, Glynn Co. (1881)

Fancy Hill, Murray Co. (1881)

Fannettwill, Clarke Co. (1920)

Fannille, Coffee Co. (1881)

Fareville, Decatur Co. (1881)

Fargo, Clinch Co. (1920)

Farley, Harris Co. (1920)

Farmdale, Coweta Co. (1920)

Framdale, Screven Co. (1920)

Farmers, Meriwether Co. (1859)

Farmers Academy, Hancock Co. (1847)

Farmers Bridge, Burke Co. (1847)

Farmersville, Chattooga Co. (1859)

Farmersville, Meriwether Co. (1847)

Farm House, Milton (Fulton) Co. (1881)

Farmington, Clarke Co. (1859)

Farmington, Oconee Co. (1920)

Farmville, Gordon Co. (1920)

Farr, Douglas Co. (1920)

Farrar, Jasper Co. (1920)

Fashion, Murray Co. (1920)

Faulkner, Pickens Co. (1920)

Fawcett, Liberty Co. (1894)

Fawn, Coffee Co. (1920)

Fay, Henry Co. (1920)

Fayette, Spalding Co. (1881); another name for Sunny Side.

Fayetteville, Fayette Co. (1920)

Feagan, Houston Co. (1920)

Fearing, Polk Co. (1920)

Featherston, Polk Co. (1920)

Federal Prison, Fulton Co. (1962); part of Atlanta.

Feensboro, Worth Co. (1870)

Felder, Turner Co. (1920)

Felix, Colquitt Co. (1920)

Fellowship Church, Hart Co. (1920)

Felsen, Oconee Co. (1920)

Felton, Haralson Co. (1920)

Fence, Gwinnett Co. (1920)

Fender, Clinch Co. (1894)

Fender, Tift Co. (1920); P.O. name for Eldorado (1962).

Fendig, Brantley Co. (1920)

Fenn, Dooly Co. (1894)

Fennell, Chatham Co. (1881); formerly known as Monteith.

Fenns Bridge, Washington Co. (1847)

Fenns Bridge, Jefferson Co. (1881); also known as Hudsonia.

Fenton, Paulding Co. (1920)

Fentress, Telfair Co. (1894)

Ferguson, Lee Co. (1894)

Fernside, Upson Co. (1894)

Fernwood, Chatham Co. (1962); part of Savannah.

Feronia, Coffee Co. (1920)

Ferrobutte, Bartow Co. (1920)

Ferry, Floyd Co. (1894)

Festus, Walker Co. (1894)

Ficklin, Wilkes Co. (1920)

Fickling, Taylor Co. (1920)

Ficklings Mill, Taylor Co. (1962)

Fidelle, Gordon Co. (1920)

Fido, Bryan Co. (1881)

Fields, Dooly Co. (1920)

Fields Crossroads, Milton (Fulton) Co. (1920)

Fields Mills, Gordon Co. (1881)

Fife, Campbell (Fulton) Co. (1920)

Fifty-Three, Warren Co. (1920)

Fig, Jones Co. (1894)

Fillmore, Whitfield Co. (1920)

Filmore, Coweta Co. (1920)

Fincher, Gordon Co. (1894)

Finchers, Pike Co. (1881); also known as Lineys Store.

Fincherville, Butts Co. (1920)

Findlay, Dooly Co. (1920)

Finleyson, Pulaski Co. (1920)

Fish, Polk Co. (1920)

Fish Creek, Polk Co. (1894)

Fishdam, Elbert Co. (1881)

Fishdam, Oglethorpe Co. (1920)

Fish Pond, Burke Co. (1847)

Fitts, Carroll Co. (1894)

Fitzgerald, Ben Hill Co. (1962)

Fitzgerald Cotton Mill, Ben Hill Co. (1962)

Fitzhugh, Early Co. (1920)

Fitzpatrick, Twiggs Co. (1920)

Five Forks, Madison Co. (1894)

Five Points, Carroll Co. (1881); also known as Sand Hill.

Five Points, Dougherty Co. (1962); part of Albany.

Five Points, Jones Co. (1881)

Five Points, Lowndes Co. (1962)

Five Points, Macon Co. (1962)

Five Points, Randolph Co. (1962)

Five Points, Taylor Co. (1962)

Five Points, Thomas Co. (1962)

Flake, DeKalb Co. (1920)

Flake Mills, DeKalb Co. (1962)

Flanders, Emanuel Co. (1894)

Flatbranch, Giler Co. (1894)

Flat Creek, Berrien Co. (1881)

Flatcreek, Fayette Co. (1920); also spelled Flat Creek (1894).

Flat Creek, Lowndes Co. (1859).

Flat Pond, Lee Co. (1881)

Flat Rock, DeKalb Co. (1894)

Flat Rock, Henry Co. (1859)

Flatrock, Muscogee Co. (1920)

Flat Rock, Pike Co. (1881)

Flat Shoals, Meriwether Co. (1881)

Flat Shoals Factory, Meriwether Co. (1847)

Flatwoods Academy, Elbert Co. (1920)

Fleehill, Camden Co. (1894)

Fleetwood, Chatham Co. (1962); part of Savannah.

Fleetwoods Mills, Wilkinson Co. (1870)

Fleming, Liberty Co. (1920)

Flemington, Liberty Co. (1920)

Fletcher, Irwin Co. (1920)

Fletcher, Taylor Co. (1894)

Fletchers, Muscogee Co. (1962)

Fletcher Spur, Muscogee Co. (1920)

Flint, Mitchell Co. (1920)

Flint Hill, Carroll Co. (1859)

Flint Hill, Talbot Co. (1894)

Flint River, Spalding Co. (1920)

Flint River Factory, Upson Co. (1881)

Flintside, Sumter Co. (1920)

Flintstone, Walker Co. (1920)

Flintsville, Franklin Co. (1859); also spelled Flintville (1881).

Flint View, Dougherty Co. (1962)

Flintville, Franklin Co. (1881); also spelled Flintsville (1859).

Flippen, Henry Co. (1920)

Flo, Floyd Co. (1920)

Flora, Monroe Co. (1920)

Floralhill, Wilkes Co. (1920)

Florence, Morgan Co. (1894)

Florence, Stewart Co. (1920)

Florenceville, Upson Co. (1881)

Florida Junction, Chatham Co. (1920)

Floss, Campbell (Fulton) Co. (1920)

Flotona, McIntosh Co. (1894)

Flournoy, Irwin Co. (1920); P.O. name is Pope

Flovilla, Butts Co. (1920)

Flower, Screven Co. (1894)

Flowery Branch, Hall Co. (1920)

Floyd, Camden Co. (1847)

Floyd, Chattooga Co. (1894)

Floyd, Cobb Co. (1920)

Floyd Mineral Springs, Floyd Co. (1870); also known as Floyd Springs (1920).

Floyd Springs, Floyd Co. (1920); also known as Floyd Mineral Springs (1870).

Fly, Bulloch Co. (1920)

Fodie, Brooks Co. (1920)

Folks, Calhoun Co. (1920)

Folkston, Charlton Co. (1920)

Folsom, Bartow Co. (1920)

Folsom, Habersham Co. (1894)

Fonthill, Wayne Co. (1847)

Ford, Bartow Co. (1920)

Ford, Glynn Co. (1920)

Fords Store, Franklin Co. (1859)

Fords Store, Hart Co. (1881)

Forest, Clayton Co. (1894)

Forest, Clinch Co. (1894)

Forest, Meriwether Co. (1920)

Forest Glen, Wilcox Co. (1920)

Forest Hall, Burke Co. (1881)

Forest Hill, Burke Co. (1847)

Forest Hills, Richmond Co. (1962); part of Augusta.

Forest Park, Clayton Co. (1920); known as Forest Station prior to 1881; name changed to Astor in March 1881 (1881).

Forest Park, Dougherty Co. (1962)

Forest Pond, Wayne Co. (1962)

Forest Station, Clayton Co. (1881); known as Forest Station prior to 1881; name changed to Astor in March 1881 (1881); now known as Forest Park (1920).

Forestville, Floyd Co. (1894)

Fork, Dawson Co. (1920)

Formyduvol, Wilcox Co. (1894)

Forrest, Catoosa Co. (1894)

Forrest, Clinch Co. (1881); P.O. name is Withers.

Forrest, Columbia Co. (1920)

Forrester, Lee Co. (1920)

Forrest Hills, Chatham Co. (1962); part of Savannah.

Forrestville, Floyd Co. (1920); another name for North Rome.

Forsyth, Monroe Co. (1920)

Fort Argyle, Bryan Co. (1881)

Fort Barrington, McIntosh Co. (1847)

Fort Benning, Chattahoochee Co. (1962)

Fort Benning Junction, Muscogee Co. (1962); part of Columbus.

Fort Buffington, Cherokee Co. (1881)

Fort Early, Dooly Co. (1847)

Fort Gaines, Early Co. (1847)

Fort Gaines, Clay Co. (1920)

Fort Gilmer, Ware Co. (1847)

Fort Gilmer, Echols Co. (1870)

Fort Gordon. Prior name was Camp Gordon; located in Richmond, McDuffie, and Jefferson Cos. (1962).

Fort Hawkins, Bibb Co. (1847)

Fort Hill, Dougherty Co. (1870)

Fort Jackson, Chatham Co. (1847)

Fort James, Appling Co. (1870)

Fort Lamar, Madison Co. (1920)

Fort McPherson, Fulton Co. (1962); part of Atlanta.

Fort Mountain, Murray Co. (1920)

Fort Mudge, Brantley Co. (1920)

Fort Mudge, Pierce Co. (1894)

Fortner, Emanuel Co. (1881)

Fort Oglethorpe, Catoosa & Walker Cos. (1962)

Fort Perry, Marion Co. (1847)

Fort Pulaski, Chatham Co. (1881)

Fort Scott, Decatur Co. (1847)

Fort Screven, Chatham Co. (1920)

Fortson, Muscogee Co. (1920)

Fortsonia, Elbert Co. (1920)

Fortsons Crossing, Muscogee Co. (1894)

Fort Stewart. Prior name was Camp Stewart; located in Liberty, Bryan, Evans, Long, & Tattnall Cos. (1962).

Fort Valley, Houston Co. (1920)

Fort Valley, Peach Co. (1962)

Fortville, Jones Co. (1920)

Fort Wilkinson, Baldwin Co. (1881)

Foster, Brooks Co. (1894)

Fosters Mill, Cherokee Co. (1859); also spelled Fosters Mills (1881).

Fosters Mill, Floyd Co. (1920)

Fosters Mill, Monroe Co. (1870)

Fosters Mills, Cherokee Co. (1881); also spelled Fosters Mill (1859).

Foster's Mills, Chattooga Co. (1894)

Foster Spur, Sumter Co. (1962)

Fosters Store, Chattooga Co. (1881)

Fosterville, Henry Co. (1881)

Fouche, Floyd Co. (1920)

Fountainville, Macon Co. (1920)

Four Oaks, McDuffie Co. (1894)

Four Points, Dougherty Co. (1962); branch of Albany.

Fowler, Chattooga Co. (1920)

Fowler, Jackson Co. (1894)

Fowler Junction, Clark Co. (1920)

Fowlstown, Decatur Co. (1920); P.O. name for Fowltown (1962).

Fowl Town, Decatur Co. (1847); located between the Chattahoochee River and Spring Creek in what later became Seminole Co.

Fowltown, Decatur Co. (1962); R.R. name for Fowlstown.

Fowl Town Academy, Decatur Co. (1847)

Fox, Floyd Co. (1920)

Fox, Upson Co. (1894)

Foxtown, Long Co. (1920)

Fragoletta, Marion Co. (1881)

Francesville, Crawford Co. (1847)

Francis, Appling Co. (1894)

Francis, Berrien Co. (1920)

Frank, Irwin Co. (1920)

Franklin, Heard Co. (1920)

Franklin Academy, Upson Co. (1847)

Franklin Mines, Cherokee Co. (1847)

Franklins Mill, Pierce Co. (1881)

Franklin Springs, Franklin Co. (1881); also known as Royston.

Franklinton, Bibb Co. (1920)

Franks, Jones Co. (1894)

Frankville, Monroe Co. (1894)

Frazier, Bleckley Co. (1920)

Frazier, Pulaski Co. (1894)

Fred, Berrien Co. (1920)

Fredel, Ware Co. (1920)

Frederica, Glynn Co. (1881)

Frederick, Oglethorpe Co. (1920)

Free, Meriwether Co. (1894)

Free Bridge, Cass (Bartow) Co. (1847)

Free Bridge, Gordon Co. (1881); also spelled Freebridge (1894).

Freedmans, Glynn Co. (1920)

Freehome, Cherokee Co. (1962); also spelled Freehomes (1920).

Freehomes, Cherokee Co. (1920); also spelled Freehome (1962).

Freeman, Early Co. (1920)

Freemans, Floyd Co. (1920)

Freemans Mill, Wilkinson Co. (1870)

Freemansville, Cherokee Co. (1859)

Freemansville, Milton (Fulton) Co. (1920)

French, Jefferson Co. (1920)

Fricks Gap, Walker Co. (1881)

Friendship, Calhoun Co. (1870)

Friendship, Stewart Co. (1859)

Friendship, Sumter Co. (1847)

Friendship Academy, Twiggs Co. (1870)

Friskey, Henry Co. (1894)

Frolona, Heard Co. (1920)

Frost, Johnson Co. (1920)

Frost, Lumpkin Co. (1920)

Fruitfarm, Worth Co. (1962)

Fruitland, Echols Co. (1920)

Fry, Fannin Co. (1920)

Frye, Clinch Co. (1962)

Fryers Pond, Burke Co. (1881); also spelled Fryers Ponds (1859).

Fryers Ponds, Burke Co. (1859); also spelled Fryers Pond (1881).

Fryes, Clinch Co. (1920)

Frys, Decatur Co. (1894)

Fulco, Fulton Co. (1962)

Fulco Junction, Fulton Co. (1962)

Fuller, Lincoln Co. (1920)

Fuller Spur, Crisp Co. (1920)

Fullerville, Carroll Co. (1920); annexed to Villa Rica since 1950 (1962).

Fullington, Dooly Co. (1894)

Fullwood, Polk Co. (1920)

Fullwood Springs, Polk Co. (1894)

Fulton, Cobb Co. (1859)

Fulton, Fulton Co. (1881); also known as Bolton and Boltonville (1881).

Fulton Copper Mines, Fulton Co. (1970)

Fulwoods Mineral Springs, Polk Co. (1881)

Funkhouser, Bartow Co. (1962)

Funston, Colquitt Co. (1920)

Furniture City, Cobb Co. (1962)

Fuqua, Dooly Co. (1920)

Furlows, Calhoun Co. (1881)

Furnace, Walker Co. (1920)

Gabbettville, Troup Co. (1920)

Gaddistown, Union Co. (1920)

Gillard, Crawford Co. (1920)

Gaines, Elbert Co. (1920)

Gaines Community, Clarke Co. (1962)

Gainesville, Hall Co. (1920)

Gainesville Cotton Mills, Hall Co. (1962)

Gains Mill, Bartow Co. (1920)

Galatia, Chatham Co. (1920)

Gallemore, Twiggs Co. (1920)

Gallimore, Twiggs Co. (1894)

Galloway, Fannin Co. (1920)

Galvans, Richmond Co. (1920)

Gamble, Jefferson Co. (1870)

Gammage, Worth Co. (1962)

Gammon, Floyd Co. (1920)

Ganor Spur, Colquitt Co. (1962)

Gantts, Worth Co. (1920)

Garbutt, Laurens Co. (1894)

Garbutts Landing, Ben Hill Co. (1920)

Garden City, Chatham Co. (1962)

Garden Lakes, Floyd Co. (1962)

Garden Valley, Macon Co. (1920)

Gardi, Wayne Co. (1920)

Gardner, Washington Co. (1920)

Garfield, Emanuel Co. (1920)

Garland, Lumpkin Co. (1920)

Garland, Upson Co. (1920)

Garlandville, Franklin Co. (1920)

Garmany, Chattooga Co. (1920)

Garnett, Houston Co. (1920)

Garrant, Coffee Co. (1894)

Garretta, Laurens Co. (1962)

Garrets, Muscogee Co. (1894)

Gartrell, Campbell Co. (1859)

Gartrell, Fulton Co. (1870)

Gartrell, Gilmer Co. (1920)

Gary, Emanuel Co. (1920)

Gary, Johnson Co. (1894)

Garys Camp, Walker Co. (1920)

Gasco, Fulton Co. (1962); part of Atlanta.

Gatesville, Early Co. (1881)

Gatewood, Sumter Co. (1920)

Gatlett, Walker Co. (1920)

Gatlin, Gilmer Co. (1920)

Gay, Meriwether Co. (1920)

Gay, Montgomery Co. (1894)

Gee, Taylor Co. (1920)

Gem, Bulloch Co. (1920)

General Knight, Berrien Co. (1870)

General Morrison, Burke Co. (1870)

Geneva, Talbot Co. (1920)

Gennett, Gilmer Co. (1962)

Genola, Carroll Co. (1920)

Gentian, Muscogee Co. (1920)

Gentry's Mills, Dawson Co. (1894)

George M. Troup, Laurens Co. (1847)

George Street, Glynn Co. (1894)

Georgetown, Randolph Co. (1847)

Georgetown, Quitman Co. (1920)

Georgian, Banks Co. (1881); also known as Jewellville.

Georgian, Franklin Co. (1859)

Georgia Railroad Junction, Richmond Co. (1894)

Georgia Southern, Bulloch Co. (1962); also known as Collegeboro.

Georgia Southwestern College, Sumter Co. (1962)

Georgia State College, Chatham Co. (1962); also known as State College and Savannah State College.

Georgia University Station, Clarke Co. (1962); part of Athens.

Geranium, Evans Co. (1920)

Gerber, Walker Co. (1881)

Germantown, Polk Co. (1881)

Germantown, Camden Co. (1894)

German Village, Glynn Co. (1962)

Germany, Rabun Co. (1962)

Gertman, Emanuel Co. (1894)

Gertman, Treutlen Co. (1920)

Gertrude, Burke Co. (1920)

Gertrude, Franklin Co. (1920)

Gertrude, Liberty Co. (1894)

Getup, Walker Co. (1920)

Ghent, Gwinnett Co. (1920)

Ghentsville, Henry Co. (1859)

Gholston, Madison Co. (1894)

Gibson, Glascock Co. (1920)

Gibson, Harris Co. (1847)

Gibson Spur, Liberty Co. (1920)

Giddens, Dodge Co. (1920)

Gignlatt, Glynn Co. (1920)

Gilbert, Clay Co. (1920)

Gilbert's Landing, Early Co. (1894)

Gilbralter, DeKalb Co. (1847)

Giles, Chattahoochee Co. (1894)

Giles, Wayne Co. (1920)

Gilesville, Bibb Co. (1894)

Gilgal, Screven Co. (1894)

Gill, Lincoln Co. (1920)

Gill, Long Co. (1920)

Gill, Meriwether Co. (1962)

Gillican, Clinch Co. (1962)

Gillionville, Baker Co. (1847)

Gillionville, Dougherty Co. (1870)

Gillis, Emanuel Co. (1847)

Gillons, Dougherty Co. (1859)

Gillsville, Hall & Banks Cos. (1962)

Gilmore, Cobb Co. (1920)

Gilmore, Washington Co. (1920)

Gintown, Worth Co. (1881); also spelled Gin Town (1870).

Gip, Irwin Co. (1894)

Girard, Burke Co. (1920); also known as Liberty Hall (1881).

Girth, Burke Co. (1894)

Glade, Oglethorpe Co. (1881); another name for Point Peter.

Glade, Hall Co. (1894)

Glade Mines, Hall Co. (1870)

Glades Cross Roads, Putnam Co. (1859)

Gladesville, Jasper Co. (1920)

Gladys, Berrien Co. (1920)

Glascock, Richmond Co. (1847)

Glasgow, Thomas Co. (1920)

Glee, Troup Co. (1920)

Glen Alta, Marion Co. (1920); also spelled Glenalta (1859).

Glencoe, Camden Co. (1920)

Glendale, Milton (Fulton) Co. (1920)

Glen Ford, Hancock Co. (1920)

Glen Grove, Fayette Co. (1881)

Glen Grove, Franklin Co. (1859)

Glen Haven, DeKalb Co. (1962)

Glenloch, Heard Co. (1920)

Glen Moore, Cass (Bartow) Co. (1847)

Glenmore, Ware Co. (1920)

Glenn, Heard Co. (1920)

Glenns, Muscogee Co. (1920)

Glenville, Tattnall Co. (1920)

Glen Willie, Floyd Co. (1847)

Glenwood, Bartow Co. (1894)

Glenwood, Montgomery Co. (1894)

Glenwood, Wheeler Co. (1920)

Glenwood Hills, DeKalb Co. (1962)

Glidden, Bibb Co. (1962)

Glory, Berrien Co. (1920)

Gloster, Gwinnett Co. (1920)

Glovers, Jones Co. (1920)

Gloverton, Coweta Co. (1962)

Glynco, Glynn Co. (1962); also known as Glynco Naval Air Station.

Glynco Naval Air Station, Glynn Co. (1962); also known as Glynco.

Glynn Haven, Glynn Co. (1962)

Gnat, Jenkins Co. (1920)

Gober, Cherokee Co. (1920)

Goddards, Polk Co. (1894)

Goddess, Gwinnett Co. (1920)

Godfrey, Morgan Co. (1920)

Godleys, Chatham Co. (1920)

Godwinsville, Dodge Co. (1920)

Goggansville, Monroe Co. (1881)

Goggansville, Lamar Co. (1920); R.R. name is Goggins.

Goggins, Lamar Co. (1920); P.O. name is Goggansville.

Goggins, Monroe Co. (1894)

Golden, Brooks Co. (1920)

Goldengate, Fulton Co. (1920); also spelled Golden Gate (1894)

Gold Hill, Meriwether Co. (1847)

Goldin, Haralson Co. (1920)

Goldmine, Hart Co. (1962); also spelled Gold Mine (1894).

Goldotha, Cobb Co. (1894)

Goldridge, Cherokee Co. (1920)

Goldsboro, Bleckley Co. (1920)

Goldsboro, Pulaski Co. (1894)

Goldsborough, Pulaski Co. (1881)

Goldsmith, Jeff Davis Co. (1920)

Goldton, McDuffie Co. (1894)

Gold Village, Carroll Co. (1894)

Goldville, Carroll Co. (1920)

Golgotha, Cobb Co. (1881)

Goloid, Screven Co. (1881)

Gomez, Wayne Co. (1920)

Gonder, Hancock Co. (1847)

Goodes, Campbell (Fulton) Co. (1920)

Good Hope, Walton Co. (1859); also spelled Goodhope (1920).

Gooding, Bulloch Co. (1920)

Goodman, Irwin Co. (1894)

Goodman, Wilcox Co. (1894)

Goodmans Cross Roads, Harris Co. (1881); another name for Chipley.

Gooseberry, Webster Co. (1894)

Goose Pond, Long Co. (1920)

Goose Pond, Oglethorpe Co. (1847)

Goodson, Fayette Co. (1881); also known as Brooks and Brooks Station.

Goodwill, Franklin Co. (1920)

Goodwins, DeKalb Co. (1881); R.R. name for Cross Keys.

Goodwins Crossing, DeKalb Co. (1920)

Gopher, Milton (Fulton) Co. (1920)

Gorday, Worth Co. (1920)

Gordon, Wilkinson Co. (1920)

Gordons, Whitfield Co. (1894)

Gordon Springs, Walker Co. (1847); also known as Medicinal Springs.

Gordon Springs, Whitfield Co. (1920); also known as Gordons Medicinal Springs (1870), & Neals Store (1881).

Gordons Medicinal Springs, Whitfield Co. (1870); another name for Gordon Springs (1920).

Gordonston, Chatham Co. (1962); part of Savannah.

Gore, Chattooga Co. (1920)

Gore, Randolph Co. (1920)

Goshen, Lincoln Co. (1920)

Goss, Elbert Co. (1920)

Gough, Burke Co. (1920)

Gould, Oconee Co. (1894)

Gould, Glynn Co. (1847)

Gower Springs, Hall Co. (1894)

Grab All, Jones Co. (1881); another name for Cornucopia.

Grace, White Co. (1881)

Grace, Lumpkin Co. (1920)

Gracewood, Richmond Co. (1920)

Grady, Polk Co. (1920)

Gradyville, Fulton Co. (1881); another name for Edwardsville.

Gradyville, Grady Co. (1920)

Graham, Appling Co. (1920)

Granberry, Harris Co. (1881)

Grand Bay, Lowndes Co. (1859)

Grange, Jefferson Co. (1920)

Grangersville, Macon Co. (1920); also spelled Grangerville (1847).

Grangerville, Macon Co. (1847); also spelled Grangersville (1920).

Grangerville, Wayne Co. (1920)

Granite Hill, Hancock Co. (1920)

Granite Spur, Madison Co. (1962)

Grants, Walker Co. (1962)

Grantville, Coweta Co. (1920)

Grapevine, Gwinnett Co. (1920)

Grassdale, Bartow Co. (1920)

Grassfield, Jasper Co. (1894)

Grassy Mountain, Murray Co. (1920)

Gratis, Walton Co. (1920)

Gravel Springs, Forsyth Co. (1920)

Graves, Terrell Co. (1881 & 1962); also known as Graves Station (1920).

Graves Station, Terrell Co. (1920); also known as Graves (1881 & 1962).

Gray, Jones Co. (1920)

Graymount, Emanuel Co. (1920); consolidated with Summit to form Twin City (1962).

Grays, Coffee Co. (1894)

Gray's Landing, Tattnall Co. (1894)

Grays Mill, Atkinson Co. (1920)

Grays Mill, Ware Co. (1881)

Grayson, Gwinnett Co. (1920)

Graysville, Catoosa Co. (1920)

Greeley, Cherokee Co. (1920)

Green, Bulloch Co. (1920)

Green Acres, Chatham Co. (1962); part of Savannah.

Greenbush, Walker Co. (1881)

Green Cut, Burke Co. (1859); also spelled Greens Cut (1962).

Greenfield, Colquitt Co. (1881)

Green Hill, Stewart Co. (1920)

Green Island Hills, Muscogee Co. (1962)

Greenough, Mitchell Co. (1920)

Greensboro, Greene Co. (1920)

Greens Cut, Burke Co. (1962); also spelled Green Cut (1859).

Greens Cut, Macon Co. (1881)

Greens Landing, Clay Co. (1870)

Greens Mill, Fannin Co. (1962)

Greens Mill, Macon Co. (1920)

Greens Station, Burke Co. (1870)

Greenville, Camden Co. (1962)

Greenville, Meriwether Co. (1920)

Greenway, Emanuel Co. (1962)

Greenway, Polk Co. (1920)

Greenwood, Catoosa Co. (1920)

Greenwood, Henry Co. (1920)

Greenwood, Mitchell Co. (1962)

Greenwood, Polk Co. (1881)

Greenwood Forest, Clinch Co. (1962)

Green Woods, Whitfield Co. (1859)

Greggs, Cook Co. (1920)

Gregory, Murray Co. (1920)

Grenada, Talbot Co. (1920)

Gresham, Walton Co. (1920)

Greshamville, Greene Co. (1920)

Gresston, Dodge Co. (1920)

Griffin, Columbia Co. (1920)

Griffin, Pike Co. (1847)

Griffin, Spalding Co. (1920)

Griffin's Landing, Burke Co. (1894)

Griffins Mills, Berrien Co. (1870)

Griffis, Ware Co. (1847)

Griffith, Lamar Co. (1962)

Grimes, Harris Co. (1920)

Grimes, Hancock Co. (1870)

Grimmets Causeway, Calhoun Co. (1870)

Grimshaw, Bulloch Co. (1920)

Grimsley, Laurens Co. (1894)

Grindle, Lumpkin Co. (1894)

Griner, Berrien Co. (1920)

Griselda, Decatur Co. (1894)

Griswold, Jones Co. (1920); P.O. name is Griswoldville.

Griswoldville, Jones Co. (1920); R.R. name is Griswold.

Grit, Hart Co. (1920)

Grogan, Peach Co. (1962)

Groganville, Cobb Co. (1881)

Groovers, Effingham Co. (1894)

Grooverville, Brooks Co. (1962); also spelled Groverville (1881).

Grooverville, Thomas Co. (1847)

Grovania, Houston Co. (1920)

Grove, Elbert Co. (1881)

Grove, Rabun Co. (1920)

Groveland, Bryan Co. (1920)

Groveland, Chatham Co. (1962); part of Savannah.

Grove Level, Banks Co. (1920)

Grove Level, Franklin Co. (1859)

Grove Mount, Burke Co. (1881)

Grove Park, Fulton Co. (1962); part of Atlanta.

Grover, Wilcox Co. (1894)

Groverville, Brooks Co. (1881); also known as Dixie (1881); also spelled Grooverville (1962).

Grovetown, Columbia Co. (1920)

Grubb, Randolph Co. (1894)

Grubbs, Chatham Co. (1962)

Gruner, Clinch Co. (1962)

Guess, Henry Co. (1881)

Guest, Colquitt Co. (1920)

Guest, Ware Co. (1847)

Guestville, Clinch Co. (1894)

Guild, Walker Co. (1920)

Guilford, Douglas Co. (1920)

Guin, Henry Co. (1920)

Gulf, Coffee Co. (1894)

Gullettsville, Monroe Co. (1881); also known as Cabonis.

Gully Branch, Coffee Co. (1881)

Gum Branch, Liberty Co. (1920)

Gum Creek, Dooly Co. (1881)

Gumlog, Towns Co. (1894)

Gumlog, Union Co. (1920); also spelled Gum Log (1962)

Gim Pond, Mitchell Co. (1881)

Gumspring, Bartow Co. (1920); also spelled Gum Springs (1881).

Gum Springs, Bartow Co. (1881); also spelled Gumspring (1920).

Gum Swamp, Pulaski Co. (1870).

Gundee, Decatur Co. (1894)

Gunns Mills, Warren Co. (1881); another name for Norwood.

Gunter, Crawford Co. (1920)

Gus, Berrien Co. (1894)

Guthrie, Emanuel Co. (1894)

Guys, Pierce Co. (1870)

Guysie, Bacon Co. (1920)

Guyton, Effingham Co. (1920); also known as Whitesville (1881).

Haasville, Fulton Co. (1894); also spelled Hasville (1920)

Habersham, Habersham Co. (1920)

Habersham Station, Habersham Co. (1920)

Hack Branch, Montgomery Co. (1920)

Hadden, Glascock Co. (1962)

Haddock, Jones Co. (1920); also known as Haddock Station (1881).

Haddock Station, Jones Co. (1881); also known as Haddock (1920).

Hagan, Evans Co. (1920)

Hagan, Tattnall Co. (1894)

Haginsville, Bulloch Co. (1881)

Hahira, Lowndes Co. (1920)

Haides, Screven Co. (1881)

Haines, Lowndes Co. (1894)

Haisting, Gwinnett Co. (1920)

Haisting, Milton (Fulton) Co. (1894)

Halcyondale, Screven Co. (1962); also spelled Halcyon Dale (1920).

Hale, Hart Co. (1920)

Hale, Catoosa Co. (1920)

Hale's, Pike Co. (1894)

Half Moon Bluff, Appling Co. (1870)

Half Moon Bluff, Glynn Co. (1847)

Halfmoon Landing, Liberty Co. (1962)

Halfway, Lumpkin Co. (1920)

Hall, Appling Co. (1859)

Hall, Madison Co. (1894)

Halley, Glascock Co. (1920)

Halleys, Screven Co. (1870)

Halloca, Muscogee Co. (1847)

Halloca, Chattahoochee Co. (1920)

Halloca Station, Chattahoochee Co. (1920)

Halls, Bartow Co. (1920); P.O. name is Linwood (1920); also known as Halls Mill (1881).

Halls Cross Roads, Hancock & Washington Cos. (1847)

Halls Mill, Bartow Co. (1881); also known as Halls (1920).

Halls Mill, Emanuel Co. (1920)

Hallwood, Putnam Co. (1962)

Hamburg, Macon Co. (1859)

Hamby, Chattooga Co. (1920)

Hambyville, Troup Co. (1920)

Hamilton, Glynn Co. (1847)

Hamilton, Harris Co. (1920)

Hamilton Cross Roads, McDuffie Co. (1881)

Hamlet, Polk Co. (1894)

Hamlet, Randolph Co. (1859)

Hammacks Grove, Crawford Co. (1847)

Hammett, Cherokee Co. (1859)

Hammett, Crawford Co. (1920)

Hammond, Fulton Co. (1920)

Hammonds Mill, Chattooga Co. (1920)

Hammonds Mill, Floyd Co. (1881)

Hamp Branch, Screven Co. (1881)

Hampton, Henry Co. (1920); also known as Bear Creek (1881).

Hampton Point, Glynn Co. (1847)

Hamptons Camp Ground, Polk Co. (1870)

Hancock, Burke Co. (1881)

Hancock, Hancock Co. (1962)

Handleys, Ben Hill Co. (1920)

Handy, Coweta Co. (1894)

Haney, Floyd Co. (1962)

Hanley, Haralson Co. (1894)

Hanlin, Paulding Co. (1920)

Hanlys Store, Hart Co. (1881)

Hannah, Douglas Co. (1920)

Hannah, Harris Co. (1894)

Hannahatchee, Stewart Co. (1881); also known as Antioch.

Hannah Mill, Upson Co. (1962)

Hannatown, Decatur Co. (1962)

Hanover, Decatur Co. (1920)

Hansell, Thomas Co. (1920)

Hansen, Irwin Co. (1920)

Hapeville, Fulton Co. (1920); R.R. name is Hassville.

Happy Valley, McDuffie Co. (1962)

Haralson, Coweta & Meriwether Cos. (1962)

Harbin, Gwinnett Co. (1920)

Hardage, Cobb Co. (1920)

Hardaway, Dougherty Co. (1920); P.O. name is Putney.

Hard Cash, Elbert Co. (1962); also spelled Hardcash (1920).

Hardeman, Harris Co. (1920)

Harding, Tift Co. (1920)

Hardins, Floyd Co. (1881)

Hard Money, Webster Co. (1870)

Hardup, Baker Co. (1894)

Hardwick, Baldwin Co. (1920); P.O. name for State Sanitarium (1962); also known as Midway (1962).

Hardwick, Bryan Co. (1881)

Hardwood, Washington Co. (1920)

Hardys, Bibb Co. (1920)

Hargett, Harris Co. (1920)

Hargrave, Catoosa Co. (1894)

Harlem, Columbia Co. (1920)

Harley, Clinch Co. (1920)

Harlow, Laurens Co. (1920)

Harman, Carroll Co. (1920)

Harmon, Upson Co. (1870)

Harmony, Elbert Co. (1881)

Harmony, Forsyth Co. (1894)

Harmony, Jackson Co. (1894)

Harmony, Putnam Co. (1881)

Harmony Grove, Jackson Co. (1881)

Harmony Junction, Jenkins Co. (1920)

Harnageville, Cherokee Co. (1847)

Harnageville, Pickens Co. (1881)

Harold, Walker Co. (1920); P.O. name is Pittsburg.

Harp, Chattahoochee Co. (1920)

Harper, Elbert Co. (1920)

Harpers, Floyd Co. (1881)

Harps, Fayette Co. (1920)

Harps, Walker Co. (1920)

Harrell, Decatur Co. (1881); another name for Whigham.

Harrietts Bluff, Camden Co. (1962)

Harrington, Glynn Co. (1962)

Harris, Douglas Co. (1881)

Harris, Meriwether Co. (1920)

Harrisburg, Richmond Co. (1881)

Harrisburg, Walker Co. (1920)

Harris City, Meriwether Co. (1894)

Harris Cross Roads, Murray Co. (1881); another name for Woodlawn.

Harrison, Washington Co. (1920)

Harrisonville, Richmond Co. (1962); part of Augusta.

Harrisonville, Troup Co. (1881); another name for Asbury.

Hart, Bibb Co. (1894)

Hart, Cherokee Co. (1920)

Hartford, Cherokee Co. (1881)

Hartford, Forsyth Co. (1881)

Hartford, Pulaski Co. (1962)

Hartley, Crawford Co. (1920)

Hartley, Peach Co. (1962)

Hartridge, Wayne Co. (1881)

Hartridgeville, Emanuel Co. (1881)

Harts, Warren Co. (1962)

Hartsfield, Colquitt Co. (1920)

Hartwell, Hart Co. (1920)

Harvest, Habersham Co. (1920)

Harvey, Morgan Co. (1920)

Harveys Mills, Henry Co. (1870)

Harville, Bulloch Co. (1920)

Haskins, Laurens Co. (1962)

Haslum, Wayne Co. (1881); also known as Satilla.

Haslum, Pierce Co. (1920)

Hassier Mill, Whitfield Co. (1962)

Hassler Mill, Murray Co. (1920); also known as Hasslers Mills (1859).

Hasslers Mills, Murray Co. (1859); also known as Hassler Mill (1920).

Hassville, Fulton Co. (1920); P.O. name is Hapeville; also spelled Haasville (1894).

Hasty, Ware Co. (1920)

Hat, Irwin Co. (1881)

Hat, Tift Co. (1920)

Hatcher, Quitman Co. (1962); another name for Hatcher Station.

Hatcher Station, Quitman Co. (1920); also known as Hatcher (1962).

Hatchet Landing, Douglas Co. (1920)

Hatfields Mills, Newton Co. (1870)

Hatley, Crisp Co. (1920)

Hatoff, Laurens Co. (1920)

Hattie, Houston Co. (1920).

Hauleiter, Pike Co. (1894)

Havana, Houston Co. (1920)

Haw Creek, Forsyth Co. (1881)

Hawkins, Walker Co. (1962)

Hawkinsville, Pulaski Co. (1920)

Haws and Hogans Mill, Lincoln Co. (1881)

Hay, Paulding Co. (1920)

Hayes, Lee Co. (1920)

Hayes, Newton Co. (1894)

Haylow, Echols Co. (1920)

Hayner, Glynn Co. (1920)

Hayneville, Houston Co. (1920)

Haynie, Floyd Co. (1894)

Hays Crossing, Stephens Co. (1920)

Hays Siding, Mitchell Co. (1920)

Hayston, Newton Co. (1920)

Haywood, Chattooga Co. (1920)

Haywood, Ware Co. (1920)

Haywood, Washington Co. (1881)

Hazard, Bibb Co. (1847)

Hazard, Washington Co. (1920)

Hazlebrand, Newton Co. (1920)

Hazlehurst, Glynn Co. (1881); also known as Bethel.

Hazlehurst, Appling Co. (1881)

Hazlehurst, Jeff Davis Co. (1920)

Hazlehurst Camp, Telfair Co. (1894)

Headlight, Clinch Co. (1920)

Head of Tennessee, Rabun Co. (1881); another name for Rabun Gap.

Headon, White Co. (1920)

Head River, Dade Co. (1920)

Head's Ferry, Habersham Co. (1894)

Heads Ferry, White Co. (1881)

Headstall, McDuffie Co. (1894)

Heard, Butts Co. (1894)

Heard, Houston Co. (1920)

Heardmont, Elbert Co. (1920)

Heardville, Forsyth Co. (1920)

Hearnville, Putnam Co. (1881)

Heartpine, Berrien Co. (1894)

Heartsease, Berrien Co. (1920)

Heath, Burke Co. (1881)

Hebardsville, Ware Co. (1920); also known as Deanwood (1962).

Hebron, Washington Co. (1920)

Hedrick, Catoosa Co. (1920)

Hedwig, Lumpkin Co. (1920)

Heflin, Heard Co. (1920)

Heidrich, Washington Co. (1962)

Helen, White Co. (1920)

Helena, Telfair Co. (1920)

Hells Gate, Baker Co. (1894)

Helmer, Fayette Co. (1920)

Help, Franklin Co. (1920)

Hematite, Polk Co. (1920)

Hembree, Douglas Co. (1894)

Hemlock, Burke Co. (1920)

Hemp, Fannin Co. (1920)

Hemphill, Fulton Co. (1920)

Hempstead, Colquitt Co. (1920)

Henderson, Houston Co. (1920)

Hendrick, Upson Co. (1962); also spelled Hendricks (1920).

Hendricks, Upson Co. (1920);
also spelled Hendrick
(1962).

Henley, Carroll Co. (1920)

Henley, Rockdale Co. (1894)

Henlys Store, Hart Co.
(1881)

Henrico, DeKalb Co. (1920)

Henry, Franklin Co. (1920)

Henry, Walker Co. (1894)

Hephzibah, Richmond Co.
(1920)

Herman, Oglethorpe Co.
(1881)

Hermitage, Chatham Co.
(1847)

Hermitage, Floyd Co.
(1920); also known as
Waters (1881).

Hermitage, Glynn Co. (1847)

Hermon, Oglethorpe Co.
(1847)

Herndon, Burke Co.
(1881)

Herndon, Jenkins Co.
(1920)

Herod, Terrell Co. (1920)

Herring, Colquitt Co.
(1920)

Hersham, Screven Co. (1920)

Hester, Jones Co. (1920)

Hewett, McIntosh Co.
(1894)

Hiawassee, Towns Co. (1962)

Hichitee, Chattahoochee
Co. (1894)

Hickman, Polk Co. (1894)

Hickman Junction, Polk Co.
(1894)

Hickmans, Hart Co. (1870)

Hickmans, Polk Co. (1920)

Hickory Bluff, Camden Co.
(1847)

Hickoryflat, Cherokee Co.
(1920); also spelled
Hickory Flat (1962).

Hickory Grove, Crawford Co.
(1920)

Hickory Level, Carroll Co.
(1920)

Hickox, Brantley Co. (1920)

Hicks, Macon Co. (1962)

Hico, Douglas Co. (1920)

Higdon, Fannin Co. (1962);
also known as Higdons
Store (1920).

Higdons Store, Fannin Co.
(1920); another name for
Higdon (1962).

Higgins, Lamar Co. (1920)

Higgins, Monroe Co. (1894)

Higgston, Montgomery Co.
(1920)

High Falls, Monroe Co. (1881);
also known as Unionville.

High Hill Fraction, Wilkinson
Co. (1881)

Highland, Cobb Co. (1920)

Highland Mills, Spalding Co.
(1962)

Highland Park, Chatham Co.
(1962) part of Savannah.

Highland Park, Muscogee Co.
(1962); part of Columbus.

Highland Pines, Muscogee Co.
(1962); another name
for Nankipooh.

High Point, Walker Co. (1920)

High Shoals, Oconee, Morgan, & Walton Cos. (1920).

Hightower, Forsyth Co. (1962); also spelled High Tower (1920).

High Towers, Johnson Co. (1881)

Hightowers Bridge, Johnson Co. (1870)

Hill, Lamar Co. (1920)

Hill City, Gordon Co. (1920)

Hilliard, Forsyth Co. (1881)

Hillis, Burke Co. (1920)

Hillman, Taliaferro Co. (1920)

Hills, Cherokee Co. (1894)

Hills, Habersham Co. (1920)

Hillsboro, Jasper Co. (1920)

Hillsdale, Worth Co. (1881)

Hillsdale, Tift Co. (1920)

Hillsdale, Walker Co. (1920)

Hillseby, Heard Co. (1894)

Hillside, Early Co. (1920)

Hills Park, Fulton Co. (1962); part of Atlanta.

Hilltonia, Screven Co. (1920)

Hillyer, Clayton Co. (1920)

Hilton, Early Co. (1920)

Hilton Heights, Muscogee Co. (1962); part of Columbus.

Hilton Station, Early Co. (1894)

Hineleys Spur, Effingham Co. (1920)

Hinely, Effingham Co. (1881)

Hines, Muscogee Co. (1881)

Hines Crossing, Harris Co. (1920)

Hinesville, Liberty Co. (1920)

Hinkles, Walker Co. (1920)

Hinson, Clinch Co. (1920)

Hinsonton, Mitchell Co. (1920)

Hinton, Pickens Co. (1962)

Hiram, Paulding Co. (1920)

Hirschmans, Screven Co. (1881)

Hitch, Madison Co. (1920)

Hix, Madison Co. (1920)

Hobbie, Dade Co. (1881)

Hobbs, Stewart Co. (1894)

Hobbs, Walker Co. (1962)

Hobby, Turner Co. (1920)

Hoboken, Pierce Co. (1881)

Hoboken, Brantley Co. (1920)

Hobson, Douglas Co. (1920)

Hodge, Carroll Co. (1920)

Hodges, Glascock Co. (1920)

Hodges' Mills, Monroe Co. (1894)

Hodo, Johnson Co. (1920)

Hoffmans Mills, Tattnall Co. (1870)

Hogan Seagor, Screven Co. (1870)

Hogansville, Troup Co. (1920)

Hog Creek, Clinch Co. (1894)

Hoggard Mill, Baker Co. (1894)

Hoggards Mill, Baker Co. (1881)

Hoggs, Marion Co. (1920)

Hog Mountain, Gwinnett Co. (1881); also known as Cains.

Hog Mountain, Hall Co. (1859)

Hoke, Telfiar Co. (1894)

Hokesboro, Irwin Co. (1920)

Holcomb, Burke Co. (1847); also spelled Holcombe (1881).

Holcomb, Pickens Co. (1920)

Holcombe, Burke Co. (1881); also known as Sebastopol (1881); also spelled Holcomb (1847).

Holden, Greene Co. (1920)

Holders, Floyd Co. (1894)

Holland, Chattooga Co. (1920)

Holland, Jasper Co. (1847)

Hollands, Pike Co. (1870)

Hollands Mills, Carroll Co. (1881)

Hollands Mills, Jasper Co. (1847)

Hollands Mills, Richmond Co. (1920)

Hollands Store, Chattooga Co. (1881)

Hollidays, Dooly Co. (1847)

Hollidays, Worth Co. (1870)

Hollingshead, Houston Co. (1920)

Hollingsworth, Banks Co. (1920)

Hollingsworth, Habersham Co. (1859)

Hollis, Thomas Co. (1920)

Hollonville, Pike Co. (1920)

Holly, Meriwether Co. (1859)

Holly, Murray Co. (1920)

Holly Creek, Murray Co. (1881)

Holly Grove, Monroe Co. (1894)

Holly Grove, Webster Co. (1870)

Holly Home, Hancock Co. (1847)

Holly Spring Church, Coweta Co. (1870)

Holly Springs, Cherokee Co. (1962); also spelled Hollysprings (1920).

Holly Springs, Campbell Co. (1870)

Holly Springs, Douglas Co. (1881); another name for Chapel Hill.

Holly Springs, Jackson Co. (1962)

Holly Springs, Madison & Elbert Cos. (1847)

Hollywood, Habersham Co. (1920)

Hollywood, Richmond Co. (1881)

Holmes, Early Co. (1859)

Holmes, Floyd Co. (1894)

Holmesville, Appling Co. (1881)

Holmesville, Early Co. (1870)

Holston, Bibb Co. (1881)

Holt, Calhoun Co. (1962)

Holt, Irwin Co. (1962)

Holt, Wilcox Co. (1894)

Holtenville, Upson Co. (1881)

Holton, Bibb Co. (1920); another name for Arkwright (1962).

Holtonville, Upson Co. (1894)

Holts, Dougherty Co. (1920)

Holts Shop, Taylor Co. (1870)

Home, Lamar Co. (1920)

Homeland, Brooks Co. (1920)

Homeland, Charlton Co. (1920)

Homer, Banks Co. (1920)

Homersville, Clinch Co. (1859); also spelled Homerville (1920).

Homerville, Clinch Co. (1920); also spelled Homersville (1859).

Homestead, Pierce Co. (1920)

Honeycreek, Rockdale Co. (1920)

Honora, Lincoln Co. (1920)

Hood, Harris Co. (1881)

Hoods, Pickens Co. (1894)

Hook, Richmond Co. (1847)

Hooker, Dade Co. (1920)

Hook's Crossing, Emanuel Co. (1894)

Hooper, Haralson Co. (1920); also spelled Hoopers (1962).

Hoopers, Haralson Co. (1962); also spelled Hooper (1920).

Hootensville, Upson Co. (1870)

Hope, Floyd Co. (1894)

Hope, Pike Co. (1920)

Hopedale, Houston Co. (1920)

Hopeful, Burke Co. (1881)

Hopeful, Mitchell Co. (1962)

Hopeton, Glynn Co. (1847)

Hopewell, Calhoun Co. (1870)

Hopewell, Cherokee Co. (1962)

Hopewell, Colquitt Co. (1881)

Hopewell, Crawford Co. (1859)

Hopewell, Dodge Co. (1881)

Hopewell, Whitfield Co. (1920)

Hopkins, Walton Co. (1894)

Hopkins, Ware Co. (1920)

Hoppsville, Wayne Co. (1894)

Horace, Carroll Co. (1920)

Horace, Emanuel Co. (1881)

Horeb, Hancock Co. (1881)

Horkan, Colquitt Co. (1920)

Horne, Monroe Co. (1920)

Horns, Crawford Co. (1962)

Horn's Cross Road, Miller Co. (1894); also spelled Horns Crossroads (1920).

Horns Crossroads, Miller Co. (1920); also spelled Horn's Cross Road (1894).

Horse Head, Houston Co. (1847)

Hortense, Brantley Co. (1920)

Hortense, Wayne Co. (1894)

Horton, Dodge Co. (1920)

Horton, Irwin Co. (1920)

Hortonville, Terrell Co. (1870)

Hoschs Store, Jackson Co. (1881)

Hochton, Jackson Co. (1920)

Hotel Tybee, Chatham Co. (1894)

Hot House, Fannin Co. (1881)

Hot House, Montgomery Co. (1859)

House Creek, Irwin Co. (1859)

House Creek, Wilcox Co. (1881)

Houston, Heard Co. (1920)

Houston Avenue, Bibb Co. (1962); part of Macon.

Houston Factory, Houston Co. (1881)

Houston Heights, Bibb Co. (1962); part of Macon.

Houston Lake, Houston Co. (1962)

Houtens, Upson Co. (1870)

Howard, Taylor Co. (1920)

Howard, Walker Co. (1894)

Howards, Bibb Co. (1870)

Howell, Columbia Co. (1962)

Howell, Echols Co. (1920)

Howell, Fulton Co. (1920)

Howells, DeKalb Co. (1881)

Howells Mills, Fulton Co. (1881)

Howells Yard, Fulton Co. (1962); part of Atlanta.

Hoyl, Gwinnett Co. (1881)

Hoys, Cherokee Co. (1894)

Hub, Grady Co. (1920)

Hubbardsville, Dawson Co. (1920)

Huber, Twiggs Co. (1962)

Hubert, Bulloch Co. (1920)

Hutching, Oglethorpe Co. (1920); R.R. name is Hutchings.

Huckabee, Harris Co. (1920)

Huckabees Spur, Jones Co. (1920)

Huckleberry, Echols Co. (1881); another name for Statenville Station.

Hudgins, Hall Co. (1920)

Hudson, Banks Co. (1881)

Hudson, Sumter Co. (1920)

Hudson, McIntosh Co. (1920)

Hudsonia, Jefferson Co. (1881); also known as Fenns Bridge.

Hudson Mill, Harris Co. (1962)

Hudson's Ferry, Screven Co. (1894)

Huey, Clinch Co. (1962)

Huff, Gwinnett Co. (1920)

Huffaker, Floyd Co. (1920)

Huffer, Coffee Co. (1920)

Hughes, Murray Co. (1920)

Hughesburg, Habersham Co. (1894); also spelled Hughesburgh (1881).

Hughesburgh, Habersham Co. (1881); also spelled Hughesburg (1894).

Hughland, Tattnall Co. (1920)

Hugo, Bartow Co. (1920)

Huguenin, Sumter Co. (1847)

Huguenot, Elbert Co. (1920)

Hulett, Carroll Co. (1920)

Huletts, Morgan Co. (1920)

Hull, Clarke Co. (1894)

Hull, Madison Co. (1920)

Hulmeville, Elbert Co. (1920)

Humber, Stewart Co. (1894)

Humboldt, Dougherty Co. (1881)

Humming, Berrien Co. (1894)

Humphreys, Clinch Co. (1894)

Hunnicut, Putnam Co. (1894)

Hunt, Towns Co. (1894)

Hunter, Screven Co. (1962); also spelled Hunters (1920).

Hunter Air Force Base, Chatham Co. (1962)

Hunters, Screven Co. (1920); also spelled Hunter (1962).

Hunters Mill, Bibb Co. (1847)

Hunters Mills, Screven Co. (1847)

Hunters Siding, Echols Co. (1920)

Huntington, Sumter Co. (1920)

Huntsville, Paulding Co. (1920)

Huntsville, Talbot Co. (1870)

Hurds Fort, Wilkes Co. (1870)

Hurley, Chattahoochee Co. (1920)

Huron, Putnam Co. (1920)

Hurricane, Appling Co. (1894)

Hurricane, Coffee Co. (1881)

Hurricane Shoals, Jackson Co. (1870)

Hurst, Bacon Co. (1920)

Hurst, Fannin Co. (1920)

Hurt, Gordon Co. (1881)

Hush, Gwinnett Co. (1920)

Huson, Baldwin Co. (1847)

Hustle, Terrell Co. (1920)

Hutching, Oglethorpe Co. (1920); another spelling of Hutchings.

Hutchings, Laurens Co. (1894)

Hutchings, Oglethorpe Co. (1920); P.O. name is Hutching.

Huttut, Gwinnett Co. (1894)

Huxford, Coffee Co. (1894)

Hyacinth, Ben Hill Co. (1920)

Hybert, Clinch Co. (1894)

Hyde, Wilkes Co. (1920)

Ice, Pierce Co. (1894)

Iceburg, Monroe Co. (1881)

Iceville, Fulton Co. (1894)

Ida, Greene Co. (1859)

Ida Cason Gardens, Harris Co. (1962)

Idavesper, Chattahoochee Co. (1920)

Ideal, Macon Co. (1920)

Idlewild Springs, Gordon Co. (1894)

Idlewood, Burke Co. (1920)

Igo, Gordon Co. (1894)

Iketon, Sumter Co. (1894)

Ila, Madison Co. (1920)

Ilco, Brooks Co. (1962)

Imlac, Meriwether Co. (1920)

Imperial, Putnam Co. (1962)

Imperial Mills, Putnam Co. (1962)

Inaha, Irwin Co. (1894)

Inaha, Turner Co. (1920)

India, Walton Co. (1920)

India, Ware Co. (1920)

Indian Hill, Elbert Co. (1881)

Indianaola, Lowndes Co. (1920)

Indian Springs, Butts Co. (1920)

Industrial College, Chatham Co. (1920)

Industry, Fulton Co. (1920)

Inez, Laurens Co. (1894)

Inez, Wayne Co. (1920)

Ingleside, Bibb Co. (1962); Part of Macon.

Ingleside, DeKalb Co. (1920)

Inglewood, Dodge Co. (1920)

Ingold, Macon Co. (1920)

Iniss, Tift Co. (1920)

Initial Point, Appling Co. (1870)

Inman, Fayette Co. (1920); R.R. name is Ackert.

Inman Park, Fulton Co. (1962); part of Atlanta.

Inston, Fannin Co. (1920)

Intal, Clinch Co. (1962)

International, Habersham Co. (1962)

Inverness, McIntosh Co. (1894)

Inwood, McIntosh Co. (1920)

Inwood, Telfair Co. (1920)

Ione, Brooks Co. (1962)

Irby, Irwin Co. (1894)

Irbyville, Fulton Co. (1881)

Irene, Washington Co. (1920)

Iric, Bulloch Co. (1920)

Irma, Schley Co. (1920)

Iron City, Decatur Co. (1894)

Iron City, Seminole Co. (1920)

Ironco, Walker Co. (1962)

Ironrock, Franklin Co. (1920); also spelled Iron Rock (1894).

Iron Spring, Butts Co. (1881)

Ironville, Bartow Co. (1894)

Irving, Spalding Co. (1920)

Irvin, Stewart Co. (1894)

Irvine, Cobb Co. (1894)

Irwin, Irwin Co. (1920)

Irwins, Washington Co. (1962)

Irwins Cross Roads, Washington Co. (1859)

Irwinsville, Irwin Co. (1859); also spelled Irwinville (1920).

Irwinton, Wilkinson Co. (1920)

Irwinville, Irwin Co. (1920); also spelled Irwinsville (1859).

Isbel, Ware Co. (1859)

Isabella, Worth Co. (1920)

Isabella Junction, Fannin Co. (1920).

Isabella Station, Worth Co. (1894)

Isbells, Polk Co. (1894)

Isla, Chatham Co. (1894)

Island Creek, Hancock Co. (1859); also spelled Islands Creek (1870).

Island Grove, Hancock Co. (1881)

Islands Creek, Hancock Co. (1870); also spelled Island Creek (1859).

Island Shoals, Henry Co. (1894)

Island Town, Chattooga Co. (1847)

Isle of Hope, Chatham Co.

Ison, Brooks Co. (1894)

Ithica, Carroll Co. (1894)

Itley, Forsyth Co. (1920)

Ivanhoe, Bulloch Co. (1920)

Ivey, Wilkinson Co. (1920)

Iveytown, Lincoln Co. (1920)

Ivy Log, Union Co. (1920)

Jackson, Butts Co. (1920)

Jackson, Houston Co. (1881); another name for Byron.

Jackson, Clarke Co. (1847)

Jackson, Oconee Co. (1881)

Jacksonboro, Screven Co. (1870); also spelled Jacksonburgh (1881).

Jacksonburgh, Screven Co. (1881); also spelled Jacksonboro (1870).

Jackson Factory, Jackson Co. (1847)

Jacksons Bluff, Sumter Co. (1847)

Jacksonville, Screven Co. (1847)

Jacksonville, Telfair Co. (1920)

Jacksonville, Towns Co. (1962)

Jacobs, Berrien Co. (1881); also known as Riverside.

Jaeckel, Emanuel Co. (1894)

Jafry, Calhoun Co. (1894)

Jake, Carroll Co. (1920)

Jakin, Early Co. (1920)

Jamaica, Glynn Co. (1920)

James, Jones Co. (1920)

James Mills, Heard Co. (1870)

Jamestown, Chattahoochee Co. (1920)

Jamestown, Muscogee Co. (1859)

Jamestown, Ware Co. (1962)

Japanese, Marion Co. (1920)

Jaroy, Cook Co. (1962)

Jarrell, Taylor Co. (1962)

Jarrels, Tattnall Co. (1920)

Jarrett, Hall Co. (1920)

Jarrett Station, Habersham Co. (1894)

Jarriel, Tattnall Co. (1894)

Jasper, Pickens Co. (1920)

Jasper, Springs, Chatham Co. (1894)

Jay, Bulloch Co. (1920)

Jay, Lumpkin Co. (1881)

Jay Bird Springs, Dodge Co. (1962)

J. Crawford, Early Co. (1847)

Jefferson, Jackson Co. (1920)

Jefferson, Putnam Co. (1962)

Jefferson Hall, Greene Co. (1847)

Jefferson Mill, Oglethorpe Co. (1962); located partly in Crawford.

Jeffersonton, Camden Co. (1859)

Jeffersonville, Camden Co. (1881)

Jeffersonville, Twiggs Co. (1920)

Jehue, Dodge Co. (1894)

Jekyl, Glynn Co. (1894)

Jekyll Island, Glynn Co. (1962)

Jenkins, Columbia Co. (1920); P.O. name is Evens.

Jenkinsburg, Butts Co. (1920)

Jenkinsville, Pike Co. (1881)

Jennings, Walker Co. (1920)

Jennings, Webster Co. (1894)

Jeptha, Madison Co. (1920)

Jernigan, Randolph Co. (1894)

Jerome, Bulloch Co. (1920)

Jerone, Heard Co. (1894)

Jerry, Dooly Co. (1920)

Jersey, Walton Co. (1920)

Jerusalem, Camden Co. (1962)

Jerusalum, Pickens Co. (1920)

Jessee, Union Co. (1920)

Jester, Stewart Co. (1894)

Jesup, Wayne Co. (1920); also known as Dradys (1881).

Jet, Carroll Co. (1920)

Jewell, Hancock Co. (1920); also known as Rock Factory (1881).

Jewells Mills, Warren Co. (1881)

Jewellville, Banks Co. (1920); also known as Georgian (1881).

Jewtown, Glynn Co. (1962); located on St. Simons Island.

Jimps, Bulloch Co. (1920)

Jincy, Wilcox Co. (1894)

Jinks, Decatur Co. (1962)

Job, Sumter Co. (1894)

Jockey, Pickens Co. (1920)

Joe, Cherokee Co. (1920)

Joel, Carroll Co. (1920)

John, Monroe Co. (1920)

Johns Creek, Gordon Co. (1881)

John's Mills, Gordon Co. (1894)

Johnson, Emanuel Co. (1881)

Johnson, Sumter Co. (1894)

Johnson Corner, Toombs Co. (1962)

Johnsons, Coweta Co. (1847)

Johnson's, Jefferson Co. (1894)

Johnsons Landing, Decatur Co. (1881); also known as Navy Yard, Steam Mill and Dickensons Store.

Johnsons Shop, Jackson Co. (1881)

Johnsons Warehouse, Emanuel Co. (1894)

Johnsonville, Appling Co. (1894)

Johnsonville, Jeff Davis Co. (1920)

Johnston Station, Liberty Co. (1881)

Johnstons Station, McIntosh Co. (1870)

Johnstonville, Monroe Co. (1881)

Johnstonville, Lamar Co. (1920)

Joice, Tattnall Co. (1920)

Joiner, Dodge Co. (1920)

Jolly, Pike Co. (1920)

Jones, McIntosh Co. (1920)

Jones, Pulaski Co. (1870)

Jones, Randolph Co. (1920)

Jones Bluff, Camden Co. (1881)

Jonesboro, Fayette Co. (1847)

Jonesboro, Clayton Co. (1920); also spelled Jonesborough (1859).

Jonesborough, Clayton Co. (1859); also spelled Jonesboro (1920).

Jones Creek, McIntosh Co. (1870)

Jones' Creek, Liberty Co. (1894)

Jones Crossing, Muscogee Co. (1881); P.O. name is Upatoie.

Jones Crossroads, Harris Co. (1962)

Jones Mills, Screven Co. (1847)

Jones Mills, Meriwether Co. (1881)

Jones Settlement, Upson Co. (1962)

Jones' Store, Gilmer Co. (1894)

Jonesville, Carroll Co. (1920)

Jonesville, McIntosh Co. (1847)

Joplin, Union Co. (1920)

Jordan City, Muscogee Co. (1962); part of Columbus.

Jordans Crossing, Baldwin Co. (1920)

Jordans Store, Pike Co. (1881)

Jordanville, Sumter Co. (1920)

Josella, Turner Co. (1920)

Joseph, Fulton Co. (1894)

Josepha, McIntosh Co. (1894)

Josephine, Early Co. (1894)

Josey, Jefferson Co. (1920)

Josh, Bulloch Co. (1894)

Josh, Candler Co. (1920)

Josselyn, Liberty Co. (1894)

Jot 'Em Down Store, Pierce Co. (1962)

Jowers, Coffee Co. (1920)

Joy, Rabun Co. (1920)

Joyce, Brooks Co. (1920)

Joys Mills, Burke Co. (1881)

Jubilee, Warren Co. (1859)

Judson, Catoosa Co. (1920)

Jug Factory, Jackson Co. (1870)

Jug Tavern, Walton Co. (1881)

Jula, Wilcox Co. (1894)

Julia, Henry Co. (1920)

Julia, Stewart Co. (1920); R.R. name is Union.

Juliette, Monroe Co. (1920)

Julinton, McIntosh C. (1920)

Julyss, Washington Co. (1920)

Junction, Clinch Co. (1894)

Junction, Dougherty Co. (1894)

Junction, Laurens Co. (1920)

Junction, Randolph Co. (1894)

Junction City, Talbot Co. (1920)

June, Dawson Co. (1881)

June, Lumpkin Co. (1859)

Junior State, Jackson Co. (1920)

Juniper, Marion & Talbot Cos. (1962)

Juniper Station, Talbot Co. (1920)

Juno, Dawson Co. (1920)

Juno Mills, Dawson Co. (1894)

Junta, Bartow Co. (1920)

Justice, Screven Co. (1894)

Kallulah Junction, Gordon Co. (1894)

Kansas, Carroll Co. (1881)

Kaolin, Washington Co. (1962)

Kartah, Chattooga Co. (1920)

Kate, Pierce Co. (1881)

Kathleen, Houston Co. (1920)

Keasley, Pickens Co. (1920); R.R. name is Carns Mill.

Kedron, Coweta Co. (1920)

Keel, Bulloch Co. (1920)

Keem, Monroe Co. (1920)

Keeter, Cherokee Co. (1894)

Keith, Catoosa Co. (1920)

Keith, Whitfield Co. (1894)

Keiths, Cherokee Co. (1894)

Keithsburg, Cherokee Co. (1920)

Kell, Tift Co. (1920)

Keller, Bryan Co. (1920)

Keller, Chatham Co. (1920)

Kellogg, Cherokee Co. (1920)

Kellog's Store, Jackson Co. (1894)

Kelly, Jasper Co. (1920)

Kellytown, Henry Co. (1962)

Kekpen, Cherokee Co. (1894)

Kelvin, Worth Co. (1920)

Kemp, Emanuel Co. (1920)

Kendall Gold Mine, Wilkes Co. (1894)

Kendrick, Walker Co. (1920)

Kenfield, Emanuel Co. (1920)

Kenna, Lincoln Co. (1920)

Kennady, Bryan Co. (1894); also spelled Kennedy (1881).

Kennedy, Brooks Co. (1920)

Kennedy, Bryan Co. (1881); also spelled Kennady (1894)

Kennedy, Tattnall Co. (1920)

Kennesaw, Cobb Co. (1920); also known as Big Shanty (1881).

Kensington, Chatham Co. (1847)

Kensington, Walker Co. (1920)

Kensington Park, Chatham Co. (1962); part of Savannah.

Kent, Montgomery Co. (1894)

Kenwood, Fayette Co. (1920)

Kenzie, Upson Co. (1920)

Kermit, Whitfield Co. (1920)

Kerns, Dooly Co. (1920)

Kerrs, Cobb Co. (1894)

Kesterton, Coweta Co. (1920)

Kestler, Early Co. (1920)

Kettle Creek, Walton Co. (1859)

Kettle Creek, Ware Co. (1870)

Ketus, Bulloch Co. (1920)

Key, Brooks Co. (1920)

Keysville, Burke Co. (1962)

Keyton, Calhoun Co. (1881)

Kibbee, Montgomery Co. (1920)

Kicklighter, Tattnall Co. (1920)

Kidron, Coweta Co. (1859)

Kiekes, Columbia Co. (1859)

Kiker, Gilmer Co. (1962)

Kilburn, Emanuel Co. (1920)

Kildare, Effingham Co. (1920)

Kildred, Emanuel Co. (1894)

Kilkenny Bluff, Bryan Co. (1847)

Killarney, Early Co. (1920)

Killen, Clay Co. (1962); also spelled Killens (1920).

Killens, Clay Co. (1920); also spelled Killen (1962).

Killian, Brooks Co. (1920)

Killkenny, Bryan Co. (1894)

Kimbell, Butts Co. (1894)

Kimbrough, Stewart Co. (1920)

Kimbrough, Webster Co. (1920)

Kincaid, Chattooga Co. (1920)

Kinchefoonee, Marion R. (1920)

Kinderlou, Lowndes Co. (1920)

Kineva, Clinch Co. (1920)

King, Chattahoochee Co. (1859)

King, Echols Co. (1894)

King, Glynn Co. (1847)

King, Newton Co. (1920); also spelled Kings (1962); also known as Cora (1962).

King Hill, Screven Co. (1894)

Kingry, Wilkinson Co. (1920)

Kings, Newton Co. (1962); also spelled King (1920); also known as Cora (1962).

Kings, Wayne Co. (1881)

Kings Bay, Camden Co. (1962)

Kingsboro, Harris Co. (1920)

Kings Gap, Harris Co. (1847)

Kingsland, Camden Co. (1920)

Kingston, Bartow Co. (1920)

Kingsville, Jones Co. (1920)

Kings Wood, Richmond Co. (1962); part of Augusta.

Kingswood, Colquitt Co. (1920)

Kinlaw, Camden Co. (1920)

Kinsey's Mills, Warren Co. (1894)

Kiokee, Columbia Co. (1881)

Kirby, Coweta Co. (1894)

Kirk, Polk Co. (1920)

Kirkland, Coffee Co. (1881)

Kirkland, Atkinson Co. (1920)

Kirkland, Jeff Davis Co. (1962)

Kirkwood, DeKalb Co. (1920); part of Atlanta.

Kiserville, Jasper Co. (1920)

Kissemee, Berrien Co. (1894)

Kite, Johnson Co. (1920)

Kittrells, Appling Co. (1894)

Kittrells, Johnson Co. (1920)

Klein, Oconee Co. (1920)

Klondike, DeKalb Co. (1920)

Klondike, Hall Co. (1920)

Klondike, Houston Co. (1962)

Knight, Worth Co. (1920)

Knights Mill, Berrien Co. (1881)

Knob, Henry Co. (1920)

Knoles, Pierce Co. (1894)

Knott, Troup Co. (1920)

Knowles, Appling Co. (1894)

Knox, Greene Co. (1962)

Knox Bridge, Hart Co. (1881)

Knoxville, Crawford Co. (1920)

Koger, Columbia Co. (1920)

Kolb, Cobb Co. (1894)

Kolb Gem, Screven Co. (1920); P.O. name is Thomasboro.

Koon, Thomas Co. (1894)

Kramer, Haralson Co. (1894)

Kramer, Wilcox Co. (1920)

Krannert, Floyd Co. (1962)

Kremlin, Emanuel Co. (1894)

Kyle, Fannin Co. (1920)

Laboon, Walton Co. (1920)

Labor, Carroll Co. (1894)

Lacey, McIntosh Co. (1920)

Laconte, Berrien Co. (1894)

Laconte, Cook Co. (1920)

LaCross, Schley Co. (1920)

Ladds, Bartow Co. (1920)

Ladson, Colquitt Co. (1962)

Laetitia, Pike Co. (1920)

LaFayette, Walker Co. (1920)

Laff, Tattnall Co. (1894)

Laff, Toombs Co. (1920)

LaGrange, Troup Co. (1920)

Laingkat, Decatur Co. (1920)

Lairdsboro, Carroll Co. (1894)

Lairdsborough, Carroll Co. (1881); formerly known as Laurel Hill.

Laird's Store, Carroll Co. (1894)

Lake, Polk Co. (1962)

Lake City, Clayton Co. (1962)

Lake Creek, Polk Co. (1962); also spelled Ladecreek (1920).

Lake Harris, Sumter Co. (1859)

Lakeland, Lanier Co. (1962)

Lakemont, Rabun Co. (1920)

Lake Park, Lowndes Co. (1920)

Lake Ravenel, Polk Co. (1920)

Lakeside, Richmond Co. (1894)

Lake Tara, Clayton Co. (1962)

Lakeview, Catoosa Co. (1962)

Lakeview, Peach Co. (1962)

Lakewood, Fulton Co. (1962); part of Atlanta.

Lakewood Heights, Fulton Co. (1962); part of Atlanta.

Lamar, Bibb Co. (1847)

Lamar, Sumter Co. (1920)

Lamara Heights, Chatham Co. (1962); part of Savannah.

Lamars Mill, Upson Co. (1881)

Lamarville, Chatham Co. (1962)

Lambert, Liberty Co. (1920); R.R. name is Palmer.

Lambs, Polk Co. (1920)

Lamkins, Columbia Co. (1894)

Lamont, Lamar Co. (1920)

Lamont, Monroe Co. (1894)

Lancaster, Marion Co. (1920)

Lancaster, Putnam Co. (1894)

Lancaster, Wayne Co. (1894)

Land, Hall Co. (1920)

Landers, Floyd Co. (1894)

Landers, Pickens Co. (1881)

Landrum, Dawson Co. (1920)

Landsberg, Montgomery Co. (1894)

Lane, Chatham Co. (1962)

Lane, Forsyth Co. (1920)

Laney, Mitchell Co. (1920)

Lang, Camden Co. (1920)

Lang, Carroll Co. (1894)

Langsbury, Camden Co. (1881)

Langston, Lincoln Co. (1920)

Langtry, Emanuel Co. (1894)

Lanier, Bryan Co. (1920)

Lanier, Macon Co. (1847)

Lanier Heights, Bibb Co. (1962)

Lannahassee, Stewart Co. (1847)

Lanton's Mills, Screven Co. (1894)

Laredo, Cherokee Co. (1920)

Larksville, Jones Co. (1847)

Laroche Park, Chatham Co. (1962); part of Savannah.

Larrett, Emanuel Co. (1894)

Lasters, Carroll Co. (1920)

Laston, Bulloch Co. (1881)

Latham, Haralson Co. (1920)

Lathemtown, Cherokee Co. (1962)

Latimer, Wilkes Co. (1894)

Latimers, DeKalb Co. (1847)

Latimores Mills, Hancock Co. (1847)

Launcelot, Irwin Co. (1920)

Laura, Union Co. (1894)

Laura, Wilkes Co. (1894)

Laurel, Dawson Co. (1920)

Laurel Hill, Carroll Co. (1881); former name of Lairdsborough.

Laurens Hill, Laurens Co. (1920)

Lavender, Floyd Co. (1920)

Lavender, Wilkinson Co. (1894)

Lavilla, Houston Co. (1920)

Lavinia, Ware Co. (1920)

LaVista, DeKalb Co. (1962)

Lavonia, Franklin Co. (1920); also known as Aquilla (1881).

Lawrenceville, Gwinnett Co. (1920)

Lawson, Colquitt Co. (1920)

Lawson, Pulaski Co. (1870)

Lawson, Wilcox Co. (1870)

Lawson Air Force Base, Chattahoochee Co. (1962); part of Fort Benning.

Lawsons Crossing, Burke Co. (1920)

Lawton, Burke Co. (1881); P.O. name is Lawtonville.

Lawton, Clinch Co. (1881); another name for DuPont.

Lawton, Jenkins Co. (1920)

Lawtonville, Burke Co. (1881); R.R. name is Lawton.

Lax, Coffee & Irwin Cos. (1962)

Layfield, Taylor Co. (1920)

Lays, Cherokee Co. (1894)

Lazaretto, Chatham Co. (1920)

Leach, Spalding Co. (1894)

Leaf, White Co. (1920)

Leah, Columbia Co. (1920)

Leake, Wayne Co. (1920)

Leakesville, Jasper Co. (1881)

Leakton, Newton Co. (1920)

Leary, Calhoun Co. (1920)

Leas Crossing, Dade Co. (1881); another name for Wildwood.

Leathers Ford, Lumpkin Co. (1847)

Leathersville, Lincoln Co. (1920)

Leatherwood, Habersham Co. (1894)

Leatherwood, Stephens Co. (1920)

Leb, Thomas Co. (1894)

Lebanon, Cherokee Co. (1920); R.R. name is Verd Antique (1920) & Toonigh (1962).

Lebanon, Cobb Co. (1847)

Lebanon, Milton (Fulton) Co. (1881)

Ledbetter, Baker Co. (1894)

Lee, Habersham Co. (1859)

Leefield, Bulloch Co. (1920)

Lee Pope, Crawford Co. (1920)

Lee Roy, Haralson Co. (1894)

Leesburg, Lee Co. (1920)

Lees Crossing, Troup Co. (1962)

Lee's Lake, Wayne Co. (1894)

Lee's Mills, Berrien Co. (1894)

Lee's Mills, Walker Co. (1894)

Lee's Store, Appling Co. (1894)

Leguin, Newton Co. (1920)

Lehigh, Jeff Davis Co. (1920)

Lehigh, Richmond Co. (1962)

Leicht, Glynn Co. (1920)

Leighton, Coffee Co. (1894)

Lela, Seminole Co. (1920)

Leland, Cobb Co. (1962)

Leland, Mitchell Co. (1920)

Lela Station, Seminole Co. (1920)

Leliaton, Coffee Co. (1881)

Leliaton, Atkinson Co. (1920)

Lelon, Berrien Co. (1894)

Leman, Emanuel Co. (1962)

Lena, Cobb Co. (1920)

Lenard, Cobb Co. (1920)

Lenas, Liberty Co. (1920)

Leno, Habersham Co. (1881)

Lenox, Berrien Co. (1894)

Lenox, Cobb Co. (1894)

Lenox, Cook Co. (1920)

Lenox Square, Fulton Co. (1962); part of Atlanta.

Lens, Colquitt Co. (1920)

Leo, White Co. (1920); R.R. name is Meldean.

Leola, Screven Co. (1920)

Leon, Dodge Co. (1920)

Leonard, Bryan Co. (1881)

Leoron, Columbia Co. (1920)

Leroy, Bacon Co. (1920)

Le Roy, Burke Co. (1920)

Leroy, DeKalb Co. (1894)

Leslie, Sumter Co. (1920)

Lester, Campbell (Fulton) Co. (1894)

Lester, Mitchell Co. (1920)

Lesters District, Burke Co. (1881); also known as Munnerlyn, Lumpkins, & Thomas Station.

Lesters Mill, Dooly Co. (1870)

Letford, Bryan Co. (1920)

Level, Monroe Co. (1894)

Levere, Ware Co. (1847)

Levere, Echols Co. (1870)

Leverett, Lincoln Co. (1920)

Leverett, Webster Co. (1962); also spelled Leveretts (1920).

Leveretts, Webster Co. (1920); also spelled Leverett (1962).

Lew, Tattnall Co. (1894)

Lewis, Macon Co. (1920)

Lewis, Screven Co. (1920)

Lewis Crossing, Emanuel Co. (1894)

Lewisianna, Hancock Co. (1847)

Lewis' Mills, Bartow Co. (1894)

Lewiston, Columbia Co. (1962)

Lewiston, Forsyth Co. (1881)

Lewiston, Wilkinson Co. (1920)

Lewner, Union Co. (1920)

Lexington, Oglethorpe Co. (1920)

Lexington Station, Oglethorpe Co. (1881); another name for Crawford.

Lexsy, Emanuel Co. (1920)

Liberty, Colquitt Co. (1920)

Liberty, Greene Co. (1894)

Liberty City, Chatham Co. (1962)

Liberty Hall, Burke Co. (1881); another name for Girard.

Liberty Hall, Taliaferro Co. (1894)

Libertyhill, Pike Co. (1881); also spelled Liberty Hill (1859).

Liberty Hill, Lamar Co. (1920)

Liclog, Gilmer Co. (1920)

Lide, Emanuel Co. (1920)

Lido, Emanuel Co. (1894)

Lifsey, Pike Co. (1920)

Light, Miller Co. (1894)

Lightfoot, Wilkinson Co. (1962)

Ligon, Bartow Co. (1920)

Lilac, Carroll Co. (1920)

Lilah, Henry Co. (1894)

Lilburn, Gwinnett Co. (1920)

Lillian, Washington Co. (1920)

Lillipond, Gordon Co. (1962); also spelled Lillypond (1920).

Lilly, Dooly Co. (1920)

Lillypond, Gordon Co. (1920); also spelled Lillipond (1962).

Lime, Hall Co. (1920)

Lime Branch, Polk Co. (1881)

Limerick, Liberty Co. (1920)

Limesink, Grady Co. (1920)

Lime Sink, Decatur Co. (1870)

Lime Sink, Laurens Co. (1859)

Limestone Spring, Hall Co. (1881); also spelled Lime Stone Spring (1894)

Lina, Wilkes Co. (1920)

Linchburg, Putnam Co. (1920)

Linco, Spalding Co. (1962)

Lincoln Mills, Muscogee Co. (1962)

Lincoln Park, Upson Co. (1962)

Lincolnton, Lincoln Co. (1920)

Lindale, Floyd Co. (1920)

Linder, Tift Co. (1962)

Lindsay's Creek, Muscogee Co. (1894)

Lindsey, Washington Co. (1920)

Lineville, Heard Co. (1894)

Lineys Store, Pike Co. (1881); also known as Finchers.

Linger, Floyd Co. (1920)

Linier, Macon Co. (1894)

Link, Stewart Co. (1920)

Linton, Hancock Co. (1920)

Linwood, Bartow Co. (1920); R.R. name is Halls.

Linwood, Muscogee Co. (1881)

Linwood, Randolph Co. (1859)

Linwood, Walker Co. (1962)

Lisbon, Lincoln Co. (1920)

Lisbon, Walker Co. (1894)

Lisco, Chattooga Co. (1920)

Listonia, Crisp Co. (1920)

Litchfield, Chatham Co. (1847)

Lithia Springs, Douglas Co. (1920)

Lithonia, DeKalb Co. (1920); also spelled Lythonia (1859)

Little Creek, Haralson Co. (1881)

Little Hell, McIntosh Co. (1847)

Littlejohn, Sumter Co. (1894)

Little Miami, Lowndes Co. (1962); located partly in Valdosta.

Little Prairie, Cass (Bartow) Co. (1859)

Little River, Chattooga Co. (1881)

Little River, Cherokee Co. (1859)

Little River, Wilkes Co. (1920)

Little Row, Gordon Co. (1894)

Littleville, Clayton Co. (1894)

Little York, Montgomery Co. (1881)

Live Oak, Decatur Co. (1894)

Liveoak, Mitchell Co. (1920)

Live Oak Gardens, Clayton Co. (1962); part of College Park.

Live Oak Grove, Mitchell Co. (1870)

Liverpool, Forsyth Co. (1920)

Livingston, Floyd Co. (1920)

Livingston, Lee Co. (1920)

Livingston, Worth Co. (1962)

Lizella, Bibb Co. (1920)

Lizzie, Cobb Co. (1920)

Lloyd, Dooly Co. (1894)

Location, Coweta Co. (1881); another name for Turin (1881); both Location & Turin shown on Map of Ga., Butts, 1870, in Coweta Co.

Lochermoss, Worth Co. (1894)

Lockair, Cobb Co. (1962)

Locket, Dougherty Co. (1920); also spelled Locketts (1962).

Lockett, Chattooga Co. (1920)

Locketts, Dougherty Co. (1962); also spelled Locket (1920).

Lockhart, Lincoln Co. (1920)

Lockville, Carroll Co. (1881)

Loco, Lincoln Co. (1920)

Locust Grove, Henry Co. (1920)

Lodi, Coweta Co. (1881); R.R. station is Sargent; also known as Wilcoxon.

Lodrick, Randolph Co. (1920)

Loftin, Heard Co. (1920); also spelled Lofton (1962).

Lofton, Butts Co. (1847)

Lofton, Heard Co. (1962); also spelled Loftin (1920)

Logan, Catoosa Co. (1920)

Loganville, Walton & Gwinnett Cos. (1962)

Lois, Berrien Co. (1920)

Lola, Lowndes Co. (1920)

Lollie, Laurens Co. (1920); R.R. name is Minter.

Loma, Appling Co. (1920)

Lombard, Emanuel Co. (1920)

Lombardy, Columbia Co. (1847)

Lombardy, McDuffie Co. (1881); also known as Dearing.

Lomonville, Hall Co. (1881); former name of Bowdre.

Lon, Bulloch Co. (1920)

Lone Oak, Meriwether Co. (1920)

Long, Polk Co. (1920)

Long Bluff, Camden Co. (1847)

Long Branch, Tattnall Co. (1881)

Long Branch, Evans Co. (1920)

Longcane, Troup Co. (1920); also spelled Long Cane (1894).

Long Island, Chatham Co. (1894)

Long Pond, Lowndes Co. (1894)

Long Pond, Montgomery Co. (1894); also spelled Longpond (1920).

Long's, Polk Co. (1894)

Longs Bridge, Hancock Co. (1859)

Longs Bridge, Washington Co. (1881)

Long Shoals, Jones Co. (1881)

Long Siding, Calhoun Co. (1962)

Longstreet, Elbert Co. (1894)

Longstreet, Pulaski Co. (1881); also spelled Long Street (1859).

Long Swamp, Pickens Co. (1881)

Longview, Banks Co. (1881)

Long View, Dodge Co. (1881)

Longview, Emanuel Co. (1894)

Longview, Habersham Co. (1894)

Longwood, Effingham Co. (1894)

Longwood, Newton Co. (1847)

Lookout, Dade Co. (1894)

Lookout, Walker Co. (1920)

Lookout Station, Dade Co. (1859)

Lorane, Bibb Co. (1920)

Lorenzo, Effingham Co. (1920)

Loretto, Screven Co. (1894)

Lost Mountain, Cobb Co. (1920)

Lota, Thomas Co. (1920)

Lothair, Montgomery Co. (1881)

Lothair, Treutlen Co. (1920)

Lothrop, Walker Co. (1920)

Lott, Montgomery Co. (1894)

Lotts, Coffee Co. (1920)

Lotus, Stewart Co. (1894)

Loudberg, Wilkes Co. (1920)

Loudsville, Habersham Co. (1859)

Loudsville, White Co. (1920)

Loughridge, Murray Co. (1847)

Louise, Troup Co. (1920)

Louisville, Jefferson Co. (1920)

Louthers Still, Coffee Co. (1920)

Louvale, Stewart Co. (1920)

Louvale Station, Stewart Co. (1920)

Lovejoy, Clayton Co. (1962); also known as Lovejoys Station (1920).

Lovejoys Station, Clayton Co. (1920); also known as Lovejoy (1962).

Lovelace, Troup Co. (1920)

Lovett, Laurens Co. (1920)

Lovette, Burke Co. (1881)

Loving, Fanning Co. (1920)

Lowe, Harris Co. (1847)

Lowe, Macon Co. (1894)

Lowell, Carroll Co. (1920)

Lowell, Randolph Co. (1847)

Lower Bluff, McIntosh Co. (1920)

Lowery, Telfair Co. (1920)

Lowry, Fayette Co. (1920)

Lowthers Still, Atkinson Co. (1920)

Loyal, Carroll Co. (1881)

Loyola, Irwin Co. (1847)

Lucile, Miller Co. (1920)

Lucile, Sumter Co. (1894)

Lucius, Gilmer Co. (1920)

Luck, Hall Co. (1894)

Luckie, Berrien Co. (1920)

Lucky, Haralson Co. (1920)

Lucky, Jefferson Co. (1894)

Lucky, Wilcox Co. (1894)

Lucy Lake, Berrien Co. (1920)

Ludovic, Bulloch Co. (1920)

Lodowici, Long Co. (1920)

Ludville, Pickens Co. (1920)

Luella, Henry Co. (1920)

Luke, Berrien Co. (1894)

Luke, Early Co. (1962)

Luke, Turner Co. (1920)

Luke, Wilcox Co. (1894)

Luke's Store, Columbia Co. (1894)

Lula, Hall & Banks Cos. (1962)

Lulah, Banks & Habersham Cos. (1881)

Lula Lake, Dade Co. (1920)

Lulaton, Wayne Co. (1881); also known as Satilla.

Lulaton, Brantley Co. (1920)

Lulaville, Ben Hill Co. (1920)

Lulaville, Wilcox Co. (1894)

Lumber City, Telfair & Wheeler Cos. (1962)

Lumberton, Wilcox Co. (1870)

Lumite, Habersham Co. (1962)

Lumpkin, Stewart Co. (1920)

Lumpkins, Burke Co. (1881); also known as Munnerlyn, Lesters District & Thomas Station.

Lumpkins Station, Burke Co. (1870)

Lupont, Effingham Co. (1920)

Lusk, Fannin Co. (1920)

Luther, Warren Co. (1920)

Luthersville, Meriwether Co. (1920); P.O. name for Lutherville (1962).

Lutherville, Meriwether Co. (1962); R.R. name for Luthersville.

Luxomni, Gwinnett Co. (1920)

Luz, Henry Co. (1920)

Lyerly, Chattooga Co. (1920)

Lyerly Junction, Chattooga Co. (1920)

Lyken, Clinch Co. (1920)

Lynch, White Co. (1920)

Lyncon, Ware Co. (1894)

Lyneville, Taliaferro Cc. (1920)

Lynhurst, Chatham Co. (1962); part of Savannah.

Lynn, Decatur Co. (1920)

Lynn, Tattnall Co. (1920)

Lyons, Montgomery Co. (1894)

Lyons, Tattnall Co. (1894)

Lyons, Toombs Co. (1920)

Lythonia, DeKalb Co. (1859); also spelled Lithonia (1920).

Lytle, Walker Co. (1920)

Mable, Camden Co. (1920)

Mable, Cherokee Co. (1894)

Mableton, Cobb Co. (1920)

Mabry, Carroll Co. (1920)

McAfee, DeKalb Co. (1962)

McArthur, Montgomery Co. (1894)

McAuthur, Wheeler Co. (1920)

McBean, Richmond Co. (1920)

McBeans Depot, Richmond Co. (1881)

McBride, Coweta Co. (1962); part of Newnan.

McBride, Montgomery Co. (1894)

McCall, Wilcox Co. (1920)

McCallie, Bartow Co. (1920)

McCarty, Johnson Co. (1920)

McCaysville, Fannin Co. (1920)

McClellans Mills, Worth Co. (1881); also known as McLellans Mills and Vines Mills.

McClure, DeKalb Co. (1894)

McCollum, Coweta Co. (1920)

McConnell, Cherokee Co. (1920)

McConnell, Walker Co. (1894)

McConnellsville, Walker Co. (1920)

McCord, Columbia Co. (1920)

McCord, Lincoln Co. (1894)

McCords, Floyd Co. (1894)

McCollin, Putnam Co. (1870)

McCormick, Pulaski Co. (1870)

McCrary, Bibb Co. (1894)

McCrary Settlement, Upson Co. (1962)

McCullough, Fannin Co. (1920)

McCutchen, Whitfield Co. (1920)

McDade, Richmond Co. (1894)

McDade's Mills, Richmond Co. (1894)

McDaniel, Pickens Co. (1920)

McDaniels, Gordon Co. (1962); also known as McHenry.

McDew, Jeff Davis Co. (1920)

McDonald, Coffee Co. (1920)

McDonald, Glynn Co. (1847)

McDonald, Thomas Co. (1881)

McDonald, Wilkinson Co. (1870)

McDonald's, Coffee Co. (1894)

McDonalds Mills, Bibb Co. (1847)

McDonalds Mill, Coffee Co. (1881); also known as Darts Mills.

McDonough, Henry Co. (1920)

McDuffie, Wilcox Co. (1870)

McEachern, Brooks Co. (1894)

Macedonia, Cherokee Co. (1881); also spelled Mascedonia (1962).

Macedonia, Miller Co. (1920)

McElhannon, Jackson Co. (1894)

McElroy, Bibb Co. (1920)

McElveensville, Baker Co. (1859)

McElvinville, Mitchell Co. (1870)

Maceo, Emanuel Co. (1920)

McGillisse's Bridge, Bryan Co. (1894)

McGinnis, Bartow Co. (1920)

McGregor, Montgomery Co. (1920)

McGriff, Bleckley Co. (1920)

McGriff, Pulaski Co. (1894)

McGillines Bridge, Bryan Co. (1881)

Mc Gruder, Burke Co. (1920)

McGuire, Floyd Co. (1881)

McGuries Store, Floyd Co. (1859)

McGruies Crossing, Bartow Co. (1920)

Machen, Jasper Co. (1920)

McHenry, Gordon Co. (1962); also known as McDaniels.

Machinery City, Cobb Co. (1920)

McIntire, Wilkinson Co. (1859)

McIntosh, Liberty Co. (1920)

McIntosh, Webster Co. (1870)

McIntosh Mill Village, Coweta Co. (1962)

McIntosh Reserve, Carroll & Coweta Cos. (1847)

McIntyre, Wilkinson Co. (1920); also spelled McIntire (1859)

McIver, McIntosh Co. (1894)

McIvoe, Cobb Co. (1894)

McKee, Dawson Co. (1920)

McKenzie, Crisp Co. (1962)

McKibben, Butts Co. (1920)

McKinney, Upson Co. (1962); also spelled McKinneys (1920)

McKinneys, Upson Co. (1920); also spelled McKinney (1962).

McKinnon, Wayne Co. (1920)

Macksville, Early Co. (1894)

Macland, Cobb Co. (1962)

McLeans, Coffee Co. (1920)

McLellans Mills, Worth Co. (1881); also known as McClellans Mills & Vines Mills.

McLemore, Walker Co. (1894)

McLemores Bridge, Emanuel Co. (1870)

McLenson, Early Co. (1920)

McLeod, Effingham Co. (1894)

McLeod, Emanuel Co. (1920)

McLeory, Clarke Co. (1894)

McManue, Glynn Co. (1962)

McNeils, Colquitt Co. (1920)

McNutt, Clarke Co. (1881)

McNutt, Oconee Co. (1894)

Macon, Bibb Co. (1920)

Macon and Augusta Junction, Bibb Co. (1894)

Macon and Northern Junction, Bibb Co. (1894)

Macon Junction, Bibb Co. (1920); another name for Central Railroad Junction.

Macon Yard, Bibb Co. (1962); part of Macon.

Macopin, Paulding Co. (1920)

McPherson, Paulding Co. (1920)

McPherson, Fulton Co. (1894)

McQueen, Chatham Co. (1894)

McQueens, Chatham Co. (1920)

McRae, Telfair Co. (1920)

McRae Junction, Telfair Co. (1962)

McRaes Mill, Montgomery Co. (1870)

McRaes Store, Telfair Co. (1870)

McRaeville, Grady Co. (1920)

McTyeire, Towns Co. (1894)

McVeigh, Pierce Co. (1894)

McVille, Telfair Co. (1881)

McVille, Hart Co. (1894)

McWhorter, Douglas Co. (1920)

Madison, Morgan Co. (1920)

Madison Springs, Madison Co. (1920)

Madola, Fannin Co. (1920)

Madras, Coweta Co. (1920)

Madray Springs, Wayne Co. (1962)

Magdalena, Meriwether Co. (1920)

Maggie, Pike Co. (1920)

Maggie, Laurens Co. (1894)

Magnes, Lowndes Co. (1894)

Magnie Gap, Dade Co. (1962)

Magnolia, Clinch Co. (1881)

Magnolia, Mitchell Co. (1920)

Magnolia, Pulaski Co. (1881)

Magnolia, Sumter Co. (1847)

Magnolia Park, Chatham Co. (1962); part of Savannah.

Magnolia Springs, Sumter Co. (1881); another name for Plains of Dura.

Magoon, Chatham Co. (1920)

Magruder, Burke Co. (1962)

Mahan, Walker Co. (1920)

Mahaers Quarry, Henry Co. (1962)

Mahoney, Brantley Co. (1962)

Major, Coweta Co. (1920)

Malbone, Bartow Co. (1920)

Malden Branch, Bryan Co. (1920)

Malinda, Barrow Co. (1920)

Malinda, Jackson Co. (1894)

Mallary, Twiggs Co. (1962)

Mallory, Morgan Co. (1920)

Mallorysville, Wilkes Co. (1881); also spelled Malloryville (1920).

Malloryville, Wilkes Co. (1920); also spelled Mallorysville (1881).

Malvern, Emanuel Co. (1920)

Manassas, Tattnall Co. (1920)

Manchester, Fulton Co. (1894)

Manchester, Meriwether Co. (1920)

Mandeville, Carroll Co. (1920)

Mangham, Glynn Co. (1847)

Manila, Monroe Co. (1920)

Manning, Laurens Co. (1920)

Manor, Ware Co. (1920)

Mansfield, Newton Co. (1920).

Manta, Chattahoochee Co. (1920)

Maple, Morgan Co. (1894)

Mapleford, Colquitt Co. (1894)

Maples, Floyd Co. (1920)

Mapleton, Mitchell Co. (1920)

Mapleville, Colquitt Co. (1881)

Maps, Greene Co. (1847)

Marble, Colquitt Co. (1920)

Marble Cliff, Gilmer Co. (1894)

Marble Head, Pickens Co. (1881)

Marblehill, Pickens Co. (1920)

Marble Works, Pickens Co. (1859)

Marco, Jasper Co. (1894)

Marcus, Jackson Co. (1920)

Marengo, Glynn Co. (1847)

Marengo, McIntosh Co. (1894)

Marevista, Glynn Co. (1894)

Margie, Floyd Co. (1920)

Margret, Fannin Co. (1920)

Marietta, Cobb Co. (1920)

Marietta East, Cobb Co. (1962)

Marion, Gilmer Co. (1920)

Marion, Irwin Co. (1920)

Marion, Lowndes Co. (1894)

Marion, Twiggs Co. (1881)

Markett, Sumter Co. (1894)

Marl, Decatur Co. (1894)

Marlow, Effingham Co. (1920)

Marquis, Decatur Co. (1894)

Mars. Lowndes Co. (1894)

Marsh, Walker Co. (1920)

Marshall, Crisp Co. (1962)

Marshallsville, Macon Co. (1859); also spelled Marshallville (1920).

Marshallville, Macon Co. (1920); also spelled Marshallsville (1859).

Marthasville, Macon Co. (1881); another name for Browns Lane.

Martin, Franklin Co. (1881)

Martin, Stephens Co. (1920)

Martindale, Walker Co. (1920)

Martinez, Columbia & Richmond Cos. (1962)

Martins, Liberty Co. (1920)

Martins, Macon Co. (1847)

Martins Bluff, Camden Co. (1881)

Martins Crossroads, Randolph Co. (1962)

Martinsville, Columbia Co. (1894)

Marvin, Washington Co. (1920)

Marysville, Johnson Co. (1881)

Mascedonia, Cherokee Co. (1962); also spelled Macedonia (1881).

Mascotte, Pickens Co. (1920)

Mash, Walker Co. (1962)

Mashes, Thomas Co. (1881)

Mason, Heard Co. (1920)

Masonville, DeKalb Co. (1894)

Massee, Cook Co. (1920)

Massey, Montgomery Co. (1894)

Massey, Walker Co. (1894)

Massey Mill, Bibb Co. (1894)

Masseys, Chattahoochee Co. (1894)

Masseys Lane, Macon Co. (1920)

Mat, Forsyth Co. (1920); also spelled Matt (1962).

Match, Elbert Co. (1962)

Math, Emanuel Co. (1881)

Mathews Spur, Upson Co. (1920)

Matlee, Emanuel Co. (1920)

Matlock, Tattnall Co. (1920)

Matt, Forsyth Co. (1962); also spelled Mat (1920).

Matthews, Jefferson Co. (1920)

Mattie, Pulaski Co. (1920)

Mattox, Charlton Co. (1962)

Mattox Mills, Tattnall Co. (1870)

Maud, Campbell (Fulton) Co. (1920)

Mauda, Hancock Co. (1881)

Mauk, Taylor Co. (1920)

Mauldin, Habersham Co. (1881); also known as Amys Creek.

Mauldins Mills, Hall Co. (1920)

Mauzy, Colquitt Co. (1920)

Max, Talbot Co. (1920)

Maxade, Macon Co. (1894)

Maxey, Oglethorpe Co. (1859); also spelled Maxeys (1920).

Maxeys, Oglethorpe Co. (1920); also spelled Maxy (1859).

Maxim, Lincoln Co. (1920)

Maxwell, Fannin Co. (1920)

Maxwell, Grady Co. (1920)

Maxwell, Jasper Co. (1920)

Maxwelton, Clayton Co. (1920)

May, Clinch Co. (1894)

Mayberry, Laurens Co. (1920)

Mayday, Echols Co. (1920)

Mayday, Henry Co. (1894)

Mayfield, Hancock Co. (1920)

Mayfield, Warren Co. (1859)

Mayhaw, Miller Co. (1920); also spelled Mayhew (1962).

Mayhew, Miller Co. (1962); also spelled Mayhaw (1920).

Maynard, Monroe Co. (1881)

Mays, Glynn Co. (1847)

Maysie, Jeff Davis Co. (1920)

Mayson, Fulton Co. (1962); part of Atlanta.

Maystown, Butts Co. (1894)

Maysville, Banks & Jackson Cos. (1920); also known as Midway (1881).

Maysville, Stewart Co. (1847)

Mayview, Washington Co. (1920)

Mayville, Columbia Co. (1894)

Mazeppa, Milton (Fulton) Co. (1881)

Mead, Bibb Co. (1962)

Meadow, Gwinnett Co. (1920)

Meadow, Johnson Co. (1962); also spelled Meadows (1920).

Meadows, Johnson Co. (1920); also spelled Meadow (1962); P.O. name is Spann (1920).

Meansville, Pike Co. (1920)

Mears, Screven Co. (1920)

Mecca, Campbell (Fulton) Co. (1894)

Mechanics Hill, Richmond Co. (1920)

Mechanicsville, Gwinnett Co. (1962)

Mechanicsville, Jasper Co. (1920)

Meda, Putnam Co. (1920)

Medders, Bacon Co. (1920)

Medicinal Springs, Walker Co. (1847); also known as Gordons Medicinal Springs (1870), Neals Store (1881), & Gordon Springs (1920).

Medicus, Madison Co. (1894)

Meeks, Johnson Co. (1920)

Megahee, McDuffie Co. (1920)

Meigs, Thomas Co. (1920)

Meinhard, Chatham Co. (1920)

Meldean, White Co. (1920); P.O. name in Leo.

Meldrim, Effingham Co. (1920)

Melley, Johnson Co. (1920)

Melrose, Echols Co. (1881)

Melrose, Lowndes Co. (1920)

Melson, Floyd Co. (1920)

Melton, Richmond Co. (1920)

Melton, Walton Co. (1920)

Melville, Chattooga Co. (1881)

Melville, Pickens Co. (1920)

Melvin, Irwin Co. (1920)

Mendes, Tattnall Co. (1920)

Menlo, Chattooga Co. (1920)

Mercer, Echols Co. (1920)

Mercer, Terrell Co. (1920)

Mercer Institute, Greene Co. (1847)

Mercer's Mills, Worth Co. (1894)

Meridian, McIntosh Co. (1920)

Meriwether, Baldwin Co. (1920)

Meriwether White Sulphur Springs, Meriwether Co. (1962); also known as White Sulphur Springs (1920).

Merle, Houston Co. (1920)

Merrell Factory, Greene Co. (1847); also spelled Merrills Factory (1881).

Merrill, Heard Co. (1894)

Merrills Factory, Greene Co. (1881); also spelled Merrell Factory (1847).

Merrillville, Thomas Co. (1920).

Merritt, Emanuel Co. (1920)

Merritts Mills Cobb Co. (1847)

Merrymans St. Mill, Tattnall Co. (1870)

Mershon, Pierce Co. (1920)

Mesena, Warren Co. (1920)

Metasville, Wilkes Co. (1920)

Metcalf, Thomas Co. (1920)

Methvins, Sumter Co. (1962)

Metter, Bulloch Co. (1894)

Metter, Candler Co. (1920)

Metzger, Effingham Co. (1881)

Mexico, Clinch Co. (1920)

Meyer, Muscogee Co. (1962)

Mica, Cherokee Co. (1920)

Mica, Pickens Co. (1881)

Middlebrooks, Upson Co. (1920)

Middle Ground, Screven Co. (1881); also spelled Middleground (1894).

Middle Ridge, Newton Co. (1881)

Middle River, Franklin Co. (1881)

Middleton, Appling Co. (1881)

Middleton, Elbert Co. (1920)

Middletons Store, Appling Co. (1859)

Midland, Muscogee Co. (1920)

Midriver, Camden Co. (1920)

Midville, Burke Co. (1920); also known as Burton (1881).

Midway, Baldwin Co. (1920); also known as Asylum (1920); Hardwick (1962) & Sanitarium (1962).

Midway, Catoosa Co. (1962)

Midway, Jackson & Banks Cos. (1881); another name for Maysville.

Midway, Jasper Co. (1894)

Midway, Liberty Co. (1962)

Midway, Meriwether Co. (1870)

Midway, Tattnall Co. (1962)

Mikado Place, Bibb Co. (1962)

Milan, Telfair & Dodge Cos. (1962)

Mildred, Taliaferro Co. (1920)

Miley, Emanuel Co. (1920)

Milford, Baker Co. (1920)

Millard, Stewart Co. (1859)

Mill Branch, Glascock Co. (1920)

Mill City, Bacon Co. (1920)

Mill Creek, Union Co. (1881)

Mill Creek, Whitfield Co. (1962)

Milldale, Crisp Co. (1920)

Milledgeville, Baldwin Co. (1920)

Millegy, Chatham Co. (1847)

Millen, Burke Co. (1881); also spelled Millin (1859).

Millen, Jenkins Co. (1920)

Millen, Screven Co. (1894)

Miller, Chatham Co. (1894)

Miller, Chattooga Co. (1920)

Miller, Gordon Co. (1894)

Millers, Chatham Co. (1920); also known as Millers Station (1881).

Millers, Gordon Co. (1881); also known as Millers Station & Blue Spring.

Millers Mills, Montgomery Co. (1870)

Millers Station, Chatham Co. (1881); also known as Millers (1920).

Millers Station, Gordon Co. (1881); also known as Millers & Blue Spring.

Millerville, Pulaski Co. (1920)

Mill Grove, Cobb Co. (1881)

Millhaven, Screven Co. (1920); also spelled Mill Haven (1859)

Millhaven Junction, Screven Co. (1962)

Millican, Catoosa Co. (1920)

Millin, Burke Co. (1859); also spelled Millen (1920).

Millner, Pike Co. (1881); also spelled Milner (1920).

Millray, Bulloch Co. (1920); also spelled Mill Ray (1859).

Mills, Whitfield Co. (1920)

Millstone, Oglethorpe Co. (1881)

Milltown, Berrien Co. (1920)

Millville, Bibb Co. (1881)

Millville, Cherokee Co. (1847)

Millwood, Dooly Co. (1859)

Millwood, Dougherty Co. (1870)

Millwood, Ware Co. (1920)

Milner, Lamar Co. (1920)

Milner, Pike Co. (1920); also spelled Millner (1881).

Milners Store, Fayette Co. (1920)

Milstead, Rockdale Co. (1920)

Milton, Spalding Co. (1920)

Milton, Wilkinson Co. (1881)

Mimosa, Walker Co. (1894)

Mims, Monroe Co. (1894)

Mims Mill, Bibb Co. (1847)

Mimsville, Baker Co. (1920)

Mina, DeKalb Co. (1894)

Mina, Fulton Co. (1920); part of Atlanta (1962).

Mineola, Lowndes Co. (1920)

Mineral Bluff, Fannin Co. (1962); also spelled Mineralbluff (1920).

Mineral Springs, Coweta Co. (1881); another name for Puckett Station.

Mineralsprings, Pickens Co. (1920); also spelled Mineral Springs (1894).

Miners Spring, Pickens Co. (1870)

Minerva, Houston Co. (1847)

Minetree, Houston Co. (1920)

Mingo, Pulaski Co. (1920)

Minisee, Colquitt Co. (1962)

Minnesota, Colquitt Co. (1962)

Minneta, Jasper Co. (1920)

Minnie, Irwin Co. (1894)

Minter, Laurens Co. (1920); P.O. name is Lollie.

Minton, Worth Co. (1920)

Minus, Screven Co. (1920)

Miona, Macon Co. (1894)

Miriam, Decatur Co. (1894)

Miriam, Seminole Co. (1920)

Mish, Forsyth Co. (1920)

Misletoe, Columbia Co. (1920); also spelled Mistletoe (1894).

Missionary Ridge, Walker Co. (1920); also known as Mission Ridge (1881).

Missionary Station, Floyd Co. (1881)

Mission Ridge, Walker Co. (1881); also known as Missionary Ridge.

Mistletoe, Columbia Co. (1894); also spelled Misletoe (1920).

Mistletow Bower, Carroll Co. (1859)

Mitchell, Charlton Co. (1870)

Mitchell, Glascock Co. (1920)

Mitchellton, Screven Co. (1881)

Mixon, Irwin Co. (1920)

Mize, Decatur Co. (1920)

Mize, Franklin Co. (1894)

Mize, Stephens Co. (1920)

Mizell, Charlton Co. (1881)

Mizell, Taylor Co. (1920)

Mizello, Charlton Co. (1894)

Mizpah, Effingham Co. (1894)

Mobile, Fannin Co. (1894)

Mobley, Screven Co. (1920)

Mobley Crossing, Bleckley Co. (1920)

Mobley Pond, Screven Co. (1881)

Moccasin, Rabun Co. (1881)

Mockville, Early Co. (1881)

Modesto, Cherokee Co. (1920)

Modoc, Emanuel Co. (1962)

Mogul, Bibb Co. (1920)

Molena, Pike Co. (1920)

Mollie, Cherokee Co. (1920)

Moniac, Charlton Co. (1920)

Monitor, Madison Co. (1920)

Monk, Campbell Fulton) Co. (1894)

Monroe, Thomas Co. (1920)

Monroe, Walton Co. (1920)

Monte, Emanuel Co. (1920)

Monteith, Chatham Co. (1920); also known as Fennell (1881).

Monteith, Effingham Co. (1870)

Montevideo, Elbert Co. (1870)

Montevideo, Hart Co. (1920); also spelled Montivedio (1962).

Montezuma, Macon Co. (1920)

Montgomery, Chatham Co. (1920)

Montgomery, Putnam Co. (1894)

Montgomery Road, Chatham Co. (1962)

Monticello, Jasper Co. (1920)

Montivedio, Elbert Co. (1847)

Montivedio, Hart Co. (1962); also spelled Montevideo (1920).

Montpelier, Bibb Co. (1920)

Montpelier, Monroe Co. (1847)

Montreal, DeKalb Co. (1920)

Montrose, Laurens Co. (1920)

Moody, Bacon Co. (1920)

Moody, Tattnall Co. (1920)

Moody Air Force Base, Lowndes & Lanier Cos. (1962); also known as Moody Field.

Moody Field, Lowndes & Lanier Cos. (1962); also known as Moody Air Force Base.

Moody's Mills, Paulding Co. (1894)

Moon, Cobb Co. (1920); also spelled Moons (1859).

Moonlight, Echols Co. (1920)

Moons, Cobb Co. (1859); also spelled Moon (1920).

Moons, Walker Co. (1962)

Moonsboro, Walker Co. (1962)

Moore, Chattooga Co. (1894)

Moore, Emanuel Co. (1881)

Moore, Laurens Co. (1920); P.O. name is Valambrosa; also spelled Moores (1962).

Moore, Upson Co. (1920)

Moores, Laurens Co. (1962); also spelled Moore (1920).

Moores, Richmond Co. (1920); part of Hephzibah (1962).

Moore's Bridge, Carroll Co. (1894)

Moores Mills, Cherokee Co. (1920)

Moore's Mills, Clayton Co. (1894)

Morea, Coffee & Atkinson Cos. (1962).

Moran, Crawford Co. (1920)

Morel, Effingham Co. (1881)

Moreland, Coweta Co. (1920)

Morgan, Calhoun Co. (1920)

Morgan, Wayne Co. (1920)

Morgan, Haralson Co. (1920)

Morgan Falls, Fulton Co. (1920)

Morgan Falls Junction, DeKalb Co. (1920)

Morganton, Fannin Co. (1920)

Morganville, Dade Co. (1920)

Morris, Franklin Co. (1881)

Morris, Quitman Co, (1962); another name for Morris Station (1920).

Morrison, Bryan Co. (1920); R.R. name is Reka.

Morrisons, Floyd Co. (1920)

Morris Siding, Fulton Co. (1962) part of Atlanta.

Morris Station, Quitman Co. (1920); also known as Morris (1962).

Morrow, Clayton Co. (1920); also known as Morrows Station (1881).

Morrows Station, Clayton Co. (1881); also known as Morrow (1920).

Morsleys Store, Franklin Co. (1881).

Mortimer, Forsyth Co. (1894)

Morton, Jones Co. (1920)

Morton Hall, Chatham Co. (1847)

Morvca, Lowndes Co. (1859)

Morven, Brooks Co. (1920)

Moselys Store, Franklin Co. (1859)

Moses, Carroll Co. (1894)

Mosley's Store, Franklin Co. (1894)

Moss, Banks Co. (1894)

Mossy, Houston Co. (1962)

Mossy Creek, White Co. (1920)

Motan, Hall Co. (1920)

Motley, Harris Co. (1920)

Motweilers Spur, Effingham Co. (1920)

Moultrie, Colquitt Co. (1920)

Mound Pond, Hancock Co. (1847)

Mountain City, Rabun Co. (1920)

Mountainhill, Harris Co. (192); also spelled Mountain Hill (1962).

Mountain House, Cass (Bartow) Co. (1859)

Mountain Park, Fulton Co. (1962)

Moutain Scene, Towns Co. (1920)

Moutaintown, Gilmer Co. (1920); also spelled Mountain Town (1859).

Mountain View, Clayton Co. (1962)

Mount Airy, Habersham Co. (1920)

Mount Airy, Harris Co. (1881)

Mount Berry, Floyd Co. (1920)

Mount Bethel, Cobb Co. (1962)

Mount Carmel, Henry Co. (1881)

Mount Carmel, Walker Co. (1962)

Mount Eolia, Towns Co. (1859)

Mount Eolia, Union Co. (1881)

Mount Gilead Cross Roads, Fulton Co. (1881); another name for Ben Hill.

Mount Gillian, Hancock Co. (1847)

Mount Hickory, Chattooga Co. (1881)

Mount Hope, Floyd Co. (1920)

Mount Horeb, Worth Co. (1870)

Mount Lake, Mitchell Co. (1870)

Mount Nebo, Baldwin Co. (1881)

Mount Pleasant, Glynn Co. (1881); also known as Dukesville.

Mount Pleasant, Laurens Co. (1847)

Mount Pleasant, Meriwether Co. (1870)

Mount Pleasant, Monroe Co. (1870)

Mount Pleasant, Newton Co. (1881)

Mount Pleasant, Wayne Co. (1881); R.R. name is Buffalo.

Mount Tabor, Forsyth Co. (1870)

Mount Vernon, Campbell (Fulton) Co. (1881)

Mount Vernon, Montgomery Co. (1920)

Mount Vernon, Polk Co. (1881)

Mount Vernon, Schley Co. (1870)

Mount Vernon, Walton Co. (1962)

Mountville, Troup Co. (1920)

Mount Yonah, White Co. (1881); another name for Cleveland; also known as Yonah.

Mount York Church, Monroe Co. (1870)

Mount Zion, Carroll Co. (1920); also known as Entrekins Mills (1881).

Mount Zion, Clay Co. (1870)

Mount Zion, Hancock Co. (1881)

Mount Zion, Meriwether Co. (1870)

Mount Zion, Spalding Co. (1881)

Moxley, Jefferson Co. (1962)

Moye, Calhoun Co. (1920)

Mozelle, Jackson Co. (1894)

Mud Creek, Clinch Co. (1894)

Mud Creek, Hall Co. (1894)

Mud Creek Mill, Clinch Co. (1881)

Mudge, Pierce Co. (1920)

Mulberry, Bartow Co. (1920)

Mulberry, Jackson Co. (1881)

Mulberry, Barrow Co. (1962)

Mulberry Grove, Harris Co. (1920)

Mule Creek, Brooks Co. (1881)

Mullinger, Dodge Co. (1894)

Mulville, Chattahoochee Co. (1881)

Mungen, Jefferson Co. (1894)

Municipal Airport, Fulton Co. (1962)

Munnerlin, Decatur Co. (1870)

Munnerlyn, Burke Co. (1920); also known as Lesters District, Lumpkins, & Thomas Station (1881).

Murchison, Bartow Co. (1920); also spelled Murchisons (1894).

Murchisons, Bartow Co. (1894); also spelled Murchison (1920).

Murphs, Houston Co. (1920)

Murphy, Colquitt Co. (1920)

Murphy, Wayne Co. (1962)

Murphy Junction, Fannin Co. (1920)

Murray, Schley Co. (1920)

Murray, Ware Co. (1920)

Murray Hill, DeKalb Co. (1920)

Murrays Cross Roads, Schley Co. (1881)

Murrayville, Hall Co. (1920)

Murryhill, Burke Co. (1920)

Muscogee, Muscogee Co. (1920); another name for Muscogee Junction (1962).

Muscogee Junction, Muscogee Co. (1962); part of Columbus; also known as Muscogee (1920).

Musella, Crawford Co. (1920)

Musgrove, Laurens Co. (1894)

Mussellwhite, Crisp Co. (1920)

Myers, Bulloch Co. (1920)

Myers, Effingham Co. (1894)

Myniks Mills, Twiggs Co. (1870)

Myra, Appling Co. (1920)

Myrick, Baldwin Co. (1847)

Myrtle, Houston Co. (1920)

Myrtle, Peach Co. (1962)

Mystic, Irwin Co. (1920)

Nacoochee, Habersham Co. (1859)

Nacoochee, White Co. (1920)

Nacora, Schley Co. (1920)

Nadine, Wilkinson Co. (1920)

Nahunta, Wayne Co. (1881)

Nahunta, Brantley Co. (1920)

Nails Bluff, Appling Co. (1870)

Nails Creek, Banks Co. (1881)

Nail's Ferry, Appling Co. (1894)

Nakomis, Crawford Co. (1920)

Nalley, Douglas Co. (1920)

Nalls Creek, Franklin Co. (1859)

Nameless, Laurens Co. (1920)

Nances, Muscogee Co. (1881)

Nankin, Brooks Co. (1920)

Nankipooh, Muscogee Co. (1962); another name for Highland Pines.

Nannie, Floyd Co. (1881); also known as Pinsons Station.

Naomi, Walker Co. (1920)

Napiers, Emanuel Co. (1920)

Naples, Pickens Co. (1920)

Napoleon, Union Co. (1920)

Narrows, Banks Co. (1920)

Nashville, Berrien Co. (1920)

Nasworthy, Johnson Co. (1894)

Natal, Union Co. (1920)

Natcheway, Randolph Co. (1881); also known as Nochway & Ward.

Nathaniel, Johnson Co. (1920)

Naval Air Station, DeKalb Co. (1962); also known as Atlanta Naval Air Station; base moved to Dobbins Air Force Base, Cobb Co. in 1959.

Naval Hospital, Laurens Co. (1962); part of Dublin.

Naval Ordinance Plant, Bibb Co. (1962); part of Macon.

Navy Supply Corps School, Clarke Co. (1962); part of Athens.

Navy Yard, Decatur Co. (1881); also known as Johnsons Landing, Steam Mill & Dickensons Store.

Naylor, Lowndes Co. (1920)

Neal, Pike Co. (1920)

Neal Dow, Cobb Co. (1881); another name for Smyrna.

Nealsboro, Floyd Co. (1894)

Neals Mills, Troup Co. (1920)

Neals Store, Whitfield Co. (1881)

Nebo, Paulding Co. (1920)

Nebraska, Columbia Co. (1859)

Nebraska, Richmond Co. (1881)

Nebula, Meriwether Co. (1920)

Neco, Richmond Co. (1920)

Needham, Ware Co. (1920)

Needmore, Brantley Co. (1920)

Needmore, Echols Co. (1962)

Neese, Madison Co. (1920)

Neills, Warren Co. (1881)

Neils, Thomas Co. (1920)

Neils, Warren Co. (1894)

Nell, Jenkins Co. (1920)

Nellieville, Dooly Co. (1920)

Nellwood, Bulloch Co. (1920)

Nelms, Dougherty Co. (1920)

Nelms, Elbert Co. (1920)

Nelson, Cobb Co. (1859)

Nelson, Pickens & Cherokee Cos. (1962)

Neon, Bryan Co. (1920)

Nesbit, Crisp Co. (1920)

Nesbit, Wayne Co. (1920)

Nesbit Place, Burke Co. (1894)

Nest, Worth Co. (1920)

Nettie, Forsyth Co. (1920)

Netts, Gilmer Co. (1894)

Nevils, Bulloch Co. (1920)

New, Chattooga Co. (1894)

New Agency, Taylor Co. (1881)

Newark, Thomas Co. (1920)

New Babylon, Paulding Co. (1881)

Newberry, Bleckley Co. (1920)

Newberry, Miller Co. (1894)

New Bethel, Floyd Co. (1894)

Newborn, Newton & Jasper Cos. (1962); also known as Sand Town (1881).

New Branch, Toombs Co. (1962)

New Bridge, Lumpkin Co. (1881); also spelled Newbridge (1894).

New Cotton Mill, Cherokee Co. (1962).

New Echota, Cass (Bartow) Co. (1847)

Newell, Charlton Co. (1920)

New Elm, Colquitt Co. (1962)

New England, Dade Co. (1920)

New England City, Dade Co. (1894)

New Era, Sumter Co. (1962)

New Georgia, Paulding Co. (1962)

Newgrade, Clinch Co. (1920)

New High Shoals, Walton Co. (1894)

New Holland, Hall Co. (1920); R.R. name is New Holland Junction.

New Holland Junction, Hall Co. (1920); P.O. name is New Holland.

New Hope, Bulloch Co. (1920)

New Hope, Glynn Co. (1847)

New Hope, Lincoln Co. (1962)

New Hope, Meriwether Co. (1870)

New Hope, Paulding Co. (1962); also spelled Newhope (1920).

New Hope, Pike Co. (1870)

New Hope Church, Douglas Co. (1920)

Newington, Screven Co. (1920)

New Lacy, Bacon Co. (1920)

New Liberty, Pickens Co. (1870)

Newman, Cobb Co. (1894)

New Manchester, Campbell Co. (1859)

New Manchester Factory, Campbell Co. (1870)

Newmarket, Monroe Co. (1920); also spelled New Market (1894)

New Mount Horeb, Worth Co. (1894)

Newnan, Coweta Co. (1920)

Newpoint, Sumter Co. (1962); also spelled New Point (1920).

Newport, Fannin Co. (1920)

New Prospect, Forsyth Co. (1881)

New Providence, Wilkinson Co. (1920)

New Rock Hill, Brooks Co. (1962)

New Rockwell, Jasper Co. (1881)

New Rockwell, Putnam Co. (1894)

New Rome, Floyd Co. (1920)

Newry, Troup Co. (1920)

New Sirmans, Clinch Co. (1962)

Newsom, Lee Co. (1920)

Newsville, Haralson Co. (1920)

New Switzerland, Habersham Co. (1962)

Newton, Baker Co. (1920)

Newton Factory, Newton Co. (1920)

Newtonville, Chatham Co. (1920)

Newtown, Cobb Co. (1859)

Newtown, Fulton Co. (1962)

Newtown, Gordon Co. (1849)

Newtown, Madison Co. (1894)

Newtown, Wilkes Co. (1962)

New York, Polk Co. (1962)

Neyami, Lee Co. (1962)

Nicholasville, Early Co. (1962)

Nicholasville, Miller Co. (1920)

Nicholls, Coffee Co. (1920)

Nicholson, Jackson Co. (1920); also known as Cooper (1881).

Nickajack, Cobb Co. (1920)

Nickelsville, Gordon Co. (1962)

Nicklesville, Wilkinson Co. (1962)

Nicklesville, Grady Co. (1962)

Nickolsonville, Chatham Co. (1962); part of Savannah.

Nickville, Elbert Co. (1881)

Nicojack, Cobb Co. (1894)

Nielly, Telfair Co. (1920)

Nile, Brooks Co. (1920); R.R. name is Spain.

Ninetyeight Mile Post, Coffee Co. (1894)

Ninnerville, Morgan Co. (1920)

Nisbets, Dade Co. (1881)

Nixon, Richmond Co. (1962)

Noah, Dawson Co. (1881)

Noah, Jefferson Co. (1920)

Noble, Walker Co. (1920)

Nochaway, Randolph Co. (1870); also spelled Nochway (1920) & Natcheway (1881); also known as Ward (1881).

Nochway, Randolph Co. (1920); also spelled Nochaway (1870) & Natcheway (1881); also known as Ward (1881).

Nochway, Terrell Co. (1870)

Noddings Point, Camden Co. (1847)

Nola, Cook Co. (1920)

Nolan, Morgan Co. (1894)

Noll, Chattooga Co. (1920)

Nona, Putnam Co. (1920); R.R. name is Dennis.

Noonday, Cobb Co. (1920)

Norcross, Gwinnett Co. (1920)

Norden, Bryan Co. (1920)

Norman, Wilkes Co. (1920)

Normandale, Dodge Co. (1894)

Norman Park, Colquitt Co. (1920)

Normans, Colquitt Co. (1920)

Normantown, Toombs Co. (1920)

Norris, Warren Co. (1962)

Norristown, Emanuel Co. (1920)

North Atlanta, DeKalb Co. (1962)

North Canton, Cherokee Co. (1962)

North Columbus, Muscogee Co. (1962); part of Columbus.

North Cornelia, Habersham Co. (1962)

Northcutt, Gilmer Co. (1920)

North Decatur, DeKalb Co. (1962)

North Druid Hills, DeKalb Co. (1962)

North Dublin, Laurens Co. (1962)

Northeast Plaza, Fulton Co. (1962)

North Elberton, Elbert Co. (1962)

Northen, Hancock Co. (1920)

North Helen, White Co. (1920); P.O. name is Robertstown.

North Highlands, Muscogee Co. (1962); part of Columbus.

North High Shoals, Oconee Co. (1962)

North Rome, Floyd Co. (1920); also known as Forrestville.

North Roswell, Fulton Co. (1962); part of Roswell.

North Side, Fulton Co. (1962); part of Atlanta.

North West Point, Troup Co. (1962)

Northwoods, DeKalb Co. (1962)

Norton, DeKalb Co. (1920)

Norton, Whitfield Co. (1920)

Norway, Harris Co. (1894)

Norwich, Taylor Co. (1920)

Norwood, Warren Co. (1920); also known as Gunns Mills (1881).

Note, Putnam Co. (1920)

Novetta, Forsyth Co. (1920)

Nuberg, Hart Co. (1920)

Nunez, Emanuel Co. (1920)

Nunn, Washington Co. (1920)

Nunnally, Walton Co. (1920); also spelled Nunnelly (1962).

Nunnelly, Walton Co. (1962); also spelled Nunnally (1920).

Nydia, Henry Co. (1920)

Nye, Milton (Fulton) Co. (1894)

Nye, Taliaferro Co. (1920)

Nyson, Fayette Co. (1920)

Oak, Cook Co. (1920)

Oak Bower, Hart Co. (1881)

Oakdale, Cobb Co. (1920)

Oakdale, Fulton Co. (1894)

Oakfield, Worth Co. (1920)

Oak Grove, Cherokee Co. (1962)

Oak Grove, DeKalb Co. (1962)

Oak Grove, Fulton Co. (1881)

Oak Grove, Hancock Co. (1847)

Oak Grove, Quitman Co. (1920)

Oak Hill, Gilmer Co. (1920)

Oak Hill, Greene Co. (1881)

Oak Hill, McIntosh Co. (1920)

Oak Hill, Newton Co. (1881)

Oakhurst, Chatham Co. (1962); part of Savannah.

Oakhurst, Cobb Co. (1920)

Oakhurst, DeKalb Co. (1962); part of Decatur.

Oakland, Gwinnett Co. (1847)

Oakland, Hall Co. (1859)

Oakland, Hancock Co. (1847)

Oakland, Lee Co. (1920)

Oakland, Meriwether Co. (1881)

Oakland, Terrell Co. (1894)

Oakland City, Fulton Co. (1962); part of Atlanta.

Oakland Heights, Bartow Co. (1962).

Oakland Institute, Cass (Bartow) Co. (1847)

Oakland Park, Muscogee Co. (1962); part of Columbus.

Oak Lawn, Baker Co. (1847)

Oaklawn, Brooks Co. (1920)

Oak Lawn, Dougherty Co. (1870)

Oaklawn, Houston Co. (1894)

Oak Level, Effingham Co. (1894)

Oakley Mill, Cobb Co. (1920)

Oakman, Gordon Co. (1920)

Oak Mountain, Harris Co. (1920); P.O. name is Cleola

Oak Park, Emanuel Co. (1920)

Oakridge, Meriwether Co. (1920); also spelled Oak Ridge (1859 & 1894).

Oak Shade, Fulton Co. (1920)

Oakwell, Camden Co. (1894)

Oakwood, Hall Co. (1920)

Oaky, Effingham Co. (1894)

Oaky Sink, Worth Co. (1870)

Oasis, Fannin Co. (1920)

Oats, Burke Co. (1920); also spelled Oatts (1962).

Oatts, Burke Co. (1962); also spelled Oats (1920).

Obe, Colquitt Co. (1881)

O'Berry, Atkinson Co. (1920)

O'Brien, Glynn Co. (1894)

Ocala, Irwin Co. (1894)

Occola, Terrell Co. (1859)

Oceana, Lowndes Co. (1894)

Ocean Wave, Ware Co. (1870)

Ocee, Fulton Co. (1962); also spelled Ocoee (1920).

Oceola, Lee Co. (1847)

Oceola, Oconee Co. (1894)

Ochillee, Chattahoochee Co. (1920); part of Fort Benning (1962).

Ochlochnee, Thomas Co. (1894)

Ochloknee, Colquitt Co. (1870)

Ockwalkee, Wheeler Co. (1920)

Ocilla, Irwin Co. (1920)

Ocmulgee, Jeff Davis Co. (1920)

Ocmulgee, Coffee Co. (1894)

Ocmulgee, Monroe Co. (1894)

Ocmulgee Bridge, Bibb Co. (1894)

Ocmulgee Mills, Butts Co. (1881); also known as Seven Islands (1881).

Ocmulgee River Bridge, Dodge Co. (1894)

Ocmulgeeville, Coffee Co. (1881)

Ocmulgee Wharf, Dodge Co. (1920)

Ocoee, Milton (Fulton) Co. (1920); also spelled Ocee (1962).

Oconee, Greene Co. (1881)

Oconee, Washington Co. (1920)

Oconee Heights, Clarke Co. (1920)

Oconee Mills, Hall Co. (1920)

Oconee River Bridge, Montgomery Co. (1894)

Oconee Siding, Baldwin Co. (1920)

Ocopilco, Lowndes Co. (1847); also spelled Okapilco (Brooks Co.) 1920).

Octagon, McIntosh Co. (1894)

Octavia, Cobb Co. (1920)

Octavia, Early Co. (1881)

Oculus, White Co. (1920)

Odchodkee, Randolph Co. (1859)

Odchodre, Quitman Co. (1894)

Odell, Forsyth Co. (1920)

Odells, Hall Co. (1881)

Odessa, Meriwether Co. (1894)

Odessa, Wayne Co. (1920)

Odessadale, Meriwether Co. (1920)

Odom, Emanuel Co. (1881)

Odomville, Emanuel Co. (1920)

Odum, Wayne Co. (1920)

Offerman, Pierce Co. (1920)

Ogden, Sumter Co. (1920)

Ogeechee, Glascock Co. (1881)

Ogeechee, Screven Co. (1920)

Ogeechee, Washington Co. (1894)

Ogeechee Church, Screven Co. (1847)

Ogeechee Road, Chatham Co. (1962)

Ogeecheeton, Chatham Co. (1962)

Oglesby, Elbert Co. (1920)

Oglethorpe, Chatham Co. (1894)

Oglethorpe, Macon Co. (1920)

Oglethorpe Bluff, Appling Co. (1870)

Oglethorpe Hotel, Glynn Co. (1894)

Oglethorpe University, Baldwin Co. (1847)

Oglethorpe University, DeKalb Co. (1920); part of North Atlanta (1962).

Ogletree Woods, Muscogee Co. (1962)

Ohio, Houston Co. (1920)

Ohoopee, Tattnall Co. (1881)

Ohoopee, Toombs Co. (1920)

Ohoopee, Emanuel Co. (1859)

Ohoopee Park, Emanuel Co. (1920)

Okapilco, Brooks Co. (1920); also spelled Ocopilco (Lowndes Co.) (1847).

Okenfenokee, Clinch Co. (1881)

Okefenokee, Ware Co. (1920)

Okloknee, Thomas Co. (1870); also spelled Oklonee (1870) & Ochlochnee (1920).

Ola, Henry Co. (1920)

Old Agency, Crawford Co. (1847)

Old Airport Community, Floyd Co. (1962)

Old Carrollton, Carroll Co. (1894)

Old Church, Burke Co. (1920)

Old Depot, Glynn Co. (1894)

Old Grade, Brantley Co. (1920)

Oldham, Ware Co. (1894)

Old Rock Hill, Brooks Co. (1962)

Old Town, Jefferson Co. (1847)

O'Learys, Chatham Co. (1920)

Olga, Stewart Co. (1920)

Olive, Ware Co. (1920)

Olive Branch, Meriwether Co. (1870)

Olive Branch, Talbot Co. (1962)

Olive Grove, Decatur Co. (1847)

Oliver, Screven Co. (1920)

Olives, Decatur Co. (1881)

Olix, Jackson Co. (1920)

Ollie, Gilmer Co. (1920)

Olliff, Brooks Co. (1894)

Olmstead, Washington Co. (1920)

Olney, Bulloch Co. (1920)

Olockochee Spring, Decatur Co. (1847)

Olympia, Lowndes Co. (1920)

Omaha, Stewart Co. (1920)

Omar, Wayne Co. (1920)

Omecron, Wilkinson Co. (1920)

Omega, Forsyth Co. (1894)

Omega, Tift Co. (1920)

Omega, Washington Co. (1894)

Omie, Bulloch Co. (1920)

O'Neals, Troup Co. (1847)

O'Neals Mills, Troup Co. (1881)

One Hundred Sixty-five Mile Post, Dougherty Co. (1894)

Onida, Liberty Co. (1920)

Ono, Campbell (Fulton) Co. (1894)

Oostanaula, Gordon Co. (1920)

Oothkaloga, Cass (Bartow) Co. (1847)

Ophelia, Wilkes Co. (1920)

Ophir, Cherokee Co. (1920)

Opossum, Madison Co. (1881)

Oran, Murray Co. (1920)

Orange, Chatham Co. (1962)

Orange, Cherokee Co. (1920)

Orchard Hill, Spalding Co. (1920); also known as Thornton Station (1881).

Ordway, Muscogee Co. (1920)

Ore Bank, Polk Co. (1894)

Oreburg, Floyd Co. (1920)

Oregon, Cobb Co. (1894)

Orel, Irwin Co. (1859)

Orel, Worth Co. (1870)

Oremont, Polk Co. (1920)

Orestes, Washington Co. (1920)

Oreta, Marion R. (1920)

Oreville, Polk Co. (1894)

Organ, Bryan Co. (1894)

Orianna, Treutlen & Laurens Cos. (1962)

Orico, Jeff Davis Co. (1920)

Orient, Gwinett Co. (1920)

Orland, Treutlen Co. (1920)

Orleans, Rockdale Co. (1920)

Orletta, Stewart Co. (1920)

Ormewood, Fulton Co. (1962); part of Atlanta.

Orr, Gilmer Co. (1920)

Orrs, Clayton Co. (1920)

Orrs, Coweta Co. (1847)

Orrsville, Gwinnett Co. (1847); also spelled Orrville (1881).

Orrville, Gwinnett Co. (1881); also spelled Orrsville (1847).

Orrville, Jackson Co. (1894)

Orrville, Washington Co. (1920)

Orser, Brantley Co. (1962)

Orsman, Floyd Co. (1920)

Orton, Floyd Co. (1920)

Osanda, Campbell (Fulton) Co. (1920)

Osborn, Towns Co. (1920)

Oscar, Telfair Co. (1920)

Oscarville, Forsyth Co. (1920)

Osceola, Oconee Co. (1881)

Osceola, Terrell Co. (1881)

Osgood, Cherokee Co. (1894)

Osgood, Cook Co. (1920)

Osierfield, Irwin Co. (1920)

Ossahatchie, Harris Co. (1920)

Osurtchee, Chattahoochee Co. (1881)

Oswald, Telfair Co. (1894)

Oswitchee, Chattahoochee Co. (1894)

Othela, Cherokee Co. (1920)

Other, Paulding Co. (1920)

Otis, Forsyth Co. (1920)

Otisca, Decatur Co. (1920)

Ottawa, Chatham Co. (1920)

Ottley, Fulton Co. (1920); part of Atlanta (1962).

Otto, Union Co. (1920)

Ousley, Lowndes Co. (1920)

Outland, Screven Co. (1894)

Oval, Paulding Co. (1920)

Overstreet, Emanuel Co. (1894)

Overton, Elbert Co. (1920)

Owen, Pierce Co. (1920)

Owens, Lee Co. (1881)

Owens, Upson Co. (1920)

Owensboro, Wilcox Co. (1920)

Owensbyville, Heard Co. (1920)

Owens Ferry, Camden Co. (1920)

Owens Mine, Carroll Co. (1847)

Owens Mine, Haralson Co. (1881)

Owlden, Coffee Co. (1894)

Owl Hollow, Walker Co. (1920)

Oxford, Newton Co. (1920)

Oxford Mills, Whitfield Co. (1894)

Oxmmor, Lowndes Co. (1894)

Ozell, Brooks Co. (1920)

Ozona, Toombs Co. (1920)

Ozora, Gwinnett Co. (1920)

Pace, Newton Co. (1920)

Pace, Twiggs Co. (1870)

Pachitla, Early Co. (1847)

Pachitla, Calhoun Co. (1881); also spelled Pachitta (1859) & Pachitala (1870).

Pachitla, Randolph Co. (1920)

Pachitta, Calhoun Co. (1859); also spelled Pachitla (1881) & Pachitala (1870).

Pachittala, Calhoun Co. (1870); also spelled Pachitta (1859) & Pachitla (1881).

Package, Macon Co. (1920)

Padena, Fannin Co. (1920)

Padgett, Jefferson Co. (1920)

Page, Cherokee Co. (1894)

Pages, Coweta Co. (1894)

Palace, Appling Co. (1894)

Palaky, Evans Co. (1920)

Palalto, Jasper Co. (1920)

Palmer, Long Co. (1920); P.O. name is Lambert.

Palmetto, was Campbell, now Fulton & Coweta (1920) & (1962).

Pametto, Oglethorpe Co. (1962)

Palmetto, Twiggs Co. (1920)

Palmour, Dawson Co. (1920)

Palmyra, Lee Co. (1920)

Palo Alto, Jasper Co. (1881)

Palos, Bleckley Co. (1920)

Pampas, Randolph Co. (1920)

Panhan, Warren Co. (1920)

Panhandle, Taylor Co. (1962)

Pannell, Walton Co. (1962)

Panola, DeKalb Co. (1920)

Pansy, Lincoln Co. (1920)

Pantertown, Fannin Co. (1962)

Panterville, Fannin Co. (1920)

Panther Creek, Habersham Co. (1881)

Panthersville, DeKalb Co. (1920)

Paoli, Madison Co. (1920)

Paper, Clarke Co. (1894)

Paradise, Barrow Co. (1920)

Paradise, Jackson Co. (1894)

Paradise, Walton Co. (1962)

Paramore, Jenkins Co. (1962); also known as Parramore Hill (1920).

Paran, Monroe Co. (1894)

Parhams, Franklin Co. (1962)

Paris, Coweta Co. (1881)

Paris Academy, Screven Co. (1870)

Parish, Bulloch Co. (1894)

Parish, Candler Co. (1920)

Parkchester, Muscogee Co. (1962); part of Columbus.

Parker, Franklin Co. (1847); also known as Parkers Store (Hart Co.) (1881) & Parkerstore (Hart Co.) (1920).

Parker, Cooly Co. (1847)

Parker, Worth Co. (1870)

Parkers, Sumter Co. (1920)

Parkersburg, Chatham Co. (1962)

Parkers Mill, Hancock Co. (1870)

Parker's Mills, Decatur Co. (1894)

Parkerstore, Hart Co. (1920); also known as Parkers Store (Hart Co.) (1881) & Parker (Franklin Co.) (1847).

Parkers Store, Hart Co. (1881); also known as Parkerstore (Hart Co.) (1920) & Parker (Franklin Co.) (1847).

Parkerville, Worth Co. (1920)

Park Hill, Hall Co. (1962); part of Gainesville.

Parkman, Chattahoochee Co. (1920)

Parkonia, Coffee Co. (1894)

Parks, Walker Co. (1894)

Parks, White Co. (1920)

Parks Bridge, Morgan Co. (1847)

Park's Mills, Greene Co. (1894)

Parkwood, Charham Co. (1962); part of Savannah.

Parnell, Columbia Co. (1894)

Parramore Hill, Jenkins Co. (1920); also known as Paramore (1962).

Parramore Hill, Screven Co. (1881)

Parrott, Terrell Co. (1920)

Parsons, Wilcox Co. (1920)

Parsons Mill, Hancock Co. (1870)

Paschal, Talbot Co. (1920)

Pasco, Thomas Co. (1920)

Passic, Wilkes Co. (1894)

Pataula, Randolph Co. (1847)

Pataula, Clay Co. (1920)

Pataula, Stewart Co. (1881)

Patesville, Dooly Co. (1894); also spelled Pateville (1881).

Pateville, Dooly Co. (1881); also spelled Patesville (1894).

Patillo, Lamar Co. (1920)

Patillo, Monroe Co. (1894)

Patrick, Spalding Co. (1920)

Patten, Thomas Co. (1920)

Patterson, Pierce Co. (1920)

Paul Echols Co. (1920)

Paulina, Harris Co. (1920)

Paulk, Coffee Co. (1894)

Pavillion, Chatham Co. (1894)

Pavo, Thomas & Brooks Cos. (1962)

Pawnee, Marion Co. (1920)

Pawnee, Grady Co. (1920)

Pax, Effingham Co. (1920)

Paxton, Liberty Co. (1894)

Paxton, Thomas Co. (1894)

Payne, Bibb Co. (1962)

Payne, Cherokee Co. (1920)

Paynes, Crawford Co. (1894)

Paynes Store, Dougherty Co. (1881)

Paynter, Fannin Co. (1920)

Pay Up, Hart Co. (1881)

Pazo, Upson Co. (1920)

Peace, Baker Co. (1920)

Peach Orchard, Richmond Co. (1962)

Peach Stone, Henry Co. (1920)

Peachstone Shoals, Henry Co. (1881); also spelled Peach Stone Shoals (1894).

Peachtree, Fulton Co. (1894)

Peachtree Park, Fulton Co. (1894)

Peachtree Station, Fulton Co. (1962); part of Atlanta.

Peacocks, Washington Co. (1920)

Peak, Taliaferro Co. (1847)

Pea Ridge, Marion Co. (1870)

Pearl, Camden Co. (1920)

Pearl, Elbert Co. (1920)

Pearl Spring, Coweta Co. (1881)

Pearly, Laurens Co. (1920)

Pearson, Atkinson Co. (1920)

Pearson, Coffee Co. (1894)

Peavine, Catoosa Co. (1894)

Pebble, Taylor Co. (1920)

Pecan, Clay Co. (1920)

Pecan City, Dougherty Co. (1920)

Peck, Glynn Co. (1847)

Peck, Worth Co. (1881); also known as Peckville.

Peckville, Worth Co. (1881); also known as Peck.

Peddy, Emanuel Co. (1920)

Pedenville, Pike Co. (1920)

Pedrick, Brooks Co. (1881)

Peeksville, Henry Co. (1920)

Peerman, Wilkes Co. (1920)

Pelham, Mitchell Co. (1920)

Pelot, Baldwin Co. (1920)

Pembroke, Bryan Co. (1920)

Pence, Cherokee Co. (1920)

Pendarvis, Wayne Co. (1870)

Pendarvis Store, Wayne Co. (1870)

Pendenville, Pike Co. (1962)

Pendergrass, Jackson Co. (1920)

Pendleton, Toombs Co. (1920)

Penfield, Greene Co. (1920); also spelled Pennfield (1847).

Penhoopee, Emanuel Co. (1920)

Penia, Crisp Co. (1920)

Penia, Dooly Co. (1894)

Pennelton, Treutlen Co. (1920)

Pennfield, Greene Co. (1847); also spelled Penfield (1920).

Pennick, Glynn Co. (1920); R.R. name is Zuta.

Pennington, Morgan Co. (1920)

Penns, Greene Co. (1894)

Pennsboro, Worth Co. (1870)

Peoples Crossing, Fayette Co. (1920)

Peoples Still, Grady Co. (1962)

Pepperton, Butts Co. (1920)

Perdue, Houston Co. (1894)

Perennial, Chattooga Co. (1962)

Perhaps, Troup Co. (1920)

Perkins, Burke Co. (1894)

Perkins, Jenkins Co. (1920)

Perkins Junction, Burke Co. (1881)

Perry, Houston Co. (1920)

Perrys Mills, Tattnall Co. (1881)

Perrys Mills, Toombs, Co. (1920)

Persia, Coffee Co. (1920)

Persico, Meriwether Co. (1920)

Persimmon, Rabun Co. (1920); also known as Blalock (1962).

Peru, Early Co. (1920)

Peru, Rockdale Co. (1894)

Pete, Dooly Co. (1920)

Peter, Chattooga Co. (1894)

Petermans, Mitchell Co. (1894)

Petersburg, Elbert Co. (1847)

Petersburg, Gordon Co. (1894)

Peterson, Montgomery Co. (1894)

Petrel, Cherokee Co. (1920)

Petross, Toombs Co. (1920); P.O. name is Edna.

Pettett, Pickens Co. (1920)

Petty, Mitchell Co. (1962)

Petty, Murray Co. (1920)

Peughs, Upson Co. (1894)

Peyton, Appling Co. (1920)

Peyton, Fulton Co. (1920)

Pfeiffer, Screven Co. (1920)

Pharr, Pickens Co. (1920)

Phelps, Whitfield Co. (1920)

Phidelta, Banks Co. (1920)

Phi Delta, Franklin Co. (1859)

Philadelphia, Jasper Co. (1881)

Philadelphia, Putnam Co. (1894)

Philema, Lee Co. (1920)

Philipi, Muscogee Co. (1920)

Phillip, Twiggs Co. (1920)

Phillips, Walker Co. (1894)

Phillipsburg, Tift Co. (1962)

Phillips Mill, Coffee Co. (1920)

Philmon, Taylor Co. (1894)

Philomath, Oglethorpe Co. (1920)

Phinizy, Columbia Co. (1920)

Phinizy, Richmond Co. (1881)

Pheonix, Putnam Co. (1920)

Phoebe, Brooks Co. (1894)

Picciola, Laurens Co. (1881)

Pickard, Upson Co. (1920)

Pickren, Coffee Co. (1881)

Pidcock, Brooks Co. (1920)

Piedmont, Forsyth Co. (1894)

Piedmont, Harris Co. (1859)

Piedmont, Lamar Co. (1920)

Piedmont, Pike Co. (1894)

Pierceville, Fannin Co. (1920)

Pierceville, Gilmer Co. (1859)

Pierceville, Heard Co. (1894)

Pike, Gilmer Co. (1920)

Pike, Montgomery Co. (1881)

Pikes Bluff, Glynn Co. (1847)

Pikes, Peak, Twiggs Co. (1920)

Piles, Glynn Co. (1847)

Pilgrim, Bleckley Co. (1920)

Pilkinton's Mills, Pike Co. (1894)

Pill, Webster Co. (1894)

Pilot, Union Co. (1920)

Pin, Paulding Co. (1920)

Pinargo, Wilcox Co. (1920)

Pickneyville, Gwinnett Co. (1881)

Pindertown, Worth Co. (1870)

Pindertown, Dooly Co. (1847)

Pinebloom, Atkinson Co. (1920)

Pine Bloom, Ware Co. (1881)

Pineboro, Colquitt Co. (1920)

Pine Chapel, Gordon Co. (1962)

Pine City, Wilcox Co. (1920)

Pinedale, Randolph Co. (1894)

Pinedale, Talbot Co. (1920)

Pine Gardens, Chatham Co. (1962); part of Savannah.

Pine Grove, Appling Co. (1920)

Pine Grove, Douglas Co. (1894)

Pine Harbor, McIntosh Co. (1962)

Pine Hill, Decatur Co. (1859)

Pine Hill, Elbert Co. (1894)

Pine Hill, Jefferson Co. (1847)

Pinehill, Laurens Co. (1920)

Pine Hill, Muscogee Co. (1962); part of Columbus.

Pine Hill, Talbot Co. (1847)

Pinehurst, Dooly Co. (1920)

Pine Knob Mills, Marion Co. (1894)

Pineknot, Chattahoochee Co. (1894)

Pine Knot Mills, Marion Co. (1881)

Pine Knot Spring, Chattahoochee Co. (1870)

Pine Lake, DeKalb Co. (1962)

Pinelevel, Crawford Co. (1920); also spelled Pine Level (1894)

Pine Log, Bartow Co. (1962); also spelled Pinelog (1920).

Pine Mountain, Harris Co. (1962); name changed from Chipley in 1950 (1962); Chipley also known as Goodmans Cross Roads (1881).

Pine Mountain, Rabun Co. (1920)

Pine Mountain Valley, Harris Co. (1962).

Pineora, Effingham Co. (1920)

Pine Park, Grady Co. (1920)

Pine Ridge, Early Co. (1881)

Pine Ridge, Twiggs Co. (1894)

Pinetta, Irwin Co. (1920)

Pinetucky, Jefferson Co. (1920)

Pine Valley, Ware Co. (1920)

Pineview, Wilcox Co. (1920)

Pine View, Jefferson Co. (1847)

Pineville, Marion Co. (1920)

Pineville, Polk Co. (1894)

Piney Grove, Harris Co. (1962)

Piney Head, Appling Co. (1870)

Piney Woods, Campbell (Fulton) Co. (1870)

Pinholloway, Wayne Co. (1894)

Pinholster, Liberty Co. (1881)

Pinia, Dooly Co. (1894)

Pinior, Randolph Co. (1870)

Pink, White Co. (1920)

Pinson, Floyd Co. (1920)

Pinsons Station, Floyd Co. (1881); also known as Nannie.

Pinson's Store, Floyd Co. (1894)

Pinta, Macon Co. (1894)

Pio Nono, Bibb Co. (1962); part of Macon.

Pippin, Jones Co. (1920)

Pirkle, Gwinnett Co. (1894)

Piscola, Brooks Co. (1920)

Piscola, Lowndes Co. (1847)

Pisgah, Gilmer Co. (1920)

Pistol, Wilkes Co. (1920)

Pistol Creek, Wilkes Co. (1847)

Pittman, Gwinnett Co. (1920)

Pitts, Wilcox Co. (1920)

Pittsburg, Fulton Co. (1894)

Pittsburg, Henry Co. (1881); also spelled Pittsburgh (1870).

Pittsburg, Walker Co. (1920); R.R. name is Harolds.

Pittsburgh, Henry Co. (1870); also spelled Pittsburg (1881).

Plainfield, Dodge Co. (1920)

Plains, Sumter Co. (1920)

Plains of Dura, Sumter Co. (1881); also known as Magnolia Springs.

Plainview, Franklin Co. (1962).

Plainville, Gordon Co. (1920)

Planter, Madison Co. (1920)

Planters Factory, Butts Co. (1847)

Planters Mills, Putnam Co. (1870)

Planters Stand, Madison Co. (1859)

Plattville, Early Co. (1894)

Plaza, Clayton Co. (1962); part of Forest Park.

Pleasant, Forsyth Co. (1920)

Pleasant Grove, Forsyth Co. (1881)

Pleasant Hill, Calhoun Co. (1870)

Pleasant Hill, Coweta Co. (1847)

Pleasant Hill, Talbot Co. (1920)

Pleasant Hill, Terrell Co. (1962)

Pleasant Level, Lee Co. (1870)

Pleasant Retreat, Lumpkin Co. (1859)

Pleasant Retreat, White Co. (1920)

Pleasant Valley, Dooly Co. (1920)

Pleasant Valley, Murray Co. (1881)

Pleasant Valley, Ware Co. (1847)

Plenitude, Jones Co. (1920)

Plowshare, Carroll Co. (1920)

Plug, Carroll Co. (1920)

Plumb, Franklin Co. (1920)

Pocataligo, Madison Co. (1920)

Picket, Gordon Co. (1894)

Poindexter, Marion Co. (1859)

Poindexter, Schley Co. (1881)

Point, Charlton Co. (1870)

Point House, Chatham Co. (1894)

Point Peter, Camden Co. (1847)

Point Peter, Oglethorpe Co. (1920); also known as Glade (1881).

Poletree, Clinch Co. (1962)

Polk, Union Co. (1894)

Polksville, Hall Co. (1881); former name of The Glades.

Polkville, Hall Co. (1894)

Pollards Corner, Columbia Co. (1962)

Pomaria, Clay Co. (1881)

Pomona, Spalding Co. (1920)

Ponce de Leon Springs, Fulton Co. (1894)

Ponder, Union Co. (1920)

Ponder, Webster Co. (1894)

Pondfork, Jackson Co. (1920); also spelled Pond Fork (1859).

Pond Spring, Walker Co. (1920)

Pond Town, Miller Co. (1881); also spelled Pondtown (1894).

Pond Town, Sumter Co. (1847); also spelled Pondtown (1859).

Pond Town, Schley Co. (1881)

Pooler, Chatham Co. (1920)

Poores Mills, Colquitt Co. (1881)

Poor Robin, Screven Co. (1870)

Poor Robin Bluff, Wilcox Co. (1870)

Pope, Jefferson Co. (1881)

Pope, Monroe Co. (1894)

Pope City, Wilcox Co. (1920)

Pope Hill, Jefferson Co. (1859)

Pope's, Oglethorpe Co. (1894)

Popes Ferry, Monroe Co. (1920)

Poplar, Talbot Co. (1920)

Poplar Hill, Telfair Co. (1881)

Poplar Spring, Hall Co. (1870); also spelled Poplar Springs (1881).

Poplar Spring Church, Laurens Co. (1870)

Poplar Springs, Hall Co. (1881); also spelled Poplar Spring (1870).

Poplar Springs, Haralson Co. (1881)

Portal, Bulloch Co. (1920)

Port Arthur, Colquitt Co. (1920)

Porter, Wilkinson Co. (1894)

Porterdale, Newton Co. (1920)

Porters, Hall Co. (1894)

Porter's Landing, Effingham Co. (1894)

Porter Springs, Lumpkin Co. (1920)

Portland, Polk Co. (1920)

Port Wentworth, Chatham Co. (1962)

Port Wentowrth Junction, Chatham Co. (1962)

Posco, Polk Co. (1920)

Possum Trot, Bartow Co. (1962)

Postell, Fannin Co. (1894)

Postell, Jones Co. (1962)

Post Oak, Catoosa Co. (1962); also spelled Postoak (1920).

Post Office, Chatham Co. (1894)

Potatoe, Pike Co. (1881)

Pothill, Monroe Co. (1920)

Pots Mountain, Dawson Co. (1920)

Potter, Echols Co. (1962)

Potterville, Taylor Co. (1920)

Poylan, Worth Co. (1920)

Pound, Upson Co. (1920)

Poverty Hill, Jones Co. (1859)

Powder Springs, Cobb Co. (1920)

Powell, Lamar Co. (1920)

Powell's, Coweta Co. (1894)

Powells, Washington Co. (1920)

Powellsville, Rabun Co. (1881); another name for Burton.

Powellton, Hancock Co. (1859); also spelled Powelton (1920).

Powellville, Coweta Co. (1881)

Powelton, Hancock Co. (1920); also spelled Powellton (1859).

Power, Cobb Co. (1920)

Powers, Terrell Co. (1881); R.R. name is Browns.

Powersville, Houston Co. (1881)

Powersville, Peach Co. (1962)

Prather, Habersham Co. (1894)

Prather, Wilkes Co. (1920)

Prattsburg, Talbot Co. (1881); also spelled Prattsburgh (1859).

Prattsburgh, Talbot Co. (1859); also spelled Prattsburg (1881).

Prattsville, Monroe Co. (1847)

Prays Church, Campbell Co. (1870)

Prenticeville, Wayne Co. (1894)

Prentiss, Appling Co. (1920)

Prescott, Echols Co. (1920)

Presley, Towns Co. (1920)

Pressley, Chatham Co. (1920)

Preston, Webster Co. (1920)

Pretoria, Bulloch Co. (1920)

Pretoria, Dougherty Co. (1920)

Prevet Heights, Cobb Co. (1962)

Price, Hall Co. (1920)

Prichards Bluff, Pulaski Co. (1870)

Prichett, Worth Co. (1920)

Pride, Hancock Co. (1920)

Pridgen, Coffee Co. (1920)

Primrose, Meriwether Co. (1920)

Prince Edward, Gilmer Co. (1881)

Princeton, Clarke Co. (1920)

Princeton, Rockdale Co. (1920)

Princeton Factory, Clarke Co. (1894)

Pringle, Washington Co. (1920)

Printup, Floyd Co. (1894)

Prior, Polk Co. (1962); also known as Priors (1920), Priors Station (1881), & Pryors (1881).

Priors, Polk Co. (1920); also known as Prior (1962), Priors Station (1881), & Pryors (1881).

Priors Station, Polk Co. (1881); also known as Priors (1920), Prior (1962) & Pryors (1881).

Pritchetts, Worth Co. (1962)

Proctor, Bulloch Co. (1920)

Proctors Store, Monroe Co. (1881)

Progress, Screven Co. (1920)

Prospect, Meriwether Co. (1870)

Prospect, Taliaferro Co. (1894)

Protection, Gilmer Co. (1920)

Providence, Meriwether Co. (1870)

Providence, Sumter Co. (1920)

Providence, Wilkinson Co. (1894)

Provo, Schley Co. (1920)

Pruit, Banks Co. (1920)

Prune, Murray Co. (1920)

Pryor, Baker Co. (1859)

Pryors, Mitchell Co. (1870)

Pryors, Polk Co. (1881); also known as Priors (1920), & Priors Station (1881).

Psalmonds, Chattahoochee Co. (1894)

Public Square, Greene Co. (1859)

Puckett, Gwinnett Co. (1920)

Puckett Station, Coweta Co. (1881); also known as Mineral Springs.

Pugh, Baldwin Co. (1920)

Pughleys Bridge, Jefferson & Burke Cos. (1847)

Pughsley, Emanuel Co. (1894)

Pulaski, Candler Co. (1920)

Pulaski, Pulaski Co. (1894)

Pulaski, Wilkinson Co. (1894)

Pultight, Decatur Co. (1894)

Pumpkin, Paulding Co. (1881)

Pumpkin Center, Columbia Co. (1962)

Pumpkin Pike, Polk Co. (1859)

Pumpkin Town, Randolph Co. (1870)

Pumpkin Vine, Paulding Co. (1859)

Purcell, Tatnall Co. (1920)

Purdyville, Dawson Co. (1881)

Purvis, Tattnall Co. (1920)

Putnam, Marion Co. (1920)

Putney, Dougherty Co. (1920); R.R. name is Hardaway.

Pye, Wayne Co. (1920)

Pyles Marsh, Glynn Co. (1920)

Pyne, Troup Co. (1920)

Quaker Spring, Columbia Co. (1847); also known as Quaker Springs (1894).

Quaker Springs, Columbia Co. (1894); also known as Quaker Spring (1847).

Quality, Thomas Co. (1962)

Quantock, Screven Co. (1881)

Quarles, Gilmer Co. (1920)

Quarries, Pickens Co. (1894)

Quarry, Walker Co. (1920)

Quartz, Rabun Co. (1920)

Quebec, Schley Co. (1881)

Quebec, Sumter Co. (1859)

Quebec, Union Co. (1894)

Queen, Candler Co. (1920)

Queenland, Wilcox Co. (1894)

Queensland, Ben Hill Co. (1920)

Quill, Gilmer Co. (1920)

Quillans, Hall Co. (1881)

Quillan's Store, Banks Co. (1894)

Quilp, Berrien Co. (1894)

Quilp, Cook Co. (1920)

Quince, Tattnall Co. (1894)

Quinsee, Lee Co. (1894)

Quitman, Brooks Co. (1920)

Quito, Talbot Co. (1881)

Rabun Gap, Rabun Co. (1920); also known as Head of Tennessee (1881).

Racoon, Chattooga Co. (1894)

Racoon Mills, Chatooga Co. (1881)

Race Pond, Charlton Co. (1962); also spelled Racepond (1920).

Rackley, Emanuel Co. (1920)

Radfords Mill, Brooks Co. (1881)

Radfords Mills, Lowndes Co. (1859)

Radium Springs, Dougherty Co. (1962)

Raes Bridge, Burke Co. (1847)

Ragan, Bibb Co. (1894)

Ragan, Mitchell Co. (1962)

Ragland, Troup Co. (1894)

Ragsdale, Dougherty Co. (1962); part of Albany

Rahn, Effingham Co. (1920)

Rahoboth, Wilkes Co. (1959)

Raiford, Mitchell Co. (1920)

Raines, Crisp Co. (1920)

Raines, Dooly Co. (1894)

Raines Store, Twiggs Co. (1870)

Rains Mills, Montgomery Co. (1870)

Raleigh, Meriwether Co. (1920)

Ralls, Lowndes Co. (1894)

Ralph, Douglas Co. (1920)

Ralterwood, Carroll Co. (1894)

Ramhurst, Murray Co. (1920)

Ramsey, Columbia Co. (1881)

Ramsey, Douglas Co. (1920)

Ramsey, Dougherty Co. (1962)

Ramsey, Murray Co. (1920)

Rancher, Hall Co. (1881)

Randa, Lumpkin Co. (1894)

Randall, Stewart Co. (1920)

Randel, Colquitt Co. (1920)

Randolph, Pierce Co. (1881); also known as Schlatterville.

Randolph, Brantley Co. (1920)

Randolph, Randolph Co. (1920)

Ranger, Gordon Co. (1920)

Rankin, Whitfield Co. (1920)

Raoul, Habersham Co. (1962)

Rape, Henry Co. (1920)

Ratcliff, Gilmer Co. (1920)

Ratio, Clinch Co. (1920)

Raulerson, Brantley Co. (1962)

Rawles Still, Brantley Co. (1920)

Rawlings, Washington Co. (1920)

Rawlins, Dodge Co. (1894)

Raybon, Brantley Co. (1920)

Ray City, Berrien Co. (1920)

Rayle, Wilkes Co. (1920)

Raymond, Coweta Co. (1920)

Rays Mill, Berrien Co. (1920); also spelled Rays Mills (1881).

Rays Mills, Berrien Co. (1881); also spelled Rays Mill (1920).

Raysville, Columbia Co. (1847)

Raysville, McDuffie Co. (1881)

Raysville, Lincoln Co. (1920)

Raytown, Taliaferro Co. (1881); R.R. name for Sharon.

Ready Creek, Jefferson Co. (1859)

Reansan's Springs, McDuffie Co. (1894)

Reason, Irwin Co. (1920)

Reavesville, Carroll Co. (1920)

Rebecca, Turner Co. (1920)

Rebie, Bleckley Co. (1920)

Recovery, Decatur Co. (1920)

Redan, DeKalb Co. (1920)

Red Belt, Catoosa Co. (1894)

Red Bluff, Appling Co. (1894)

Red Bluff, Coffee Co. (1870)

Red Bluff, Montgomery Co. (1881)

Red Bluff, Treutlen Co. (1920)

Red Bone, Marion Co. (1894)

Redding, Harris Co. (1847)

Reddish, Wayne Co. (1894)

Red Hill, Franklin Co. (1920)

Red Hill, Liberty Co. (1881)

Red Hill, Murray Co. (1847)

Red Hill, Whitfield Co. (1881); another name for Varnells Station.

Red Hill Mills, Burke Co. (1894)

Red Land, Polk Co. (1894)

Redland, Wayne Co. (1920)

Red Lane, Hall Co. (1962)

Redlevel, Wilkinson Co. (1920); also spelled Red Level (1894).

Red Level Church, Wilkinson Co. (1870)

Red Oak, Campbell (Fulton) Co. (1920)

Red Oak, Fayette Co. (1859)

Red Ore, Polk Co. (1894)

Red Rock, Worth Co. (1962)

Red Rock, Paulding Co. (1962); also known as Terry.

Red Stone, Jackson Co. (1920)

Reed, Haralson Co. (1920)

Reed, Harris Co. (1894)

Reed Creek, Hart Co. (1920)

Reed Mountain, Carroll Co. (1920)

Reeds, Twiggs Co. (1894)

Reedy Creek, Jefferson Co. (1881); also spelled Reidy Creek.

Reedy Springs, Laurens Co. (1920); also known as Blue Water (1881).

Reesburg, Floyd Co. (1920)

Reese, Morgan Co. (1920)

Reese, Warren Co. (1962)

Reeves, Gordon Co. (1920); also known as Reeves Station (1881).

Reeve's Mills, Paulding Co. (1894)

Reeves Station, Gordon Co. (1881); also known as Reeves (1920).

Reform, Effingham Co. (1847)

Refuge, Camden Co. (1920)

Refuge, Decatur Co. (1894)

Refuge Mountain, Camden Co. (1894)

Register, Bulloch Co. (1920)

Regnant, Johnson Co. (1894)

Rehobeth, Harris Co. (1962)

Rehoboth, DeKalb Co. (1962)

Rehoboth, Morgan Co. (1920); also known as Rehobothville (1847).

Rehoboth, Wilkes Co. (1847)

Rehobothville, Morgan Co. (1847); also known as Rehoboth (1920).

Reid, Twiggs Co. (1920); also spelled Reids (1962).

Reids, Pike Co. (1894)

Reids, Twiggs Co. (1962); also spelled Reid (1920).

Reidsboro, Pike Co. (1920)

Reidsfield, Wilcox Co. (1894)

Reidsville, Tattnall Co. (1920)

Reidy Creek, Jefferson Co. (1881); also spelled Reedy Creek.

Reka, Bryan Co. (1920); P.O. name is Morrison.

Relay, Floyd Co. (1962)

Remerton, Lowndes Co. (1920)

Remus, Paulding Co. (1920)

Renfroe, Chattahoochee Co. (1962); also spelled Renfroes (1894).

Renfroes, Chattahoochee Co. (1894); also spelled Renfroe (1962).

Renfroes, Stewart Co. (1920)

Reno, Grady Co. (1920)

Rentz, Laurens Co. (1920)

Renwick, Lee Co. (1881); another name for Smithville.

Reo, Walker Co. (1920)

Repose, Haralson Co. (1881)

Reppards Mill, Clinch Co. (1881)

Republican, Warren Co. (1847)

Republican, McDuffie Co. (1881)

Resaca, Gordon Co. (1920)

Resaca, Hancock Co. (1847)

Resource, Screven Co. (1894)

Resseaus Crossroads, Putnam Co. (1962).

Rest, Fayette Co. (1920)

Rest Haven, Gwinnett Co. (1962)

Rest Haven, Upson Co. (1920)

Retreat, Clinch Co. (1894)

Retreat, Glynn Co. (1847)

Retreat, Liberty Co. (1920)

Retreat, Wayne Co. (1847)

Rett, Carroll Co. (1894)

Reuben, Chattooga Co. (1881)

Revere, Lamar Co. (1920)

Rex, Clayton Co. (1920)

Reynolds, Bartow Co. (1920)

Reynolds, Burke Co. (1881)

Reynolds, Taylor Co. (1920)

Reynolds' Mills, Fulton Co. (1894)

Reynoldsville, Seminole Co. (1920)

Reynoldsville, Warren Co. (1894)

Rheneyville, Burke Co. (1894)

Rhine, Dodge Co. (1920)

Rhodesville, Decatur Co. (1894)

Rice, Cobb Co. (1920)

Riceboro, Liberty Co. (1920)

Riceboro Station, Liberty Co. (1894)

Richardson, Rockdale Co. (1920)

Richfield, Chatham Co. (1962)

Richland, Glynn Co. (1847)

Richland, Stewart Co. (1920)

Richland, Twiggs Co. (1881)

Richland Academy, Twiggs Co. (1870)

Richland Farms, Greene Co. (1920)

Richmond, Richmond Co. (1894)

Richmond Factory, Richmond Co. (1881)

Richmond Hill, Bryan Co. (1962)

Richmond Hill, Richmond Co. (1881)

Rich Mountain, Pickens Co. (1881)

Richwood, Dooly Co. (1920)

Ricksville, Emanuel Co. (1894)

Rico, Campbell (Fulton) Co. (1920)

Riddles, Montgomery Co. (1894)

Riddleville, Washington Co. (1920)

Ridge, McIntosh Co. (1920)

Ridge, Richmond Co. (1920)

Ridge Valley, Floyd Co. (1881)

Ridgeville, McIntosh Co. (1920)

Ridgeway, Harris Co. (1920)

Ridgewood, Chatham Co. (1962); part of Savannah.

Ridgwood, Muscogee Co. (1870)

Rift, Lee Co. (1920)

Riggton, Tattnall Co. (1920)

Rile, Hart Co. (1894)

Riley's Mill, Habersham Co. (1894)

Rilla, Carroll Co. (1894)

Rincon, Effingham Co. (1920)

Ring, Telfair Co. (1894)

Ringgold, Catoosa Co. (1920)

Rio, Coweta Co. (1881)

Rio, Oglethorpe Co. (1894)

Rio, Spalding Co. (1962)

Rio Vista, Dougherty Co. (1962)

Rip, Appling Co. (1894)

Ripley, Madison Co. (1894)

Ripley, Twiggs Co. (1920)

Rising Fawn, Dade Co. (1920)

Ritch, Wayne Co. (1920)

Ritt, Carroll Co. (1920)

Riverdale, Clayton Co. (1920)

River Junction, Cherokee Co. (1894)

Riverland Terrace, Muscogee Co. (1962); part of Columbus.

Riverside, Berrien Co. (1881); also known as Jacobs.

Riverside, Colquitt Co. (1920)

Riverside, Greene Co. (1920)

Riverside, Heard Co. (1894)

Riverside, Troup Co. (1894)

River Swamp, Long Co. (1920)

Rivertown, Campbell (Fulton) Co. (1920); also spelled River Town (1847).

Riverturn, Seminole Co. (1962)

Riverview, Meriwether Co. (1920)

Rives, Dawson Co. (1894)

Rives, Dougherty Co. (1881)

Rivoli, Bibb Co. (1920); part of Macon (1962).

Rixville, Emanuel Co. (1894)

Rixville, Treutlen Co. (1920)

Roadside, Upson Co. (1962)

Roanoak, Stewart Co. (1847)

Roanoke, Milton (Fulton) Co. (1920)

Rober, Pickens Co. (1920)

Roberson, Baldwin Co. (1962)

Roberta, Crawford Co. (1920)

Roberts, Jones Co. (1920)

Robertsons, Troup Co. (1920)

Robertsons Store, Gordon Co. (1881)

Roberts Station, Jones Co. (1881)

Robertstown, White Co. (1920); R.R. name is North Helen.

Robertsville, Jones Co. (1894)

Robins Air Force Base, Houston Co. (1962)

Robinson, Taliaferro Co. (1920)

Robinson, Floyd Co. (1920)

Robison, Washington Co. (1881)

Robley, Crawford Co. (1920)

Robuck, Gilmer Co. (1920)

Rochelle, Wilcox Co. (1920)

Rockalo, Heard Co. (1920)

Rock Branch, Elbert Co. (1962)

Rock Bridge, Gwinnett Co. (1849)

Rock City, Gordon Co. (1962)

Rock Comfort, Jefferson Co. (1920)

Rock Creek, Murray Co. (1894)

Rock Creek, Walker Co. (1920)

Rock Cut, Clayton Co. (1962); part of Lake City.

Rockdale Paper Mills, Rockdale Co. (1881)

Rock Factory, Hancock Co. (1881); another name for Jewell.

Rockfence, Elbert Co. (1920); also spelled Rock Fence (1894).

Rock Hill, Gilmer Co. (1859)

Rockingham, Bacon Co. (1920)

Rockingham, Chatham Co. (1847)

Rockledge, Laurens Co. (1920)

Rockmart, Polk Co. (1920)

Rock Mills, Hancock Co. (1847)

Rockpile, Dawson Co. (1920)

Rock Pond, Decatur Co. (1881)

Rock Spring, Murray Co. (1881)

Rock Spring, Walker Co. (1920)

Rockville, Putnam Co. (1920)

Rockwell, Jasper Co. (1894)

Rocky Creek, Gordon Co. (1920)

Rock Creek, Laurens Co. (1894)

Rocky Creek Church, Burke Co. (1870)

Rocky Face, Whitfield Co. (1920)

Rocky Ford, Screven Co. (1920)

Rocky Mount, Meriwether Co. (1920)

Rocky Plains, Newton Co. (1920)

Roddenbery, Grady Co. (1962)

125

Roderick, Liberty Co. (1894)

Roody, Dodge Co. (1920)

Roderick, Long Co. (1920)

Roding, Bryan Co. (1920)

Rogers, Bartow Co. (1920)

Rogers, Burke Co. (1881)

Rogers, Jenkins Co. (1920)

Rogers, Walker Co. (1894)

Rogersville, Mitchell Co. (1962); also spelled Rogerville (1920)

Rogerville, Mitchell Co. (1920); also spelled Rogersville (1962).

Roland, Upson Co. (1962)

Rolands Mineral Spring, Bartow Co. (1881)

Rollersville, Richmond Co. (1894)

Rollin, Fannin Co. (1859)

Rollins, Paulding Co. (1920)

Rollo, Crawford Co. (1920)

Rollo Sand Pit, Crawford Co. (1962)

Rolston, Gilmer Co. (1920)

Rome, Floyd Co. (1920)

Rome and Decatur Crossing, Floyd Co. (1894)

Roney, Sumter Co. (1920)

Rooney's Mills, Chattahoochee Co. (1894)

Roopville, Carroll Co. (1920)

Roosevelt, Gilmer Co. (1920)

Roosterville, Heard Co. (1962)

Roper, Jeff Davis Co. (1920)

Rosa, Johnson Co. (1894)

Roscoe, Coweta Co. (1920)

Rose, Lamar Co. (1920)

Rosebud, Gwinnett Co. (1920)

Rosebud, Heard Co. (1894)

Rosedale, Floyd Co. (1920)

Rose Dew, Chatham Co. (1847)

Rose Hill, Chatham Co. (1962); part of Savannah.

Rose Hill, Muscogee Co. (1881); part of Columbus (1962).

Rose Hill, Oconee Co. (1962)

Rose Hill, Pike Co. (1962)

Rose Hill, Union Co. (1881)

Rose Hill Heights, Muscogee Co. (1962); part of Columbus.

Roseland, Fulton Co. (1920)

Roseland, Decatur Co. (1920)

Rose Lawn, Clinch Co. (1894)

Rosemont, Columbia Co. (1962)

Rose Mount, Montgomery Co. (1870)

Rosemont, Muscogee Co. (1962); part of Columbus.

Rosemont Park, Floyd Co. (1962)

Rosendale, Berrien Co. (1881)

Roseville, Richmond Co. (1894)

Rosewood, Cobb Co. (1920)

Rosier, Burke Co. (1920)

Ross, Crisp Co. (1920)

Ross, Wayne Co. (1920)

Rosser, Wayne Co. (1962)

Rosser Dale, Hancock Co. (1847)

Rossignol Hill, Chatham Co. (1962); part of Garden City.

Rossville, Walker Co. (1920)

Rosswell, Walker Co. (1881)

Rosswell Junction, DeKalb Co. (1894)

Roswell, Fulton Co. (1962)

Roswell Station, Milton (Fulton) Co. (1920).

Rotherwood, Carroll Co. (1881)

Rothwell, Chatham Co. (1920)

Rough and Ready, Fayette Co. (1847)

Rough and Ready, Clayton Co. (1881)

Roundabout, Coffee Co. (1870)

Round Bluff, Appling Co. (1870)

Round Hill, Dawson Co. (1881)

Round Hill, Lumpkin Co. (1859)

Round Lake, Brooks Co. (1894)

Round Oak, Jones Co. (1920)

Round Top, Dawson Co. (1870)

Roundtop, Gilmer Co. (1920); also spelled Round Top (1894)

Rounsaville, Floyd Co. (1894)

Rountree, Emanuel Co. (1894)

Rouse, Worth Co. (1881)

Routhwell, Chatham Co. (1894)

Rover, Spalding Co. (1920)

Rowan, Berrien Co. (1894)

Rowell, Chattooga Co. (1920)

Rowena, Early Co. (1920)

Rowland, Upson Co. (1894)

Rowlands Mineral Spring, Cass (Bartow) Co. (1847)

Rowland Springs, Bartow Co. (1894)

Roxana, Paulding Co. (1920); also spelled Roxanna (1962).

Roxanna, Paulding Co. (1962); also spelled Roxana (1920).

Roxie, Berrien Co. (1920)

Roy, Bibb Co. (1962)

Roy, Gilmer Co. (1920)

Royal, Taylor Co. (1894)

Royster, Bibb Co. (1920)

Royston, Hart, Franklin & Madison Cos. (1962); also known as Franklin Springs (1881).

Ruark, Dougherty Co. (1920)

Ruby, Irwin Co. (1894)

Ruby, Jones Co. (1962)

Ruckerville, Elbert Co. (1920)

Rudden, Putnam Co. (1920)

Ruden, Pickens Co. (1962)

Rudisils Mill, Hancock Co. (1847)

Rue, Telfair Co. (1920)

Ruff, Cobb Co. (1881); another name for Smyrna (1881); also known as Neal Dow (1881).

Ruff, Gilmer Co. (1894)

Ruffs, Cobb Co. (1894)

Rufus, Bulloch Co. (1920)

Rugby, Union Co. (1920)

Rumphs, Houston Co. (1920)

Runnymead, Burke Co. (1894)

Rupert, Taylor Co. (1920)

Rural, Taylor Co. (1894)

Rural Vale, Whitfield Co. (1920)

Rush, Webster Co. (1962)

Rushville, Appling Co. (1870)

Rushville, Banks Co. (1881)

Rushville, Franklin Co. (1894)

Ruskin, Ware Co. (1920)

Russell, Barrow Co. (1920)

Russellville, Monroe Co. (1920)

Rustic, Floyd Co. (1920)

Rustic, Liberty Co. (1894)

Rustic City, Liberty Co. (1881)

Ruth, Greene Co. (1920)

Rutherford, Oconee Co. (1920)

Rutland, Bibb Co. (1920)

Rutledge, Morgan Co. (1920)

Rydal, Bartow Co. (1920)

Ryley, Macon Co. (1920)

Ryo, Gordon Co. (1920)

Ryonville, Liberty Co. (1894)

Rysh, Clay Co. (1920)

Sabine, Twiggs Co. (1920)

Sackville, Carroll Co. (1920)

Saco, Mitchell Co. (1920)

Saffold, Early Co. (1920)

Sahara, Richmond Co. (1847)

Saint Augustine, Chatham Co. (1920)

St. Bernard, Irwin Co. (1847)

Saint Charles, Coweta Co. (1920)

Saint Clair, Burke Co. (1920)

St. Clair Village, Glynn Co. (1847)

Saint Cloud, Heard Co. (1881)

Saint Elmo, Schley Co. (1881)

Saint George, Charlton Co. (1920)

Saint Illa, Coffee Co. (1920)

St. Joseph, Fulton Co. (1894)

Saint Marks, Meriwether Co. (1920)

Saint Marys, Camden Co. (1920)

Saint Marys Hills, Muscogee Co. (1962); part of Columbus.

St. Mill, Decatur Co. (1870)

St. Mill, Mitchell Co. (1870)

St. Patrick, Irwin Co. (1847)

St. Saville, Wayne Co. (1847)

Saint Simons, Glynn Co. (1920); census name for Saint Simons Island (1962).

Saint Simons Island, Glynn Co. (1962); census name is Saint Simons.

Saint Simons Mills, Glynn Co. (1920)

St. Stanislaus, Bibb Co. (1894)

Salacoa, Bartow Co. (1870)

Salacoa Spring, Cass (Bartow) Co. (1847)

Salacoa Spring, Gordon Co. (1870)

Sale City, Mitchell Co. (1920)

Salem, Calhoun Co. (1870)

Salem, Clarke Co. (1847)

Salem, Lincoln Co. (1894)

Salem, Oconee Co. (1962)

Salem, Rockdale Co. (1920)

Salem, Talfair Co. (1870)

Salem, Walker Co. (1894)

Salem Camp Ground, Heard Co. (1870)

Salem Creek, Telfair Co. (1881)

Sallacoa, Cherokee Co. (1920)

Sallylu, Habersham Co. (1920)

Salmon, Oglethorpe Co. (1920)

Salmonville, Oglethorpe Co. (1870)

Salter, Sumter Co. (1894)

Salters, Sumter Co. (1920)

Salt Springs, Cambpell Co. (1859)

Salt Springs, Douglas Co. (1881)

Saluda, Coweta Co. (1881)

Saluda Farm, Dade Co. (1859)

Sam, Bulloch Co. (1920)

San Bar Ferry, Richmond Co. (1894)

Sanborns Mills, Decatur Co. (1847)

Sanders, Hancock Co. (1847)

Sanderstown, Pickens Co.

Sandersville, Washington Co. (1920)

Sandfly, Chatham Co. (1920)

Sand Hill, Carroll Co. (1962); also spelled Sandhill (1920); also known as Five Points (1881)

Sand Hill, Chattahoochee Co. (1920)

Sand Hill, Glynn Co. (1894)

Sand Hill, Muscogee Co. (1962); part of Fort Benning.

Sand Hill, Telfair Co. (1870)

Sand Hills, Glynn Co. (1847)

Sand Hills, Richmond Co. (1894)

Sandsprings, Floyd Co. (1920)

Sand Town, Baldwin Co. (1881); also spelled Sandtown (1847).

Sandtown, Campbell (Fulton) Co. (1920); also spelled Sand Town (1847).

Sand Town, Newton Co. (1881); another name for Newborn.

Sandtown, Wilkes Co. (1962)

Sandy, Butts Co. (1920)

Sandy, Jefferson Co. (1920)

Sandy Bottom, Clinch Co. (1920)

Sandy Cross, Franklin Co. (1962)

Sandycross, Oglethorpe Co. (1920); also spelled Sandy Cross (1894).

Sandy Cross Roads, Oglethorpe Co. (1870)

Sandy Hill, Coffee Co. (1894)

Sandypoint, Crawford Co. (1920); also spelled Sandy Point (1870).

Sandyridge, Henry Co. (1920); also spelled Sandy Ridge (1962).

Sandy Slue, Coffee Co. (1881)

Sandy Springs, Fulton Co. (1962)

Sanford, Madison Co. (1962)

Sanford, Stewart Co. (1920)

Sanitarium Junction, Baldwin Co. (1962)

Santa Claus, Toombs Co. (1962)

Santa Luca, Gilmer Co. (1920); also spelled Santa Lucah (1859); also known as Buckhorn & Boardtown (1881).

Santa Lucah, Gilmer Co. (1859); another spelling of Santa Luca (1920).

Santilla, Wayne Co. (1870)

Sanvalda, Mitchell Co. (1881)

Sap, Thomas Co. (1894)

Sapello, McIntosh Co. (1894); another spelling of Sapelo (1920).

Sapelo, McIntosh Co. (1920); also spelled Sapello (1894).

Sapelo Island, McIntosh Co. (1962)

Sapelo Spur, McIntosh Co. (1920)

Sapp, Burke Co. (1847)

Sapp, Whitfield Co. (1920)

Sapps Still, Coffee Co. (1962)

Sappville, Ware Co. (1920)

Sarah, Union Co. (1920)

Sardis, Burke Co. (1920)

Sarepta, Dawson Co. (1920)

Sargent, Coweta Co. (1920); R.R. name for Lodi (1881); also known as Wilcoxon (1881).

Sasnett, Hancock Co. (1847)

Sasser, Terrell Co. (1920)

Saterfield, DeKalb Co. (1894)

Satilla, Appling Co. (1870)

Satilla, Wayne Co. (1881); also known as Haslum.

Satilla, Pierce Co. (1920)

Satilla Bluff, Camden Co. (1920)

Satilla Mills, Camden Co. (1894)

Satolah, Rabun Co. (1920)

Sanders Town, Pickens Co. (1881)

Saussy, Clinch Co. (1894)

Sautee, White Co. (1962); also known as Sautee-Nacoochee.

Sautee-Nacoochee, White Co. (1962); another name for Sautee.

Savannah, Chatham Co. (1920)

Savannah and Atlanta Junction, Warren Co. (1962)

Savannah Beach, Chatham Co. (1962)

Savannah Junction, Chatham Co. (1894)

Savannah State College, Chatham Co. (1962); also known as Georgia State College & State College.

Savilles, Stewart Co. (1920)

Savilles, Webster Co. (1894)

Savoy, Wilkes Co. (1920)

Sawalds, Mitchell Co. (1894)

Saw Dust, Columbia Co. (1920)

Saw Mill, Chattooga Co. (1894)

Sawneys Mountain, Forsyth Co. (1859)

Sawtell, Fulton Co. (1962); part of Atlanta.

Saw Tooth, Rabun Co. (1962)

Saxon, Liberty Co. (1894)

Scale Works, Floyd Co. (1894)

Scarboro, Jenkins Co. (1920)

Scarboro, Screven Co. (1894); also spelled Scarborough (1859).

Scarborough, Screven Co. (1859); also spelled Scarboro (1894).

Scarlett, Camden Co. (1894)

Scearcorn, Pickens Co. (1894)

Schatulga, Muscogee Co. (1920)

Schlatterville, Pierce Co. (1881); also known as Randolph.

Schlatterville, Brantley Co. (1920)

Schley, Colquitt Co. (1920)

Schley, Schley Co. (1920)

Schoen, Fulton Co. (1962); part of Atlanta.

Schrenkville, Bryan Co. (1920)

Scienceville, Stewart Co. (1920)

Scogin, Meriwether Co. (1920)

Scotchville, Camden Co. (1920)

Scotland, Telfair & Wheeler Cos. (1962).

Scott, Habersham Co. (1894)

Scott, Johnson Co. (1920)

Scott, Walker Co. (1894)

Scottdale, DeKalb Co. (1920)

Scott's, Taylor Co. (1894)

Scotts, Walker Co. (1962)

Scottsboro, Baldwin Co. (1920)

Scotts Mill, Bibb Co. (1847)

Scova, Berrien Co. (1894)

Screven, Appling Co. (1870)

Screven, Wayne Co. (1920)

Scruggs, Brooks Co. (1920)

Scruggsville, Glascock Co. (1894)

Scull Shoals, Greene Co. (1859)

Seabolt, Union Co. (1920)

Seabolt, Liberty Co. (1920)

Seaford, Lowndes Co. (1920)

Seago, Bibb Co. (1881); R.R. name for Walden.

Sea Island, Glynn Co. (1962)

Seals, Camden Co. (1920)

Seals, Sumter Co. (1894)

Searcy, Gilmer Co. (1920)

Searsville, Stewart Co. (1847)

Seaverton, Dougherty Co. (1881)

Sebastopol, Burke Co. (1881); also known as Holcombe.

Seborn, Fulton Co. (1920)

Sectionville, Tattnall Co. (1894)

Seed, Habersham Co. (1920)

Seidell, Hart Co. (1894)

Seila, Habersham Co. (1894)

Selton, Cherokee Co. (1920)

Selina, Clayton Co. (1920)

Sellers, Appling Co. (1881)

Sells, Jackson Co. (1920)

Seminole, Wilcox Co. (1920)

Semper, Spalding Co. (1920)

Seney, Polk Co. (1920)

Senoia, Coweta Co. (1920)

Senrab, Macon Co. (1920)

Sepel's Island, McIntosh Co. (1894)

Sessoms, Appling Co. (1894)

Sessoms, Bacon Co. (1920)

Settendown, Forsyth Co. (1881)

Seven Islands, Butts Co. (1881); another name for Ocmulgee Mills.

Seventy-four Mile Post, Glynn Co. (1894)

Sevier, Forsyth Co. (1920)

Seville, Wilcox Co. (1920)

Seward, Montgomery Co. (1881)

Seymour, Jackson Co. (1920)

Seymour, Putnam Co. (1962)

Shack, Chattahoochee Co. (1920)

Shackleford, Dougherty Co. (1920)

Shackleton, Chattooga Co. (1920)

Shad, Floyd Co. (1894)

Shades, Polk Co. (1894)

Shadow Brook, Gwinnett Co. (1920)

Shady Dale, Jasper Co. (1920)

Shady Grove, Carroll Co. (1920)

Shady Grove, Forsyth Co. (1894)

Shady Grove, Union Co. (1859)

Shafter, Bleckley Co. (1920)

Shakerag, Milton (Fulton) Co. (1894)

Shannon, Floyd Co. (1920)

Shannon's Mills, Franklin Co. (1894)

Shanty 29, Clay Co. (1894)

Sharon, Taliaferro Co. (1920); R.R. name is Raytown (1881).

Sharon, Telfair Co. (1870)

Sharpe, Walker Co. (1920)

Sharpes, Lowndes Co. (1847)

Sharpes, Creven Co. (1870)

Sharpes Store, Brooks Co. (1870)

Sharphagen, Seminole Co. (1962)

Sharpsboro, Coweta Co. (1920); P.O. name is Sharpsburg.

Sharpsburg, Coweta Co. (1920); R.R. name is Sharpsboro.

Sharp's Landing, Tattnall Co. (1894)

Sharps Spur, Montgomery Co. (1920).

Sharpstown, DeKalb Co. (1894)

Sharp Top, Cherokee Co. (1962); also spelled Sharptop (1920).

Shaw, Pierce Co. (1894)

Shaw, Walker Co. (1920); R.R. name is Estelle.

Shawnee, Effingham Co. (1920)

Shaws Mill, Pierce Co. (1881)

Shaws Still, Atkinson Co. (1920)

Shea, Brantley Co. (1920)

Sheba, Hancock Co. (1920)

Sheffield, Camden Co. (1894)

Sheffield, Early Co. (1920)

Sheffield, Newton Co. (1881)

Shellbluff, Burke Co. (1920); also spelled Shell Bluff (1847).

Shell Bluff, Lee Co. (1847)

Shell Creek, Muscogee Co. (1847)

Shellman, Randolph Co. (1920)

Shellman Bluff, McIntosh Co. (1962)

Shellmans, Bartow Co. (1920)

Shell Mound Mine, Dade Co. (1894)

Shelly, Thomas Co. (1920)

Sheltonville, Forsyth Co. (1859)

Sheltonville, Milton (Fulton) Co. (1920)

Shepards, Screven Co. (1920); also spelled Sheppards (1962).

Shepherd, Coffee Co. (1894)

Sheppards, DeKalb Co. (1962)

Sheppards, Houston Co. (1920)

Sheppards, Screven Co. (1962); also spelled Shepards (1920).

Sherly, Charlton Co. (1894)

Sherman, Pickens Co. (1920)

Sherm Siding, Clarke Co. (1962)

Sherwood Lodge, Wayne Co. (1847)

Shewmake, Laurens Co. (1920)

Shilling, Pulaski Co. (1894)

Shiloh, Harris Co. (1920)

Shiloh, Jasper Co. (1894)

Shingler, Worth Co. (1920)

Shipps Spur, Sumter Co. (1962)

Shipyard, Chatham Co. (1962)

Shirley Park, Chatham Co. (1962)

Shiver, Brooks Co. (1962)

Shivers, Dooly Co. (1894)

Shoal Creek, Cherokee Co. (1894)

Shoal Creek, Hall Co. (1859)

Shoal Creek, Hart Co. (1920)

Shoals, Glascock Co. (1920); also known as Shoals of Ogeechee (1881); [Note: This town was located at the intersection of Glascock, Warren, & Hancock Counties, on both sides of the Ogeechee River.]

Shoals, Warren Co. (1894); [See next above.]

Shoals of Ogeechee, Hancock Co. (1881); also known as Shoals (1920) [See entry for Shoals above].

Shoo Fly Mills, Burke Co. (1894)

Shopes, Union Co. (1881)

Shore, Brooks Co. (1920); R.R. name is Empress.

Shot, Emanuel Co. (1894)

Shoulder, Hancock Co. (1920)

133

Shurlington, Bibb Co. (1962); part of Macon.

Sibbie, Ben Hill Co. (1920)

Sibbie, Wilcox Co. (1894)

Sibley, Dooly Co. (1894)

Sibley, Turner Co. (1920)

Sidney, Emanuel Co. (1894)

Sidney, Jenkins Co. (1920)

Sidney, Oconee Co. (1920)

Sigma, Liberty Co. (1894)

Signboard, Liberty Co. (1894)

Sigbee, Colquitt Co. (1920)

Sigurd, Dodge Co. (1920)

Sikes, Pierce Co. (1920)

Siko, Bulloch Co. (1894)

Silar, Colquitt Co. (1920)

Silas, Washington Co. (1920)

Silco, Camden Co. (1920)

Silk Hope, Chatham Co. (1962)

Silk Mills, Elbert Co. (1962)

Siloam, Greene Co. (1920)

Silverberg, Chatham Co. (1894)

Silver City, Forsyth Co. (1920)

Silver Creek, Floyd Co. (1920)

Silver Hill, Chattooga Co. (1920)

Silvershoal, Banks Co. (1920); also spelled Silver Shoal (1894).

Silvertown, Upson Co. (1962); annexed to Thomaston in 1950.

Silvey, Meriwether Co. (1894)

Simeon, Dooly Co. (1894)

Simmons, Effingham Co. (1920)

Simpson, Brooks Co. (1920)

Simpson, Heard Co. (1920)

Sims, Lowndes Co. (1894)

Simsville, Carroll Co. (1881)

Simsville, Emanuel Co. (1894)

Sink, Bulloch Co. (1894)

Sink Hole, Bulloch Co. (1894)

Sion Hill, Screven Co. (1881)

Sirmans, Clinch Co. (1920)

Sirmans, Lanier Co. (1962)

Sirrom, Emanuel Co. (1894)

Sisson, Wilkes Co. (1920)

Sisters Ferry, Effingham Co. (1859)

Sittons, Chattooga Co. (1894)

Siver, Carroll Co. (1920)

Six Mile, Floyd Co. (1920)

Six Mile Station, Floyd Co. (1881); another name for Vans Valley.

Sixteen Mile Spur, Chattahooche Co. (1920)

Skeinah, Fannin Co. (1881)

Skeins, Coweta Co. (1847)

Skelleys, Gordon Co. (1881)

Skelton, Milton (Fulton) Co. (1894)

Skidaway, Chatham Co. (1881)

Skipperton, Bibb Co. (1920)

Skitts Mountain, Habersham Co. (1847)

Skitts Mountain, Hall Co. (1859)

Skyland, DeKalb Co. (1962)

Slackville, Whitfield Co. (1881); another name for Starks.

Slade, Washington Co. (1920)

Slappey, Houston Co. (1920)

Slate, Hart Co. (1920)

Slate Rock, Columbia Co. (1881)

Slattings, Montgomery Co. (1870)

Sleepy Hollow, Early Co. (1847)

Sloans, Hall Co. (1920)

Slocumb, Jones Co. (1894)

Slover, Wayne Co. (1920)

Small, Johnson Co. (1920)

Smarrs, Monroe Co. (1920); also known as Smarrs Station (1881).

Smarrs Station, Monroe Co. (1881); also known as Smarrs (1920).

Smiley, Liberty Co. (1894)

Smiley, Long Co. (1920)

Smith, Burke Co. (1894)

Smith, Dade Co. (1881)

Smith Academy, Upson Co. (1962)

Smithboro, Jasper Co. (1894); also spelled Smithborough (1881).

Smithborough, Jasper Co. (1881); also spelled Smithboro (1894).

Smithfield, Hancock Co. (1847)

Smithsonia, Oglethorpe Co. (1920)

Smiths, Colquitt Co. (1920)

Smiths, Irwin Co. (1962)

Smiths, Jefferson Co. (1894)

Smiths Crossroads, Harris Co. (1962)

Smiths Mills, Jasper Co. (1920)

Smith's Mills, Monroe Co. (1894)

Smiths Siding, Whitfield Co. (1920)

Smithsonia, Bibb Co. (1962)

Smith's Store, Tattnall Co. (1894)

Smithton, DeKalb Co. (1881)

Smithton, Jasper Co. (1894)

Smithville, Dawson Co. (1870)

Smithville, Lee Co. (1920); also known as Renwick (1881).

Smyrna, Cobb Co. (1920); also known as Neal Dow & Ruff (1881).

Smyrna, Greene Co. (1881)

Snake, Fannin Co. (1920)

Snake Nation, Fannin Co. (1962)

Snap, Bulloch Co. (1920)

Snapfinger, DeKalb Co. (1920)

Snapping Shoals, Newton Co. (1920)

Snead, Columbia Co. (1962); also spelled Sneads (1920).

Sneads, Columbia Co. (1920); also spelled Snead (1962).

Sneed, Lee Co. (1881)

Sneed, Berrien Co. (1920)

Snells Bridge, Johnson Co. (1881)

Snellville, Gwinnett Co. (1920)

Smelson, Meriwether Co. (1894); also spelled Snelsons (1920).

Snelsons, Meriwether Co. (1920); also spelled Snelson (1894).

Snider, Gilmer Co. (1920)

Snidersville, Pike Co. (1894)

Sniff, Berrien Co. (1894)

Snipesville, Jeff Davis Co. (1962)

Snow, Dooly Co. (1920); also known as Snow Springs (1881).

Snow Hill, Walker Co. (1847)

Snow Hill, Catoosa Co. (1881)

Snow Springs, Dooly Co. (1881); also known as Snow.

Snyder, Chatham Co. (1920)

Social Circle, Walton Co. (1920)

Social Hill, Cherokee Co. (1881)

Socrates, Lamar Co. (1920)

Sofkee, Bibb Co. (1920)

Sofkee, Grady Co. (1920)

Sofkey, Decatur Co. (1959)

Solmonville, Oglethorpe Co. (1894)

Solo, Forsyth Co. (1894)

Solomon, Twiggs Co. (1894)

Solomonville, Oglethorpe Co. (1881); also known as Antioch.

Sonora, Gordon Co. (1881); another name for Sonoraville (1920).

Sonoraville, Gordon Co. (1920); also known as Sonora (1881).

Soperton, Treutlen Co. (1920)

Sophia, Bartow Co. (1894)

Soque, Habersham Co. (1920); known as Batesville prior to 1881 (1881).

Soreca, Oconee Co. (1920)

Sorrells, Madison Co. (1920)

Southard, Forsyth Co. (1894)

South Atlanta, Fulton Co. (1920); part of Atlanta (1962).

South Augusta, Richmond Co. (1962)

Southbend, Fulton Co. (1920)

South Decatur, DeKalb Co. (1962)

South End, Chatham Co. (1920); P.O. name is Tybee.

Southern Junction, Glynn Co. (1920)

South Gate, Richmond Co. (1962)

South Georgia, Coffee Co. (1962); part of Douglas.

South LaGrange, Troup Co. (1920)

Southland, Taylor Co. (1920)

South Macon, Bibb Co. (1962); part of Macon.

South Millem, Screven Co. (1894)

South Moultrie, Colquitt Co. (1962)

South Nellsville, Richmond Co. (1962)

South Newport, McIntosh Co. (1881).

Southover, Chatham Co. (1962)

Southover Junction, Chatham Co. (1920)

South Rome, Floyd Co. (1894)

South Valdosta, Lowndes Co. (1962)

Southwell, Bryan Co. (1920)

South Western Junction, Laurens Co. (1920)

Sowhatchee, Early Co. (1920)

Spain, Brooks Co. (1920); P.O. name is Nile.

Spalding, McIntosh Co. (1847)

Spanish Creek, Charlton Co. (1894)

Spann, Johnson Co. (1920); R.R. name is Meadows.

Sparks, Berrien Co. (1894)

Sparks, Cook Co. (1920)

Sparta, Hancock Co. (1920)

Speer, Habersham Co. (1881)

Speirs, Bryan Co. (1920)

Speirs, Jefferson Co. (1870)

Speirs Turnout, Jefferson Co. (1859); also known as Spiers & Bartow (1881).

Spence, Crady Co. (1962)

Spence, Mitchell Co. (1962)

Spencer, Appling Co. (1894)

Sperry, Houston Co. (1920)

Spiers, Jefferson Co. (1881); another name for Bartow (1881); also known as Speirs Turnout (1859).

Spilo, Union Co. (1920)

Spivey, Putnam Co. (1920)

Split Silk, Walton Co. (1962)

Spooner, Miller Co. (1920)

Spoonville, Houston Co. (1881)

Spot, Forsyth Co. (1920)

Spread, Jefferson Co. (1920); also known as Spread Oak prior to 1881 (1881).

Spread Oak, Jefferson Co. (1881); former name of Spread.

Sprewell, Carroll Co. (1894)

Spriggs, Whitfield Co. (1894)

Spring, Henry Co. (1859)

Spring Bluff, Camden Co. (1847)

Spring Creek, Decatur Co. (1881)

Spring Creek, Early Co. (1859)

Springfield, Effingham Co. (1920)

Spring Garden, Walker Co. (1962)

Spring Grove, Stewart Co. (1847)

Springhaven, Laurens Co. (1920)

Spring Head, Atkinson Co. (1920)

Spring Hill, Monroe Co. (1847)

Spring Hill, Montgomery Co. (1894)

Springhill, Wheeler Co. (1920)

Spring Place, Murray Co. (1920)

Spring Town, Cass (Bartow) Co. (1847)

Springvale, Randolph Co. (1920)

Springvale Station, Randolph Co. (1920)

Springwood, Thomas Co. (1881)

Sprite, Floyd Co. (1894)

Sprite Station, Chattooga Co. (1920); P.O. name is Tulip.

Sproule, Pierce Co. (1920)

Spruce, Rabun Co. (1920)

Squatt, Crawford Co. (1894)

Stacer, Toombs Co. (1920)

Staffords, Upson Co. (1920)

Stalco, Screven Co. (1962)

Staley Heights, Chatham Co. (1962); part of Savannah.

Stallings, Morgan Co. (1847)

Stallings, Walton Co. (1881)

Stamp Creek, Bartow Co. (1920)

Stamperville, Early Co. (1859)

Stamps, Upson Co. (1920)

Stanford's Mill, Harris Co. (1894)

Stanfordville, Putnam Co. (1920)

Stanhope, Screven Co. (1894)

Stanley, Screven Co. (1894)

Stanley's Mills, Laurens Co. (1894)

Stanleys Store, Toombs Co. (1962)

Stansell, Elbert Co. (1920)

Stapleton, Jefferson Co. (1920)

Stapleton, Johnson Co. (1894)

Stapleton Station, Jefferson Co. (1962); R.R. station for Stapleton.

Star, Bulloch Co. (1920)

Stark, Butts Co. (1920)

Starks, Whitfield Co. (1881); also known as Slackville.

Starkville, Lee Co. (1881)

Starr, Habersham Co. (1847)

Starr, White Co. (1881)

Starr Farm, Lee Co. (1920)

Starrsville, Newton Co. (1920)

State College, Chatham Co. (1962); also known as Georgia State College & Savannah State College.

State Farm, Baldwin Co. (1920)

State Line, Fannin Co. (1894)

State Line, Heard Co. (1920)

State Line, Whitfield Co. (1881); also known as County Line & Red Clay.

Staten, Lowndes Co. (1962); another name for Statenville.

Statenville, Echols Co. (1920)

Statenville, Lowndes Co. (1962); also known as Staten.

Statenville Station, Echols Co. (1881); also known as Huckleberry.

State Rights, Oglethorpe Co. (1847)

State Sanitarium, Baldwin Co. (1962); R.R. name for Hardwick; also known as Midway.

Statesboro, Bulloch Co. (1920)

Statham, Jackson Co. (1894)

Stathem, Barrow Co. (1920)

Station, Thomas Co. (1859)

Staunton, Berrien Co. (1894)

Staunton, Cook Co. (1920)

Stay, Lumpkin Co. (1920)

Steadman, Newton Co. (1870)

Steam Factory, Muscogee Co. (1859)

Steam Mill, Decatur Co. (1894)

Steam Mill, Paulding Co. (1870)

Steam Mill, Seminole Co. (1920); also known as Navy Yard, Johnsons Landing, & Dickensons Store (1881).

Stearnesville, Pike Co. (1881)

Stedman, Haralson Co. (1920)

Steed, Upson Co. (1920)

Stegall, Bartow Co. (1894); also spelled Stegalls (1881).

Stegalls, Bartow Co. (1881); also spelled Stegall (1894).

Stell, Carroll Co. (1920)

Stella, Berrien Co. (1894)

Stella, Elbert Co. (1920)

Stella, Lowndes Co. (1881)

Stellaville, Jefferson Co. (1920); R.R. name is Zebina.

Stephens, Oglethorpe Co. (1920)

Stephens Bluff, Pulaski Co. (1870)

Stephens Pottery, Baldwin Co. (1894) [See Stevens Pottery below].

Stephensville, Wilkinson Co. (1920)

Stephenton, Lowndes Co. (1920)

Sterling, Glynn Co. (1920); also spelled Stirling (1847).

Sterling, Houston Co. (1920)

Sterling, Montgomery Co. (1870)

Sterling Station, Glynn Co. (1894)

Stevens, Terrell Co. (1920)

Stevens Crossing, Emanuel Co. (1920)

Stevens Pottery, Baldwin Co. (1920); also known as Whiting (1881); [See Stephens Pottery above].

Stewart, Atkinson Co. (1920)

Stewart, Newton Co. (1920)

Stewart, Sumter Co. (1881)

Stewart Mill, Jones Co. (1894)

Stewarts Mill, Schley Co. (1881)

Stewartville, Lamar Co. (1920)

Stewartville, Pike Co. (1894)

Stiger, Ware Co. (1894)

Stilesboro, Bartow Co. (1920); also spelled Stilesborough (1859).

Stilesborough, Bartow Co. (1859); also spelled Stilesboro (1920).

Stillmore, Emanuel Co. (1920)

Stillwater, Irwin Co. (1894)

Stillwell, Effingham Co. (1920)

Stilson, Bulloch Co. (1920)

Stinson, Meriwether Co. (1894)

Stirling, Glynn Co. (1847); also spelled Sterling (1920).

Stirling, Montgomery Co. (1881)

Stithville, Campbell (Fulton) Co. (1881)

Stobo, Hall Co. (1920)

Stockbridge, Henry Co. (1920)

Stock Hill, Fannin Co. (1881)

Stocks, Lee Co. (1920)

Stockton, Clinch Co. (1894)

Stockton, Lanier Co. (1920)

Stogner, Carroll Co. (1920)

Stokesville, Charlton Co. (1920)

Stokesville, Coffee Co. (1894)

Stone Creek Church, Twiggs Co. (1870)

Stoneham, Jackson Co. (1962)

Stone Mountain, DeKalb Co. (1920)

Stonewall, Campbell (Fulton) Co. (1920)

Stonewall, Monroe Co. (1894)

Stoney Bluff, Burke Co. (1847)

Stono, Milton (Fulton) Co. (1920)

Stonyhead, Toombs Co. (1920)

Stony Point, Wilkes Co. (1881)

Stop, Fayette Co. (1894)

Storeville, Forsyth Co. (1920)

Story, Cobb Co. (1920)

Storys Mill, Chattooga Co. (1920)

Stovall, Habersham Co. (1962); part of Cornelia.

Stovall, Meriwether Co. (1920)

Strange, Chattooga Co. (1881)

Strannahan, Meriwether Co. (1920)

Strapton, Pierce Co. (1894)

Stratford, Fulton Co. (1920); part of Atlanta (1962).

Streator, Columbia Co. (1894)

Stricklan, Decatur Co. (1920); R.R. name is Whites Mill.

Strickland, Hall Co. (1894)

Strickland, Henry Co. (1894)

Strickland, Pierce Co. (1870)

Stricklands, Decatur Co. (1920)

Stricklands, Lowndes Co. (1962)

Stricklands, Ware Co. (1859)

Stricklands Mills, Tattnall Co. (1870)

Strickland Springs, Gwinnett Co. (1962)

Strom, Dougherty Co. (1962); also spelled Stroms (1920).

Stroms, Dougherty Co. (1920); also spelled Strom (1962).

Strother, Houston Co. (1920)

Strothers Siding, Clarke Co. (1962)

Strouds, Monroe Co. (1920)

Stroup's Furnace, Walker Co. (1894)

Strumbay, Liberty Co. (1920)

Stubbs, Mitchell Co. (1920)

Stubbs, Washington Co. (1894)

Stuckey, Montgomery Co. (1894)

Stuckey, Wheeler Co. (1920)

Stuttsville, Habersham Co. (1894)

Subligna, Chattooga Co. (1920)

Suburban, Houston Co. (1920)

Success, Screven Co. (1920)

Suches, Union Co. (1920)

Sudie, Paulding Co. (1920)

Sugar Creek, Telfair Co. (1881)

Sugar Hill, Gwinnett Co. (1962)

Sugar Hill, Hall Co. (1920)

Sugar Pit, Early Co. (1894)

Sugar Valley, Murray Co. (1847)

Sugar Valley, Gordon Co. (1920)

Sulphur Springs, Chattahoochee Co. (1894)

Sulphur Springs, Dade Co. (1920)

Sulphur Springs, Hall Co. (1881)

Sumach, Murray Co. (1920)

Sumerlins Mill, Heard Co. (1870)

Sumer's Store, Screven Co. (1894)

Summerfield, Bibb Co. (1881)

Summerfield, Stewart Co. (1847)

Summer Hill, Thomas Co. (1894)

Summertown, Emanuel Co. (1920)

Summervale, Elbert Co. (1881)

Summerville, Chattooga Co. (1920)

Summerville, Richmond Co. (1920)

Summit, Emanuel Co. (1920); consolidated with Graymount to form Twin City (1962).

Summit, Harris Co. (1894)

Summit, Henry Co. (1894)

Sumner, Worth Co. (1920)

Sumter, Sumter Co. (1920)

Sumterville, Lee Co. (1859)

Sunbery, Liberty Co. (1894); also spelled Sunbury (1881).

Sunbury, Liberty Co. (1881); also spelled Sunbery (1894).

Sun Hill, Washington Co. (1962); also spelled Sunhill (1920).

Sunnydale, Chattooga Co. (1881)

Sunnydale, Richmond Co. (1894)

Sunny Side, Spalding Co. (1920); corporate name is spelled Sunnyside (1962); also known as Fayette (1881).

Sunset, Colquitt Co. (1920)

Sunset Park, Chatham Co. (1962); part of Savannah.

Sunshine, Douglas Co. (1920)

Sunsweet, Tift Co. (1962)

Sunup, Newton Co. (1894)

Suomi, Dodge Co. (1920)

Surrency, Appling Co. (1920)

Susina, Thomas Co. (1894)

Sutalee, Cherokee Co. (1962); also spelled Sutallee (1920).

Sutallee, Cherokee Co. (1920); also spelled Sutalee (1962).

Sutherland, Dodge Co. (1920)

Sutherlands Bluff, McIntosh Co. (1847)

Sutton, Irwin Co. (1894)

Sutton, Tift Co. (1920)

Suttons, Berrien Co. (1920)

Suttons Corner, Clay Co. (1962)

Suttons Mill, Emanuel Co. (1920)

Suwanee, Gwinnett Co. (1920)

Suwanoochee, Clinch Co. (1881)

Swains, Telfair Co. (1870)

Swainsboro, Emanuel Co. (1920)

Swamp, Bulloch Co. (1894)

Swan, Fannin Co. (1920)

Swan, Irwin Co. (1894)

Sweden, Pickens Co. (1920)

Sweetgum, Fannin Co. (1920); also spelled Sweet Gum (1962).

Sweet Hill, Bryan Co. (1894)

Sweetwater, Gwinnett Co. (1920); also spelled Sweet Water (1859).

Sweet Water Factory, Campbell Co. (1847)

Sweet Water Town, Cobb Co. (1847); also spelled Sweetwater Town (1881).

Swift, Colquitt Co. (1962)

Swift, Elbert Co. (1920)

Swift, Thomas Co. (1920)

Swiftcreek, Bibb Co. (1920); also spelled Swift Creek (1894).

Swifton, Upson Co. (1920)

Swindel, Liberty Co. (1894)

Swindel, Long Co. (1920)

Swords, Morgan Co. (1920)

Sybert, Lincoln Co. (1920)

Sycamore, Irwin Co. (1881)

Sycamore, Turner Co. (1920)

Sycorax, Oglethorpe Co. (1920)

Syllsfork, Oglethorpe Co. (1894)

Sylvan Grove, Jefferson Co. (1847)

Sylvan Hill, Hancock Co. (1847)

Sylvania, Screven Co. (1920)

Sylvester, Worth Co. (1920)

Tabor, Forsyth Co. (1881)

Tabor, Franklin Co. (1920)

Tahoma, Richmond Co. (1920)

Tailscreek, Gilmer Co. (1920); also spelled Tails Creek (1859).

Talasee, Jackson Co. (1920)

Talbotton, Talbot Co. (1920)

Taliaferro, Chattooga Co. (1920)

Talking Rock, Pickens Co. (1920)

Talking Rock Mills, Pickens Co. (1894)

Tallahassee, Appling Co. (1870)

Tallakas, Brooks Co. (1881)

Tallapoosa, Carroll Co. (1847)

Tallapoosa, Haralson Co. (1920)

Tallapoosa Mines, Haralson Co. (1894)

Tallman, Decatur Co. (1894)

Tallokas, Lowndes Co. (1859)

Tallulah, Habersham Co. (1881)

Tallulah, Rabun Co. (1894)

Tallulah Falls, Rabun and Habersham Cos. (1962)

Tallulah Lodge, Habersham Co. (1920); part of Tallulah Falls but has separate post office (1962).

Tallulah Park, Habersham Co. (1920)

Tally, Fannin Co. (1920)

Talmadge, Baldwin Co. (1881)

Talmadge, Richmond Co. (1962); part of Augusta.

Talmadge, Wilcox Co. (1920)

Talmage, Pickens Co. (1920)

Talmo, Jackson Co. (1920)

Talona, Gilmer Co. (1920)

Tamworth, Bibb Co. (1920)

Tenery, Gwinnett Co. (1920)

Tangent, Taylor Co. (1920)

Tanner, Coffee Co. (1894)

Tannville, Warren Co. (1859)

Tapley, Irwin Co. (1920)

Tarboro, Camden Co. (1920)

Tarrytown, Treutlen Co. (1920)

Tarrytown, Montgomery Co. (1962)

Tarver, Echols Co. (1920)

Tarvers, Twiggs Co. (1870)

Tarversville, Twiggs Co. (1881)

Tarverville, Burke Co. (1894)

Tate, Pickens Co. (1920)

Tate Station, Pickens Co. (1920)

Tatesville, Thomas Co. (1859)

Tatum, Dade Co. (1920)

Tatum, Forsyth Co. (1894)

Tatumsville, Chatham Co. (1962); part of Savannah.

Tax, Henry Co. (1894)

Tax, Talbot Co. (1894)

Taylor, Crawford Co. (1920)

Taylor, Dooly Co. (1894)

Taylor Creek, Liberty Co. (1881); also spelled Taylors Creek (1920).

Taylors, Colquitt Co. (1920)

Taylors, Glynn Co. (1920)

Taylors, Pulaski Co. (1870)

Taylors Creek, Liberty Co. (1920); also spelled Taylor Creek (1881).

Taylor's Mills, Madison Co. (1894)

Taylorsville, Bartow Co. (1920)

Taylorsville, Laurens Co. (1881)

Taylorsville, Madison Co. (1881)

Taylor Town, Appling Co. (1894)

Tazewell, Marion Co. (1920)

Teagle, Gwinnett Co. (1920)

Teague, Cherokee Co. (1962)

Tebeauville, Ware Co. (1881)

Tedy, Calhoun Co. (1894)

Teelga Springs, Chattooga Co. (1859)

Teem, Gilmer Co. (1920)

Telfair Junction, Chatham Co. (1920)

Telfairville, Burke Co. (1894)

Tell, Campbell (Fulton) Co. (1920)

Teloga, Chattooga Co. (1920)

Teloga Springs, Chattooga Co. (1894)

Temperance, Screven Co. (1870)

Temperance, Telfair Co. (1920)

Temple, Carroll Co. (1920)

Templegrove, Murray Co. (1920)

Tempora, Floyd Co. (1920)

Tennega, Murray Co. (1920)

Tennille, Washington Co. (1920)

Teria, Campbell (Fulton) Co. (1920)

Terrace, Colquitt Co. (1920)

Terra Cotta, Bibb Co. (1920); part of Macon (1962).

Terrell, Worth Co. (1920)

Terrell's Creek, Cobb Co. (1894)

Terry, Paulding Co. (1962); also known as Red Rock.

Tesnatee, White Co. (1920)

Texas, Chattooga Co. (1870)

Texas, Heard Co. (1920)

Texas, Meriwether Co. (1847)

Thad, Chattahoochee Co. (1894)

Thalmann, Glynn Co. (1920)

Thames, Clayton Co. (1920)

Tharin, Camden Co. (1920)

Tharp, Bibb Co. (1870)

Tharpe, Houston Co. (1920)

Thaxton, Wilkes Co. (1920)

Thebes, Liberty Co. (1920)

The Cedars, Effingham Co. (1894)

The Cove, Meriwether Co. (1894)

The Glades, Hall Co. (1920); also known as Polksville prior to 1881 (1881).

The Hill, Richmond Co. (1962); part of Augusta.

Thelma, Clinch Co. (1920)

Thena, Washington Co. (1920)

The Pines, Effingham Co. (1894)

The Rock, Upson Co. (1920)

Thigpen, Lanier Co. (1920)

Thigpen, Clinch Co. (1894)

Thomas, Burke Co. (1894)

Thomas, Floyd Co. (1920)

Thomasboro, Screven Co. (1920); R.R. name is Kolb Gem.

Thomas Mill, Terrell Co. (1870)

Thomas Mills, Floyd Co. (1881)

Thomason, Decatur Co. (1920)

Thomas Station, Burke Co. (1881) also known as Lesters District, Munnerlyn & Lumpkins.

Thomaston, Upson Co. (1920)

Thomasville, Thomas Co. (1920)

Thompson, Columbia Co. (1859)

Thompson Mills, Jackson Co. (1920); also spelled Thompsons Mills (1962).

Thompsons Bridge, Burke Co. (1847)

Thompsons Mills, Jackson Co. (1962); also spelled Thompson Mills (1920).

Thompson's Mills, Pike Co. (1894)

Thompson's Store, Laurens Co. (1894)

Thoms, Montgomery Co. (1894)

Thomson, McDuffie Co. (1920)

Thornton Station, Spalding Co. (1881); another name for Orchard Hill.

Thorntonville, Marion Co. (1920)

Thrift, Emanuel Co. (1894)

Thrift, Jenkins Co. (1920)

Thunder, Upson Co. (1920)

Thunderbolt, Chatham Co. (1920)

Thundering Springs, Upson Co. (1894)

Thunder Springs, Upson Co. (1847)

Thurman, Meriwether Co. (1920)

Thurman, Irwin Co. (1920)

Thurston, Greene Co. (1962)

Thyatira, Jackson Co. (1920)

Tibet, Long Co. (1920)

Tickanetley, Gilmer Co. (1920)

Ticknor, Colquitt Co. (1920)

Tidings, Chattooga Co. (1920)

Tifton, Berrien Co. (1881)

Tifton, Tift Co. (1920)

Tiger, Rabun Co. (1920)

Tignall, Wilkes Co. (1920)

Tilda, Milton (Fulton) Co. (1920)

Tillman, Brooks Co. (1920)

Tillman, Lowndes Co. (1962)

Tillmans Bridge, Tattnall Co. (1847)

Tilly, Polk Co. (1894)

Tilton, Whitfield Co. (1920)

Time, Hall Co. (1894)

Timms, Gwinnett Co. (1920)

Timothy, Campbell (Fulton) Co. (1920)

Timothy, Clarke Co. (1962)

Timson, Rabun Co. (1881)

Tingle, Laurens Co. (1920)

Tinkle, Tattnall Co. (1920)

Tinsley, Bibb Co. (1920)

Tippen's Mills, Floyd Co. (1894)

Tippettville, Dooly Co. (1920)

Tiptop, Harris Co. (1920)

Tierd Creek, Decatur Co. (1859)

Tison, Tattnall Co. (1920)

Titus, Towns Co. (1920)

Titus Hill, Burke Co. (1847)

Tivola, Houston Co. (1920)

Tobesofkee, Bibb Co. (1894)

Tobler, Upson Co. (1920)

Toccoa, Fannin Co. (1870)

Toccoa, Habersham Co. (1894)

Toccoa, Stephens Co. (1920)

Toccoa Falls, Habersham Co. (1894)

Toccoa Falls, Stephens Co. (1962)

Toco Hills, DeKalb Co. (1962)

Todd, Jones Co. (1920)

Todd's Mills, Whitfield Co. (1894)

Toland, Jasper Co. (1894)

Toledo, Charlton Co. (1920)

Toll Gate, White Co. (1881); also spelled Tollgate (1894).

Tolona, Gilmer Co. (1894)

Tom, Brooks Co. (1894)

Tom, Johnson Co. (1920)

Tomato, Bulloch Co. (1894)

Tombs, Hart Co. (1920)

Tomlinson, Ware Co. (1847)

Tomlinson, Clinch Co. (1920)

Tompkins, Camden Co. (1894)

Toombs, Richmond Co. (1870)

Toomsboro, Wilkinson Co. (1920); also spelled Toomsborough (1859).

Toomsborough, Wilkinson Co. (1859); also spelled Toomsboro (1920).

Toonigh, Cherokee Co. (1920); R.R. name for Lebanon (1962); another name for Lebanon (1881).

Tootle, Tattnall Co. (1920)

Top, Jenkins Co. (1920)

Top, Screven Co. (1894)

Topeka Junction, Upson Co. (1920)

Torbit, Burke Co. (1962)

Tosh, Montgomery Co. (1894)

Touchton, Echols Co. (1920)

Touraine, Thomas Co. (1920)

Tournapull, Stephens Co. (1962)

Towalaga, Henry Co. (1920)

Towalaga, Spalding Co. (1962)

Towaliga, Butts Co. (1920)

Towanda, Atkinson Co. (1920)

Tower, Union Co. (1920)

Town and Country, Cobb Co. (1962); part of Marietta.

Town and Country Acres, Dougherty Co. (1962).

Town Creek, Gilmer Co. (1920)

Town Bluff, Appling Co. (1894)

Town Creek, Gilmer Co. (1920)

Towns, Telfair Co. (1920)

Townsend, McIntosh Co. (1920)

Toy, Houston Co. (1920)

Track Rock, Union Co. (1920)

Tracy, Meriwether Co. (1894)

Traders Hill, Charlton Co. (1920)

Trammell, Troup Co. (1920)

Tram Road Mills, Telfair Co. (1894)

Tranquilla, Jones Co. (1881)

Trans, Walker Co. (1920)

Transferville, Bartow Co. (1894)

Travellers Rest, Dooly Co. (1847)

Travis, Habersham Co. (1894)

Travisville, Clinch Co. (1920)

Tray, Habersham Co. (1881)

Trebor, Macon Co. (1920)

Tredwell, Butts Co. (1894)

Tree, Towns Co. (1920)

Tremont Park, Chatham Co. (1962)

Trenton, Dade Co. (1920)

Trevard's Mills, Murray Co. (1894)

Tribble, Troup Co. (1920)

Trible, Clarke Co. (1894)

Trice, Upson Co. (1962)

Trickem, Jasper Co. (1847)

Trickum, Carroll Co. (1870)

Trickum, Whitfield Co. (1920)

Tricum, Gwinnett Co. (1962)

Trimble, Lincoln Co. (1920)

Trimble, Troup Co. (1962)

Trinity, Liberty Co. (1920)

Trion, Chattooga Co. (1920); also known as Trion Factory (1881).

Trion Factory, Chattooga Co. (1881); also known as Trion (1920).

Trip, Gwinnett Co. (1894)

Triplett, Wilkes Co. (1920)

Tripoli, Whitfield Co. (1920)

Tropic, Sumter Co. (1920)

Troublesome, Clinch Co. (1859)

Troublesome, Echols Co. (1894)

Troup Factory, Troup Co. (1920)

Troup's Old Mills, Laurens Co. (1894)

Troupville, Lowndes Co. (1881)

Troutman, Stewart Co. (1920)

Troy, Cherokee Co. (1881)

Troy, Colquitt Co. (1920)

Troy, Milton (Fulton) Co. (1894)

Truckers, Bulloch Co. (1920)

Trudie, Brantley Co. (1920)

Truett, Emanuel Co. (1894)

Truitt, Colquitt Co. (1920)

Truman, Walton Co. (1894)

Trust, Hall Co. (1894)

Tubize, Floyd Co. (1962)

Tuckahoe, Screven Co. (1920)

Tucker, DeKalb Co. (1920)

Tucker, Sumter Co. (1894)

Tuckers Cabin, Henry Co. (1847)

Tugalo, Stephens Co. (1920)

Tugaloo, Habersham Co. (1962); part of Tallulah Falls.

Tugby, Screven Co. (1894)

Tulip, Chattooga Co. (1920); R.R. name is Sprite Station.

Tullis, Marion Co. (1894)

Tulsa, Bryan Co. (1920)

Tump, Emanuel Co. (1894)

Tunis, Henry Co. (1920)

Tunnel Camp, Paulding Co. (1894)

Tunnel Hill, Whitfield Co. (1920); also spelled Tunnelhill (1894).

Tupper, Montgomery Co. (1894)

Turia, Coweta Co. (1859)

Turin, Coweta Co. (1920); also known as Location (1881) [Note: Both Turin & Location are shown on Map of Georgia, Butts, 1870].

Turkey, Laurens Co. (1894)

Turkey Creek, Carroll Co. (1894)

Turkey Creek, Dooly Co. (1881)

Turkey Creek, Laurens Co. (1894)

Turkey Creek Mills, Carroll Co. (1881)

Turman, Calhoun Co. (1920)

Turner, Floyd Co. (1920)

Turner Air Force Base, Dougherty Co. (1962)

Turner City, Dougherty Co. (1962); part of Albany.

Turner's Chapel, Macon Co. (1894)

Turners Chapel, Taylor Co. (1881)

Turners Rock, Chatham Co. (1962)

Turner's Store, Calhoun Co. (1894)

Turnerville, Habersham Co. (1920)

Turnpike, Calhoun Co. (1894)

Turnpike, Cherokee Co. (1894)

Turpentine Farm, Worth Co. (1881)

Tusculum, Effingham Co. (1920)

Tutenia, Liberty Co. (1920)

Tuton, Mitchell Co. (1894)

Tweed, Laurens Co. (1920)

Twiggsville, Twiggs Co. (1920)

Twilight, Miller Co. (1920)

Twin City, Emanuel Co. (1962); formed by consolidation of Graymont & Summit.

Twin Lakes, Lowndes Co. (1962)

Two Hundred and Eight Mile Siding, Thomas Co. (1894)

Two Run, Lumpkin Co. (1881)

Tybee, Chatham Co. (1920); R.R. name is South End.

Tybee Island, Chatham Co. (1894)

Tyner, Meriwether Co. (1881)

Tyre, Douglas Co. (1920)

Tyrone, Fayette Co. (1920)

Tyrone, Wilkes Co. (1920)

Tysonville, Troup Co. (1894)

Ty Ty, Worth Co. (1881)

Ty Ty, Tift Co. (1920)

Tyrus, Carroll Co. (1920)

Unadilla, Dooly Co. (1920)

Underwood, Dougherty Co. (1962)

Undine, Evans Co. (1920)

Union, Dooly Co. (1870)

Union, Meriwether Co. (1870)

Union, Putnam Co. (1881)

Union, Quitman Co. (1962)

Union, Stewart Co. (1920);
P.O. name is Julia.

Union, Talbot Co. (1847)

Union City, Campbell (Fulton) Co. (1920)

Union Hill, Upson Co. (1847)

Union Junction, Chatham Co. (1920)

Union Mill, Morgan Co. (1847)

Union Mills, Heard Co. (1881)

Union Point, Greene Co. (1920)

Unionville, Bibb Co. (1962); part of Macon.

Unionville, Lamar Co. (1920)

Unionville, Monroe Co. (1881); another name for High Falls (1881); [NOTE: Both Unionville and High Falls are shown on Map of Ga., Bonner, 1847].

Unionville, Tift Co. (1920)

United States Marine Corps Supply Center, Dougherty Co. (1962).

Unity, Franklin Co. (1962)

Unity, Harris Co. (1920)

University, Bibb Co. (1962); part of Macon.

Univeter, Cherokee Co. (1920)

Uno, Chattahoochee Co. (1920)

Upatoi, Muscogee Co. (1962); also spelled Upatoie (1920).

Upatoie, Muscogee Co. (1920); also spelled Upatoi (1962); R.R. name was Jones Crossing in 1881 (1881).

Uphaupee, Bryan Co. (1894)

Upper Kings Bridge, Whitfield Co. (1859)

Upshaw, Cobb Co. (1920)

Upson, Upson Co. (1920)

Upton, Coffee Co. (1920)

Upton Mill, Taylor Co. (1962)

Uptonville, Charlton Co. (1920)

Urbana, Tift Co. (1920)

Urbs, Randolph Co. (1920)

Urena, Banks Co. (1920)

Ursula, Troup Co. (1920)

Utica, Worth Co. (1920)

Utoy, DeKalb Co. (1859)

Utoy, Fulton Co. (1859)

Uvalda, Montgomery Co. (1920)

Vada, Decatur & Mitchell Cos. (1962)

Valambrosa, Laurens Co. (1920); R.R. name is Moore.

Valdosta, Lowndes Co. (1920)

Valentine, Echols Co. (1894)

Valley, Talbot Co. (1881)

Valley Plains, Harris Co. (1881)

Valley Store, Chattooga Co. (1920)

Valley View, Habersham Co. (1894)

Valley View Orchard, Peach Co. (1962)

Valona, McIntosh Co. (1920)

Van, Ben Hill Co. (1920)

Van Buren, Jones Co. (1920)

Van Buren, Pike Co. (1894)

Vance, Tattnall Co. (1920)

Vanceville, Berrien Co. (1881)

Vanceville, Tift Co. (1920)

Vandiver, Franklin Co. (1962)

Vandiver, Rabun Co. (1894)

Vanna, Hart Co. (1920)

Vanns Valley, Floyd Co. (1859); also spelled Vans Valley (1920).

Vanoy, Crawford Co. (1920)

Vansandts Store, Fannin Co. (1859); also spelled Vanzants Store (1881).

Vans Valley, Floyd Co. (1920); also spelled Vanns Valley (1859); also known as Six Mile Station (1881).

Van Wert, Polk Co. (1920)

Vanzant, Douglas Co. (1920)

Vanzants Store, Fannin Co. (1881); also spelled Vansandts Store (1859).

Varn, Ware Co. (1894)

Varnell, Whitfield Co. (1962); also known as Varnells Station (1920); also known as Red Hill (1881).

Varnells Station, Whitfield Co. (1920); also known as Varnell (1962); also known as Red Hill (1881).

Vasons, Dougherty Co. (1920)

Vaudelt, Clayton Co. (1920)

Vaughn, Spalding Co. (1920); also known as Creswell (1881).

Vaughns Mills, Heard Co. (1870)

Vauns, Putnam Co. (1870)

Vayles, Union Co. (1920)

Veal, Carroll Co. (1962)

Veazey, Greene Co. (1920)

Vega, Pike Co. (1920)

Velma, Appling Co. (1920)

Venice, Jefferson Co. (1920)

Venture, Monroe Co. (1920)

Venus, Stewart Co. (1894)

Verbena, Montgomery Co. (1894)

Verd Antique, Cherokee Co. (1920); P.O. name is Lebanon.

Verdis, Camden Co. (1920)

Vernal, Randolph Co. (1920)

Vernon, Troup Co. (1920)

Vernonburg, Chatham Co. (1962)

Vernon View, Chatham Co. (1962)

Verona, Randolph Co. (1859)

Vesta, Oglethorpe Co. (1920)

Veterans Hospital, Richmond Co. (1962; part of Augusta).

Vic, Irwin Co. (1894)

Vickers, Coffee Co. (1920)

Vickery, Forsyth Co. (1920)

Vickerys Creek, Forsyth Co. (1881)

Victoria, Cherokee Co. (1920)

Victory, Carroll Co. (1920)

Victory Heights, Chatham Co. (1962); part of Savannah.

Vidalia, Montgomery Co. (1894)

Vidalia, Toombs Co. (1920)

Vidette, Burke Co. (1920)

Vienna, Dooly Co. (1920)

View, Habersham Co. (1920)

Vildo, Berrien Co. (1894)

Villa, Bleckley Co. (1920)

Villana, Hancock Co. (1847)

Villanow, Walker Co. (1920)

Villa Rica, Carroll & Douglas Cos. (1962)

Villa School, Hancock Co. (1847)

Vincent, Laurens Co. (1920)

Vine Cottage, Dawson Co. (1894)

Vines Mills, Worth Co. (1881); also known as McClellans Mills & McLellans Mills.

Vineville, Bibb Co. (1920); part of Macon (1962).

Vineyard, Irwin Co. (1859)

Vineyard, Spalding Co. (1920)

Vineyard, Wilcox Co. (1894)

Vinings, Cobb Co. (1920); also known as Vining Station (1881) and Vinings Bridge (1847).

Vinings Bridge, Cobb Co. (1847); also known as Vining Station (1881) and Vinings (1920).

Vining Station, Cobb Co. (1881); also known as Vinings Bridge (1847) and Vinings (1920).

Vinson, Paulding Co. (1920)

Viola, Heard Co. (1894)

Viola, Mitchell Co. (1859)

Violet, Meriwether Co. (1894)

Virgil, Jackson Co. (1881)

Virgin, Bibb Co. (1920)

Virginia-Carolina Chemical Company, Carroll Co. (1920)

Visage, Towns Co. (1920)

Vivian, Screven Co. (1894)

Vogel, Clinch Co. (1962)

Von, Candler Co. (1920)

Vulcan, Walker Co. (1962)

Waco, Haralson Co. (1920)

Wacoville, Haralson Co. (1894)

Waddell's, Polk Co. (1894)

Wade, Emanuel Co. (1920)

Wades, Randolph Co. (1920)

Wadespark, Brook Co. (1894)

Wade's Store, Brooks Co. (1894)

Wadley, Jefferson Co. (1920); also known as Bethany (1881).

Wahoo, Lumpkin Co. (1920)

Wahoo Mills, Lumpkin Co. (1894)

Wainright, Charlton Co. (1894)

Walburg, Glynn Co. (1920)

Walden, Bibb Co. (1920); R.R. name is Seago Station (1881).

Walden, Washington Co. (1894)

Walesca, Cherokee Co. (1859); also spelled Waleska (1920).

Waleska, Cherokee Co. (1920); also spelled Walesca (1920).

Walkee, Laurens Co. (1920)

Walker, Dougherty Co. (1962)

Walker, Echols Co. (1920)

Walker Park, Walton Co. (1920)

Walkers, Cobb Co. (1894)

Walkers, Twiggs Co. (1870)

Walkers Bridge, Burke Co. (1847)

Walker Station, Dougherty Co. (1881)

Walkersville, Pierce Co. (1920)

Walkinshaw, Richmond Co. (1962)

Wallace, DeKalb Co. (1920)

Wallace, Jones Co. (1859)

Wallace, Pulaski Co. (1920)

Wallaces Mill, DeKalb Co. (1962)

Wallaceville, Walker Co. (1962)

Walls Crossing, Schley Co. (1920)

Walnut, Jackson Co. (1881)

Walnut, Lumpkin Co. (1920)

Walnutgrove, Walton Co. (1920); corporate name spelled Walnut Grove (1962).

Walnut Hill, Franklin Co. (1920)

Walrick, Crawford Co. (1920)

Walter, Burke Co. (1920)

Walter, Gwinnett Co. (1962)

Walters, Lee Co. (1920)

Walter Station, Dougherty Co. (1920)

Waltertown, Ware Co. (1920)

Waltham, Butts Co. (1920)

Walthoursville, Liberty Co. (1859); also spelled Walthourville (1881).

Walthourville, Liberty Co. (1920); also spelled Walthoursville (1859).

Walthourville Station, Long Co. (1920).

Walthrall, Polk Co. (1920)

Waltons Ford, Habersham Co. (1881)

Wampun, Haralson Co. (1920)

Wano, Henry Co. (1881)

Ward, Douglas Co. (1920)

Ward, Randolph Co. (1881); also known as Natcheway & Nochway (1881); also spelled Wards (1870).

Wardin, Charlton Co. (1920)

Wards, Randolph Co. (1870); also spelled Ward (1881).

Ward Station, Randolph Co. (1894)

Warco, Ware Co. (1962)

Waresboro, Ware Co. (1920)

Wares Crossroads, Troup Co. (1962)

Waresville, Heard Co. (1962)

Warfield, Putnam Co. (1920)

Warhill, Dawson Co. (1920)

War Hill, Hall Co. (1881)

Waring, Whitfield Co. (1920)

Waring, Morgan Co. (1920)

Warmank's Mills, Whitfield Co. (1894)

Warm Springs, Meriwether Co. (1920)

Warner Robins, Houston Co. (1962)

Warnerville, Meriwether Co. (1881)

Warrens, Walker Co. (1920)

Warrens Mill, Early Co. (1920)

Warren Springs, Upson Co. (1870)

Warrens Switch, Early Co. (1920)

Warrenton, Warren Co. (1920)

Warrior, Bibb Co. (1847)

Warrior, Worth Co. (1920)

Warsaw, Chatham Co. (1870)

Warsaw, McIntosh Co. (1920)

Warsaw, Forsyth Co. (1847)

Warsaw, Milton (Fulton) Co. (1920)

Warthen, Washington Co. (1920)

Watherns Store, Washington Co. (1859)

Warwick, Worth Co. (1920)

War Woman, Rabun Co. (1881)

Washington, Wilkes Co. (1920)

Wassaw, Chatham Co. (1920)

Wataga, Decatur Co. (1920)

Waterloo, Burke Co. (1847)

Waterloo, Clinch Co. (1894)

Waterloo, Columbia Co. (1920)

Waterloo, Irwin Co. (1920)

Waterloo, Polk Co. (1894)

Waterman, Cobb Co. (1894)

Watermelon, Tattnall Co. (1859); also spelled Water Melon (1894).

Waterport, Walton Co. (1920)

Waters, Floyd Co. (1881); another name for Hermitage.

Waters, Screven Co. (1920)

Waters Station, Screven Co. (1894)

Watersville, Bulloch Co. (1920)

Waterville, Walker Co. (1920)

Watkinsville, Clarke Co. (1859)

Watkinsville, Oconee Co. (1920)

Watlee, Chatham Co. (1920)

Watson, Cherokee Co. (1920)

Watson, Thomas Co. (1894)

Watson's Spring, Greene Co. (1894)

Watters, Newton Co. (1847)

Wauhatchee, Dade Co. (1847)

Waverly, Camden Co. (1920)

Waverly Hall, Harris Co. (1920)

Wax, Floyd Co. (1920)

Way Back, Calhoun Co. (1920); also spelled Wayback (1962).

Waycross, Ware Co. (1920)

Wayland, Liberty Co. (1920)

Waynesboro, Burke Co. (1920)

Wayne's Mills, Oconee Co. (1894)

Waynesville, Wayne Co. (1881)

Waynesville, Brantley Co. (1920)

Waynmanville, Upson Co. (1920)

Wayside, Jones Co. (1920)

Ways Station, Bryan Co. (1920)

Weatherford, Meriwether Co. (1920)

Weaver, Pike Co. (1920)

Webb, Milton (Fulton) Co. (1920)

Webbs Creek, Franklin Co. (1859)

Webbs Spur, Johnson Co. (1920)

Webbville, Gwinnett Co. (1920)

Webbville, Newton Co. (1847)

Weber, Berrien Co. (1920)

Webster Place, Elbert Co. (1920)

Websterville, Bibb Co. (1847)

Weddington, Douglas Co. (1894)

Weeda, Washington Co. (1920)

Weefanie, Long Co. (1920)

Weisman, Screven Co. (1920)

Welch, Towns Co. (1920)

Welcome, Coweta Co. (1920)

Weldon, Colquitt Co. (1920)

Wellborn Mills, Houston Co. (1859); also spelled Wellborns Mill (1859).

Wellborns Mill, Houston Co. (1859); also spelled Wellborn Mills (1881).

Wellington, Morgan Co. (1881)

Wells, Murray Co. (1894)

Wellscott, Fannin Co. (1881)

Wells Mill, Sumter Co. (1920)

Wells Mills, Berrien Co. (1881)

Wellston, Houston Co. (1920)

Wendell, Warren Co. (1920)

Wenona, Crisp Co. (1920)

Wenona, Dooly Co. (1894)

Weracoba Heights, Muscogee Co. (1962); part of Columbus.

Wesley, Emanuel Co. (1920)

Wesley, Oconee Co. (1894)

Wesley, Taylor Co. (1962)

Wesley, Walton Co. (1894)

Wesleyan, Bibb Co. (1962)

Wessboro, Walker Co. (1894)

West, Haralson Co. (1920)

West Atlanta, Fulton Co. (1894)

West Bainbridge, Decatur Co. (1920); P.O. name is Diffie (1920); part of Barinbridge (1962).

West Bowersville, Franklin Co. (1881)

West Bremen, Haralson Co. (1962)

Westbrook, Laurens Co. (1894)

Westbrook, Pickens Co. (1920)

West Camilla, Mitchell Co. (1962)

West Cordele, Crisp Co. (1962); part of Cordele.

West Crossing, Haralson Co. (1962)

West End, Douglas Co. (1920)

West End, Floyd Co. (1962); part of Rome.

West End, Fulton Co. (1894); station of Atlanta.

Wester, Elbert Co. (1962); part of Elberton.

Westeria, Richmond Co. (1894)

West Georgia College, Carroll Co. (1962); part of Carrollton.

West Green, Coffee Co. (1920)

Westlake, Twiggs Co. (1920)

West Newnan, Coweta Co. (1962)

Westoak, Cobb Co. (1962)

Weston Mills, Berrien Co. (1894)

Westover, Baldwin Co. (1847)

Weston, Webster Co. (1920)

Westonia, Coffee Co. (1881); also known as Westons Mill.

Westons Mill, Coffee Co. (1881); another name for Westonia.

Westover, Richmond Co. (1920)

West Point, Glynn Co. (1847)

West Point, Troup & Harris Cos. (1962)

West Rome, Floyd Co. (1920)

Wests, Walker Co. (1920)

West Savannah, Chatham Co. (1962); part of Savannah.

Westside, Hall Co. (1962)

Wests Mill, Macon Co. (1881)

West View, DeKalb Co. (1920)

West Waycross, Ware Co. (1920)

Westwood, Ben Hill Co. (1962)

Whaley, Hancock Co. (1920)

Whaleys, Wayne Co. (1920)

W. H. Crawford, Oglethorpe Co. (1847)

Wheat City, Chatham Co. (1962); part of Garden City.

Wheat Hill, Chatham Co. (1894)

Wheaton, Appling Co. (1920)

Wheeler, Gordon Co. (1920)

Wheeler Heights, Bibb Co. (1962)

Whelchel, Hall Co. (1920)

Wheless, Richmond Co. (1920); part of Augusta (1962).

Whidden Mills, Irwin Co. (1894)

Whigham, Decatur Co. (1881); also known as Harrell.

Whigham, Grady Co. (1920)

Whistleville, Barrow Co. (1962)

White, Bartow Co. (1920)

White Bluff, Chatham Co. (1881); part of Savannah (1962).

White Chimney, McIntosh Co. (1894)

White City, Cherokee Co. (1962)

White Cut, Whitfield Co. (1920)

White Hall, Clarke Co. (1920); corporate name is spelled Whitehall (1962).

Whiteheads, Jeff Davis Co. (1920)

White Hill, Fulton Co. (1881)

Whitehill, Screven Co. (1920)

Whitehouse, Henry Co. (1920); also spelled White House (1859).

White House, Randolph Co. (1920)

White Oak, Camden Co. (1920)

White Oak, Columbia Co. (1847)

White Oak, McDuffie Co. (1894)

White Oak Camp Ground, Columbia Co. (1847)

Whitepath, Gilmer Co. (1920); also spelled White Path (1859); also known as Cherry Log (1881).

White Path Mines, Gilmer Co. (1894)

White Plains, Greene Co. (1920)

White Plains Junction, Greene Co. (1920)

Whites, Berrien Co. (1920)

Whites, Elbert Co. (1847)

Whites, Montgomery Co. (1870)

White's Bridge, Jackson Co. (1894)

Whitesburg, Carroll Co. (1920); also spelled Whitesburgh (1881).

Whitesburgh, Carroll Co. (1881); also spelled Whitesburg (1920).

White's Factory, Newton Co. (1894)

White's Hill, Troup Co. (1894)

Whites Mill, Decatur Co. (1920); P.O. name is Stricklan.

Whitestone, Gilmer Co. (1920)

White Sulphur, Hall Co. (1920)

White Sulphur Springs, Meriwether Co. (1920); also known as Meriwether White Sulphur Springs (1962).

Whitesville, Effingham Co. (1881); another name for Guyton.

Whitesville, Elbert Co. (1894)

Whitesville, Harris Co. (1920)

Whitewater, Crawford Co. (1920)

White Water, Fayette Co. (1881)

White Water Mills, Taylor Co. (1894)

Whitey, Calhoun Co. (1870)

Whitfield, Pulaski Co. (1894)

Whitfield, Troup Co. (1894)

Whiting, Baldwin Co. (1881); another name for Stevens Pottery.

Whitley, Irwin Co. (1920)

Whitney, Calhoun Co. (1894)

Whitney, Walton Co. (1920)

Whitsett, Dooly Co. (1894)

Whitsett, Lee Co. (1894)

Whittaker Springs, Burke Co. (1894)

Whittington, Worth Co. (1894)

Whittle, Washington Co. (1881)

Whittles, Cook Co. (1920)

Wicker, Washington Co. (1894)

Wier, Dawson Co. (1894)

Wier, Lumpkin Co. (1920)

Wigginsville, Marion Co. (1881)

Wiggs, Madison Co. (1920)

Wilburn, Franklin Co. (1894)

Wilburville, Macon Co. (1881)

Wilcox, Coffee Co. (1920)

Wilcox, Telfair Co. (1920)

Wilcoxon, Coweta Co. (1881); also known as Lodi; R.R. name is Sargent.

Wildborn, Chatham Co. (1847)

Wild Cat, Forsyth Co. (1894)

Wildwood, Dade Co. (1920); also known as Leas Crossing (1881).

Wiley, Rabun Co. (1920)

Wiliford, Dooly Co. (1894)

Wilkerson's, Dooly Co. (1894)

Wilkins, Floyd Co. (1920)

Wilkinson, Liberty Co. (1894)

Wilkinsons, Lamar Co. (1920)

Willacoochee, Coffee Co. (1881)

Willacoochee, Atkinson Co. (1920)

Willard, Putnam Co. (1920)

Willeo Mills, Cobb Co. (1881)

Willett, Muscogee Co. (1920); part of Columbus (1962).

Williams, Butts Co. (1894)

Williams, Cass (Bartow) Co. (1847)

Williams, Chatham Co. (1920)

Williams, Crisp Co. (1920)

Williams, Thomas Co. (1920)

Williams, Troup Co. (1962)

Williams, Wilcox Co. (1894)

Williamsburg, Calhoun Co. (1920); also spelled Williamsburgh (1881).

Williamsburgh, Calhoun Co. (1881); also spelled Williamsburg (1920).

Williamson, Pike Co. (1920)

Williamson's Mills, Wilcox Co. (1894)

Williamson Station, Screven Co. (1894)

Williams Store, Berrien Co. (1881); another name for Afton.

Williamsville, Pike Co. (1870)

Willie, Liberty Co. (1920)

Willingham, Macon Co. (1920)

Willingham, Worth Co. (1920)

Willis, Terrell Co. (1894)

Willis, Twiggs Co. (1920)

Willis' Mills, Cobb Co. (1894)

Willow, Lumpkin Co. (1920)

Willow Dell, Coweta Co. (1859)

Willow Grove, Coweta Co. (1881)

Willow Lake, Houston Co. (1920)

Willow Pond, Berrien Co. (1894)

Willsbank's Store, Habersham Co. (1894)

Wilma, Houston Co. (1870)

Wilma Junction, Mitchell Co. (1920)

Wilmington, Chatham Co. (1962)

Wilmington Island, Chatham Co. (1962)

Wilmot's Store, Banks Co. (1894)

Wilner, Jackson Co. (1920)

Wilscot, Fannin Co. (1920)

Wilson, Appling Co. (1894)

Wilson, Peach Co. (1962)

Wilsons, Chattooga Co. (1920)

Wilson's, Hancock Co. (1894)

Wilsons, Screven Co. (1894)

Wilsons Church, Jackson Co. (1920)

Wilsons Mill, DeKalb Co. (1920)

Wilson's Mills, Douglas Co. (1894)

Wilson's Store, Effingham Co. (1894)

Wilsonville, Coffee Co. (1920)

Wilsonville, Douglas Co. (1881)

Wimberly, Carroll Co. (1859)

Wimberly, Chatham Co. (1847)

Wimberly, Muscogee Co. (1881)

Winburn, Evans Co. (1920)

Winchester, Macon Co. (1920)

Winder, Barrow Co. (1920)

Winder, Jackson Co. (1894)

Windsor, Walton Co. (1920)

Windsor Forest, Chatham Co. (1962); part of Savannah.

Winfield, Columbia Co. (1920)

Winfield, Hancock Co. (1894)

Winfred, Jasper Co. (1920)

Winkles, Polk Co. (1894)

Winn, Douglas Co. (1894)

Winns Spur, Gwinnett Co. (1920)

Winokur, Charlton Co. (1920)

Winston, Douglas Co. (1920)

Winter, Laurens Co. (1920)

Winter's Oglethorpe Co. (1894)

Winterville, Oglethorpe Co. (1881)

Winterville, Clarke Co. (1920)

Winton, Newton Co. (1894)

Wire Bridge, Quitman Co. (1920)

Wiregrass, Clinch Co. (1920)

Wisdom Cross Roads, Harris Co. (1870)

Wisdoms Store, Harris Co. (1920)

Wise, Bibb Co. (1920)

Wise, Oglethorpe Co. (1920)

Wise, Webster Co. (1920)

Wisenbaker, Lowndes Co. (1920)

Wishart, Wilcox Co. (1894)

Withers, Clinch Co. (1920); R.R. name is Forrest (1881).

Withoft, Houston Co. (1920)

Woffords, Pickens Co. (1894)

Wolk Creek, Wilcox Co. (1881)

Wolfden, Forsyth Co. (1894)

Wolffork, Rabun Co. (1920)

Wolf Island, McIntosh Co. (1894)

Wolf Pen, Bartow Co. (1894)

Wolf Pen Cross Roads, Haralson Co. (1881); also known as Dean.

Wolf Skin, Oglethorpe Co. (1881)

Womack, Clay Co. (1894)

Womack's, Washington Co. (1894)

Wood, Warren Co. (1920)

Woodacre, Mitchell Co. (1962)

Woodberry, Meriwether Co. (1859); also spelled Woodbury (1920).

Woodbine, Camden Co. (1920)

Woodburn, Jefferson Co. (1881)

Woodburn, Walker Co. (1920)

Woodbury, Meriwether Co. (1920); also spelled Woodberry (1859).

Woodcliff, Screven Co. (1920)

Woodfin, Jasper Co. (1920)

Woodhouse, Meriwether Co. (1847)

Woodhull, Decatur Co. (1894)

Woodland, Talbot Co. (1920)

Woodland, Decatur Co. (1894)

Woodlands, Cass (Bartow) Co. (1847)

Woodlawn, Habersham Co. (1894)

Woodlawn, Lincoln Co. (1962)

Woodlawn, Murray Co. (1881); also known as Harris Cross Roads.

Woodlawn, Richmond Co. (1894)

Woodlawn Terrace, Chatham Co. (1962)

Woodruff, Walton Co. (1920)

Woods, Houston Co. (1920)

Wood's Mill, Heard Co. (1894)

Woods Station, Catoosa Co. (1859); also spelled Wood Station (1920).

Woods Station, Walker Co. (1847)

Wood Station, Catoosa Co. (1920); also spelled Woods Station (1859).

Woodstock, Cherokee Co. (1920)

Woodstock, Floyd Co. (1870)

Woodstock, Oglethorpe Co. (1881)

Woodstock, Polk Co. (1920)

Woodstock Mills, Appling Co. (1881)

Woodstown, Henry Co. (1920)

Woodsville, Camden Co. (1962)

Woodville, Baldwin Co. (1881)

Woodville, Chatham Co. (1962)

Woodville, Greene Co. (1920)

Woodward, Fulton Co. (1920)

Woodyard, Chattooga Co. (1920)

Wooleys, Bartow Co. (1920)

Wooley's Ford, Hall Co. (1894); also spelled Woolleys Ford (1859).

Woolfolk, Chattahoochee Co. (1870)

Woolleys, Hall Co. (1920)

Woolleys Ford, Forsyth Co. (1881)

Woolleysford, Hall Co. (1859); also spelled Wooleys Ford (1894).

Woolsey, Fayette Co. (1920)

Woolseyville, Fayette Co. (1894)

Wooster, Meriwether Co. (1920)

Wootens, Lee Co. (1870); also known as Wooten Station (1881).

Wooten Station, Lee Co. (1881); also known as Wootens (1870).

Wooten's Mill, Telfair Co. (1894)

Wormsloe, Chatham Co. (1962); part of Isle of Hope.

Worner, Terrell Co. (1920)

Worrill, Randolph Co. (1920)
Worsham, Monroe Co. (1894)
Worten, Lee Co. (1894)
Worth, Turner Co. (1920)
Worth, Worth Co. (1894)
Worthville, Butts Co. (1920)
Wray, Irwin Co. (1920)
Wrayswood, Greene Co. (1920)
Wrens, Jefferson Co. (1920)
Wright, Ben Hill Co. (1920)
Wright, Houston Co. (1920)
Wrights, Terrell Co. (1870)
Wrightsboro, McDuffie Co. (1920)
Wrightsville, Johnson Co. (1920)
Wriley, Wilkinson Co. (1962)
Wyats, Chattooga Co. (1920)
Wych, Elbert Co. (1894)
Wye, Pike Co. (1894)
Wylly, Laurens Co. (1920)
Wyna, Talbot Co. (1920)
Wynns Mill, Henry Co. (1881)
Wynnton, Muscogee Co. (1962); part of Columbus.
Wynern, Bartow Co. (1920)

Xerxes, Meriwether Co. (1894)

Yacht, Screven Co. (1894)
Yahoola, Lumpkin Co. (1920)
Yana, Upson Co. (1920)
Yancey, Floyd Co. (1920)
Yankee Town, Ware Co. (1847)
Yarborough, Floyd Co. (1881)
Yarbrough, Gordon Co. (1920)
Yates, Coweta Co. (1962)
Yates, Douglas Co. (1920)
Yatesville, Upson Co. (1920)
Yaw, Sumter Co. (1920)
Yellow Bluff, Camden Co. (1881)
Yellow Bluff, Telfair Co. (1894)
Yellow Creek, Dawson Co. (1920)
Yellowdirt, Heard Co. (1920); also spelled Yellow Dirt (1962).
Yellow River, Gwinnett Co. (1920)
Yellow Stone, Polk Co. (1881)
Yeomans, Emanuel Co. (1881); also spelled Youmans (1962).
Yeomans, Terrell Co. (1920)
Yonah, Banks Co. (1894)
Yonah, Hall Co. (1962)
Yonah, White Co. (1920); also known as Mount Yonah (1881); another name for Cleveland (1881).
Yonkers, Dodge Co. (1920); P.O. name is Younker.
Yopp's Store, Laurens Co. (1894)
York, Houston Co. (1881)
York, Rabun Co. (1962)
York, Spalding Co. (1859)
Yorkville, Paulding Co. (1920)
Youley, Burke Co. (1894)
Youley, Jenkins Co. (1920)
Youmans, Emanuel Co. (1962); also spelled Yeomans (1881).

Young, Washington Co. (1894)

Youngcane, Union Co. (1920); also spelled Young Cane (1859)

Young Harris, Towns Co. (1920)

Youngs, Hall Co. (1881)

Youngs, Polk Co. (1920)

Youngsville, Thomas Co. (1859)

Younker, Dodge Co. (1920); R.R. name is Yonkers.

Youth, Walton Co. (1920)

Ypsilanti, Talbot Co. (1920)

Uykon, Gilmer Co. (1920)

Zachry, Morgan Co. (1894)

Zaidee, Montgomery Co. (1894)

Zaidee, Treutlen Co. (1920)

Zana, Ben Hill Co. (1920)

Zarax, Crawford Co. (1920)

Zebina, Jefferson Co. (1920)

Zebulon, Pike Co. (1920)

Zeigler, Screven Co. (1920)

Zeke, Cherokee Co. (1920)

Zeland, Irwin Co. (1894)

Zellner, Lamar Co. (1920)

Zellobee, Marion Co. (1962); also spelled Zelobee (1920).

Zelobee, Marion Co. (1920); also spelled Zellobee (1962).

Zenith, Crawford Co. (1920)

Zero, Miller Co. (1894)

Zero, Pierce Co. (1859)

Zetella, Spalding Co. (1920)

Zetto, Clay Co. (1920)

Zidon, Franklin Co. (1920)

Zingara, Rockdale Co. (1920)

Zirkle, Pierce Co. (1920)

Zoar, Bulloch Co. (1920)

Zone, Walker Co. (1920)

Zulu, Chattooga Co. (1920)

Zuta, Glynn Co. (1920); P.O. name is Pennick.

Zyrza, Putnam Co. (1894)

www.ingramcontent.com/pod-product-compliance
Lightning Source LLC
Chambersburg PA
CBHW031420290426
44110CB00011B/457